Acknowledgements

This new edition of *The Good Trustee Guide* has been co-ordinated by Anne Moynihan and has been made possible by the generous contributions of a number of people who have helped ensure that it reflects the many changes in law and best practice since 2008.

Huge thanks go to:
Lindsay Driscoll, charity governance consultant, and Andrew Studd, Russell-Cooke Solicitors, for contributing to the legal aspects of the guide.

Linda Laurance, governance consultant, for contributing to the sections on handling conflict and relations with staff and volunteers.

Oonagh Smyth, director of governance and strategy at Mencap, for her contribution on risk.

NCVO staff members, including Georgina Anstey for her contributions to the sections on strategic planning and making a difference; Hannah Kowszun for her assistance with the sections on information technology and data; Michael Scott and Kristen Stephenson in respect of volunteering and Myles Kunzli for his work on the equalities section and for his invaluable assistance with project managing all of the activity that has been required to produce this latest edition of the guide.

We would also like to recognise Peter Dyer's contribution to the previous edition, a great deal of which lives on, in this sixth edition of *The Good Trustee Guide*.

Contents

Part One: The essentials   1

Foreword

We are delighted to be sponsoring this new edition of *The Good Trustee Guide*. In an environment of increased focus on governance and the effective management of charities, we are sure that trustees will find this guide invaluable. As investors, good governance and financial management remains at the forefront of our minds. As the largest charity investment manager in the UK, we also understand the responsibilities placed on trustees and recognise this in our interaction with our charity clients and the sector.

If there is anything that we can do to support your charity in the management of its investments, please get in touch. Whether you are writing your investment policy, identifying an appropriate spending rate or wrestling with the challenges of investing responsibly, we hope that our thoughtful approach can help you find the best solution for your charity.

Kate Rogers
Head of Policy, Cazenove Charities

kate.rogers@cazenovecapital.com
www.cazenovecharities.com

CAZENOVE
CAPITAL MANAGEMENT

Charity Investment from Schroders

Introduction

The Good Trustee Guide is aimed at trustees of charities. As a charity trustee you can use the guide to find out more about your duties and responsibilities, as a reference guide to check individual issues as they arise, or as a guide to develop your board or review its effectiveness.

The guide is also useful for individuals supporting trustees, for example chief executives, staff, advisers, trainers and consultants, as a tool to develop good governance practice in organisations.

Who is a trustee and what is a trustee board?

In *The Good Trustee Guide*, a trustee is a member of a group of people, the board of trustees or governing body, who take ultimate responsibility for a charity.

In *The Good Trustee Guide*, these individuals are referred to as trustees or board members, and the trustee group referred to as a trustee board or 'the board'. It is recognised that some charities use other terms to describe their trustees, such as management committee members.

About *The Good Trustee Guide*

This sixth edition of *The Good Trustee Guide* has been updated to reflect the many changes in law, regulation and best practice affecting trustees since 2008. Changes include the introduction of charitable incorporated organisations (CIOs), the consolidation of the 2006 and 2011 Charities Acts and publication of the second edition of *Good Governance: A Code for the Voluntary and Community Sector* in October 2010.

Part One of the guide deals with the essentials. It introduces the role of the trustee and where they fit into the charity, including guidance on legal structures and charitable status.

Part Two of the guide, Good Governance, aims to explore the many and varied issues that may come to a trustee's attention. This section of the guide aims to provide essential information on a range of topics, along with guidance on the role of the board in relation to each issue – from planning, to health and safety, to relations with staff and volunteers. This large section necessarily contains a significant amount of detail on some technical issues and the resources section is intended to signpost to further reading and sources of support where required.

Parts Three and Four of the guide concentrate on the role of the board itself and how it can be supported and developed. Part Three, Developing the Board, covers key aspects of board practice from recruitment to board composition. Part Four, Improving Governance, explores how trustees can undertake a review of their charity's governance and reflect on their own individual role as trustees.

The Good Trustee Guide is comprehensive and wide-ranging, but it is not exhaustive. Over recent years many sources of information on trusteeship and good governance have been developed, and a number of organisations provide support and information to trustees at national, regional and local level. Part Five, Further Information and Support, aims to signpost you to these key resources and support bodies.

Features of the guide

Throughout the guide you will find references to further sources of information, either within other parts of the guide or from external sources.

Each chapter or section of the guide ends with a checklist to help you identify action points for your trustee board. You may wish to add your own notes after the checklists.

We hope you find the guide useful and welcome your comments. Your feedback and ideas are extremely valuable to help plan future editions.

Part One:

The essentials

1

1.1

Introducing the role

What is trusteeship?

The concept of trusteeship has evolved over many centuries and broadly means that a donor gives or settles property on the trustees for the benefit of a third party.

This basic concept is still valid today. Charity trustees are people who are entrusted to look after money (or other resources such as land or property) given to a charity by a person or group of people. As a charity trustee, you must ensure that these resources are used effectively to achieve the particular purpose for which they were given (e.g. money donated by the public to cure heart disease should be spent on this area of work).

Trustees act within charities that generally have a formal structure and a set of rules and often delegate many day-to-day tasks to staff or volunteers. This structure will vary depending on your charity, and will affect your responsibilities and eligibility as a trustee.

This relationship works as follows:

FUNDERS
(donors, charitable trusts, etc.)

BENEFICIARIES OR SERVICE USERS

TRUSTEES

- act in the best interests of beneficiaries
- make sure assets are used exclusively to further the objects of the charity
- operate within an organisational structure that sets out its purposes and rules
- avoid conflicts of interest

DAY-TO-DAY TASKS
often delegated to staff or volunteers

1.2

Who are trustees (and who aren't)?

Who are trustees?

Section 177 of the Charities Act 2011 defines charity trustees as: 'the persons having the general control and management of the administration of a charity'. (See section 2 to find out more about charitable status.)

Trustees may also be called:

• members of the committee

• management committee members

• council members

• executive committee members

• governors.

No matter what title you are given, if you are a member of the governing body of a charity and you are entitled to take part in the decision-making process and vote at meetings, then you are a charity trustee.

NCVO recommends that charities call the people with the legal responsibility for trusteeship 'trustees' and refer to the committee or council on which they sit as the 'board of trustees'. These titles are used throughout *The Good Trustee Guide*.

In a charitable company, are trustees and company directors the same?

Yes. Trustees are members of the governing body of the charity. If the charity is also a company, then they will also be company directors (see section 1.4).

Can I be a trustee even if another group in my organisation is known as 'the trustees'?

In some charities, those known as 'the trustees', and perhaps listed as such in the annual report, are actually patrons (see page 54) or, in the case of unincorporated charities, merely hold the trust's property (see section 7.2). Those who take responsibility for controlling the management and administration of the charity may be known by some other term, such as 'the management committee'; this is the group that the law recognises as the trustees.

Can staff of charitable companies be 'shadow' directors?

Under company law, a shadow director is someone in accordance with whose directions the directors of a company (in this instance the trustees of a charitable company) are accustomed to act. If someone is a shadow director, then he or she might be held to be a trustee for certain purposes, sharing the responsibilities and liabilities of trusteeship (for instance, in relation to liability for wrongful trading).

Further Information:
ACEVO (2006) *Guidance on the Legal Status of Charity Chief Executives.* London: ACEVO.

Senior staff of charitable companies might be deemed to be shadow directors in circumstances where they dominate a passive board of trustees, for example where the management not only advises the trustees but also tells them what to do. Trustees should ensure that they do not simply 'rubber stamp' decisions made by senior staff, but make independent decisions, albeit with the advice of senior staff.

Am I a trustee if I am a member of the committee of a local branch?

Some national charities have groups or branches with local committees.

If the branch is constitutionally part of the national charity, then the members of the local committee are not trustees. The trustees are the members of the national governing body, and it is they who ultimately bear responsibility for the effective governance and conduct of the charity, including the work of the local branches. Some charities allocate places on their board of trustees for representatives of local groups.

If each local group is independent, with its own governing document, separately registered as charities but affiliated to a national charity, then the members of the local committees will be trustees of that local group. Age UK is an example of a charity with this structure (see section 2.3 for more information on branches).

1.3

Can a user of a charity's services
be a trustee?

Yes. In most cases, nothing prevents
users from acting as trustees. Service
users, or beneficiaries, can bring a vital
perspective to the work of the board.
Service user involvement can
demonstrate that your charity takes
an inclusive approach to involving users
in decision-making. It can give your
charity greater credibility or legitimacy.

On the other hand, involving service
users at board level, if unplanned, can
sometimes risk being tokenistic – that
is, simplistic assumptions can be made
that a service user speaks for or
represents all users (see section 19.3).
Some charities find that there are
more effective ways of involving
service users as well as, or instead of,
board membership, such as advisory
groups (see section 21.8). Conflicts
of interest can occur between the
user's trustee role and service user
role and these must be managed
(see section 3.5).

Further Information:
Charity Commission (2012) *Users
on Board* (CC24). London: Charity
Commission.

How do I become
a trustee?

Trustees are elected or appointed in
many different ways. These include:

Election	Individuals may be elected at an annual general meeting and/or by post. Individuals may be elected by, for example:
	• the entire membership
	• an 'electoral college' where the right to appoint trustee(s) rests with a specific group of members or stakeholders, eg volunteers, interest groups, geographical areas
Co-option	A number of trustees may be appointed by the board of trustees themselves
Appointed from outside	One or more trustees may be appointed by an external organisation, eg. a local authority
Ex Officio	One or more trustees may be appointed by virtue of the office they hold, eg. a mayor or vicar

Check your governing document to
see what it says about your charity's
procedures for electing or appointing
trustees (see section 2.2).

Tip: Part Three contains practical
suggestions for improving your
recruitment practices and information
about governance arrangements for
membership organisations.

If a trustee is appointed by an outside organisation, do they have the same responsibilities as other trustees?
Yes. Some charities have a provision in their governing document that gives the right for another organisation to appoint a trustee or trustees. These trustees are sometimes known as representative or nominative trustees and may be appointed for a number of reasons.

- To ensure that vacancies on the trustee board can be easily filled.

- To ensure that outside bodies that have an interest in the work of the charity can have an association with it.

- To ensure that the charity has a well-balanced cross section of either the community or service users.

No matter how you are elected or appointed, you have the same responsibilities as other trustees.

If you are appointed by a nominating organisation, you are not there to represent that organisation; you are there to act in the best interests of the charity to which you have been appointed.

If you are appointed by a nominating organisation, you are personally responsible for fulfilling your duty as a trustee – this means that, for example, the nominating organisation cannot send alternative people if you cannot attend a board meeting, nor will the responsibility as a trustee rest with them.

There may be occasions when your duty to act in the best interests of the charity is in conflict with the best interests of the organisation that appointed you as a trustee. If this happens, you should follow an agreed policy on how to deal with conflicts of interest. In the absence of an existing policy, you should remove yourself from discussion of the item concerned and your absence should be minuted. This may not, however, absolve you from being jointly responsible and liable for any decision made (see section 3.6).

Note:
There are certain circumstances when the governing document of a charity allows an organisation to be appointed as a 'corporate trustee'. However, this is a specific situation and will be clearly set out in your governing document.

See section 21.7 for further guidance on the role of trustees nominated by outside organisations.

Can individuals attend a board meeting but not be a trustee?
Yes, it is quite common for individuals who are not trustees to attend all or part of board meetings, either occasionally or regularly, but it is important to be clear about their role being distinct from the role of a trustee. These individuals are sometimes called observers or representatives, or may be members of staff, such as in the following examples.

- In charities that employ staff, it is usual for a chief executive to attend board meetings to report on day-to-day issues. A member of staff may take the minutes of a meeting.

- Some charities allow an individual to be elected by service users as a 'representative' to attend all or part of board meetings but not as a trustee (it is quite common for service users to act as trustees – see above).

- A member of an outside organisation – an officer or member of a local authority, for example – may regularly attend board meetings in an advisory capacity but not as a trustee.

- A person with particular expertise or experience may sometimes attend board meetings to provide advice on a one-off or regular basis.

There can be confusion about whether these individuals are trustees; for example a local authority member may be a trustee in one charity but not in another.

If individuals are attending board meetings as something other than a trustee, it should be made explicit that they are not trustees and do not take part in decision making to ensure they are not found to be liable for decisions taken. This can be shown in the meeting minutes (eg by listing non-trustees as 'in attendance' in a different list from trustees) or via a provision in the governing document.

Case study
A local community support centre

The centre is a small charity with a small staff team (manager, finance officer and caretaker) supported by many volunteers. The trustees are elected by members at the annual general meeting. The centre manager attends every board meeting to report on day-to-day issues. A member of the local authority attends board meetings as an observer, and this is made clear in the minutes. A representative of service users, elected by service users but not a trustee, also attends part of every meeting to discuss service user issues. Again, their role as 'in attendance' is made clear in the minutes. However, service users are encouraged to join the board as full trustees and sometimes a service user has moved from being the 'representative' to being elected as a trustee.

1.4

Who can and can't be a trustee?

The Charities Act 2011 sets out who is disqualified from acting as a charity trustee. This applies to all charities including excepted and exempt charities.

Company law sets out who is disqualified from acting as a company director. These provisions apply to charities formed as a company limited by guarantee (as well as all other companies).

Who is disqualified from acting as a charity trustee?

Section 178 of the Charities Act 2011 disqualifies people who:

- have unspent convictions for offences involving deception or dishonesty (unless 'spent'), eg theft, fare evasion or falsely claiming benefit

- are undischarged bankrupts

- have been, at any time, removed from trusteeship of a charity by the Charity Commission or the court in England, Wales or Scotland, because of misconduct or mismanagement

- are disqualified from being company directors under the Company Directors Disqualification Act 1986

- have failed to make payments under county court administration orders

- have made compositions (ie. come to an arrangement) with their creditors and have not been discharged.

As soon as someone comes within section 178 (eg the day they are convicted of an offence involving dishonesty), he or she is automatically disqualified from acting as a trustee. It is a criminal offence to act as a charity trustee while disqualified.

Charities can apply to the Charity Commission for a waiver of disqualification under section 181 of the Charities Act 2011, either generally or in relation to a charity or a specific class of charities. The Commission will consider what, if any, benefit is likely to result from an applicant acting as a trustee. Under the Charities Act 2011, if the ground for disqualification was removal from the trusteeship by the Charity Commission or the court in England, Wales or Scotland, and five years has passed, then the application for waiver must normally be granted unless there are special circumstances that would justify refusal.

Further information:

Charity Commission (2011) *Finding New Trustees: What charities need to know* (CC30). London: Charity Commission.

Charity Commission (2012) *Users on Board* (CC24). London: Charity Commission.

Who is disqualified from acting as a company director?

Under the Company Directors Disqualification Act 1986, the court may disqualify people:

- who have been convicted of criminal offences relating to the promotion, formation, management or liquidation of a company

- who have been persistently in default of company legislation for filing accounts and other documents

- who have been found guilty of fraudulent trading or fraud

- whose conduct as a director has made them unfit to be involved in the management of a company.

Are there any other factors affecting eligibility?

- Trustees of unincorporated charities cannot be under the age of 18. Under the Companies Act 2006, it is possible for a director of a charitable company to be 16, and under the Charities Act 2011, it is possible for a trustee of a charitable incorporated organisation (CIO) to be 16. In some circumstances, parents can be liable for the actions of their children; parents of people who are under 18 and considering becoming trustees should be made aware of the duties and responsibilities.

- The governing document of a charity may include restrictions on who may become a trustee of that charity, for example requiring them to live in a certain area or to be of a particular religious denomination.

- The Charity Commission states that:

  'It is important that anyone appointed as a trustee is made fully aware of his or her responsibilities and liabilities. It is unfair to impose on someone a range of duties that that person cannot properly understand and cannot, or does not want to, carry out.'

- The Safeguarding Vulnerable Groups Act 2006 bans certain individuals from being a trustee of children's charities or vulnerable adults' charities. Further information on this can be obtained from the Disclosure and Barring Service (DBS).

- Since September 2012, the position of a trustee of a children's or vulnerable adult's charity is no longer a regulated activity unless the trustees have close and unsupervised contact with the beneficiaries. However, a trustee who does not fall within this definition is still eligible to obtain an enhanced DBS check, and the Charity Commission strongly recommends that trustees of charities working with children and vulnerable adults who are eligible to obtain disclosures from DBS should do so. Further information on this can be found in Charity Commission (2011) *Finding New Trustees: What charities need to know* (CC30). London: Charity Commission.

- All prospective charity trustees should sign a declaration of eligibility to act, which should also cover DBS checks. (See section 19.6 for a model declaration.)

Further information:
Further advice on the appointment of under 18s can be found on the Charity Commission website Finding and Supporting Young Trustees: A checklist for charities and Charity Commission (2011) *Finding New Trustees: What charities need to know* (CC30) London: Charity Commission).

Remember that there are other ways of involving people in the work of a charity besides becoming a trustee.

Checklist

Have you considered asking your board or committee to review the names it uses for the people and the committees, so that those who are the trustees in law understand their status?

Have you checked your governing document to see what it says about your charity's procedures for electing/appointing trustees?

Are any members of your trustee board appointed by outside organisations?

If so, are they clear that they must act in the best interests of your charity?

If individuals who are not trustees attend your board meetings do you make this clear in the minutes of the meeting?

Are you a trustee of a national charity with local branches?

Are the local branches separate legal entities?

If your charity has local branches, does your board need to review how it exercises its responsibilities for the activities of the local branches and how the local branches ensure their accountability to the national trustees?

Has your board checked that your trustees are eligible for trusteeship under the terms of your governing document, and that these disqualify only those you would wish to exclude?

Is there someone in your charity who is responsible for checking that trustees are not disqualified?

Do you ask new trustees to sign a declaration of commitment to the charity and eligibility to act as a charity trustee? (See section 19.6)

If your charity works with children, young people or vulnerable adults, have you obtained a DBS check for trustees if required by law or if eligible to do so?

1.5

What do trustees do?

Although many day-to-day tasks can be delegated to staff (where they are employed) or to individual board members, volunteers or others, the central responsibilities of trustee boards are the same whatever the size of the board or the nature of the charity. These responsibilities are taken up in other parts of this book in more detail but can be summarised into 12 essential areas (see box).

The 12 essential board responsibilities at a glance

1. Set and maintain vision, mission and values
The trustee board is responsible for establishing the essential purpose of the charity as set out in the objects of its governing document. The board is also responsible for guarding the ethos and values of the charity.

2. Develop strategy
Together, the trustees (and chief executive where employed) should develop a long-term strategy. Meeting agendas need to reflect the key points of the strategy in order to keep the organisation on track.

3. Establish and monitor policies
The trustee board creates a wide range of policies to govern organisational activity. These may include human resources, financial controls, safeguarding, risk management, volunteer management and selection of beneficiaries.

4. Ensure compliance with the governing document
The governing document is the rulebook for the charity, and the trustees must ensure it is followed. In particular, the charity's activities must comply with the charitable objects in the governing document.

5. Ensure accountability
The trustees should ensure that the charity fulfils its legal requirements to be accountable. This will include publishing annual reports and accounts. The charity should also be accountable to other groups that are sometimes known as stakeholders: donors, beneficiaries, staff, volunteers and the general public.

6. Ensure compliance with the law
Trustees are responsible for checking that all the charity's activities are legal.

7. Maintain proper fiscal oversight
Trustees are responsible for effectively managing the charity's resources and funding so it can meet its charitable objects. The trustee board secures sufficient resources to fulfil the mission; monitors spending in the best interests of the charity; approves the annual financial statement and budget; protects the charity against liability by providing insurance; seeks to manage risk for the charity; ensures compliance with the law.

(Note: continued on following page)

8. Respect the role of staff/volunteers

The trustee board recognises and respects the domain of staff and/or volunteer responsibility. It also creates policy to guide staff and/or volunteer activities and safeguard the interests of the charity.

9. Maintain effective board performance

The board keeps its own house in order. It engages in productive meetings, effective committees with adequate resources, development activities and regular reviews of its role. The board is also responsible for overseeing trustee board recruitment.

10. Promote the organisation

Through their own behaviour, their governance oversight and their activities on behalf of the charity, trustees enhance and protect the reputation of their charity. They are good ambassadors for the charity.

Where staff are employed:

11. Set up employment procedures

The trustee board creates comprehensive, fair and legal personnel policies. These protect the charity and those who work for it. They cover recruitment, support, appraisal, remuneration and discipline.

12. Select and support the chief executive

If necessary, the trustee board creates policy covering the employment of a chief executive. It also selects and supports the chief executive and reviews their performance.

What is governance?

Governance is about leadership and ensuring that an organisation is effectively and properly run. The 12 responsibilities are based on principles of good governance.

Good governance is the board's responsibility, but governance covers more than the board's duties and responsibilities: governance includes how the board is appointed and supported and how it works to ensure decisions are taken properly and the work of the charity is effective and furthers its purposes.

Governance is distinct from day-to-day management and operations delegated to staff and volunteers. Sandy Adirondack in *The Good Governance Action Plan for Voluntary Organisations* (NCVO, 2002) wrote that 'governance is not necessarily about doing; it is about ensuring things are done'.

Governance has been high on the agenda for charities in recent years. A very useful framework of good governance developed to help guide trustees and organisations is *Good Governance: A code for the voluntary and community sector* (the Code), Second Edition, 2010.

The first version of the Code was drawn up in 2005 and this was revised in 2010 with a further version for smaller organisations published in 2011. The steering group now responsible for the Code consists of the Association of Chief Executives of Voluntary Organisations (ACEVO), the Institute of Chartered Secretaries and Administrators (ICSA), the National Council for Voluntary Organisations (NCVO), the Small Charities Coalition and Wales Council for Voluntary Action (WCVA), with the Charity Commission. The Code sets out a statement of best practice in governance, designed around six principles. The six principles, explored in Chapter 5, are useful in understanding more about what a well-governed organisation should look like, and are good starting points to review the board and organisation's effectiveness, and put in place good practice.

Further information:
Good Governance: A code for the voluntary and community sector is available from the Code website (see Part Five).

Another useful resource to help trustees understand their roles and responsibilities is the *National Occupational Standards for Trustees and Management Committee Members*, which was drawn up in 2005. These standards set out the competencies that all trustees should develop to ensure that they are able to carry out their role effectively. They are particularly useful for helping individual trustees to understand their duties and responsibilities and for helping boards to plan training and development. The standards (sometimes referred to as 'NOS') are explored further in Chapter 23.

Further information:
National Occupational Standards for Trustees and Management Committee Members, available from Skills for Health.

I am a new trustee.
How can I find out more about my roles and responsibilities?
The Good Trustee Guide covers all of the main areas of a trustee's responsibility. You can use the Guide to find out more about your responsibilities, to check individual issues as they arise or to develop your board or review its effectiveness. It also provides links to more detailed and comprehensive sources of guidance – for example, the Charity Commission provides more detailed advice on some of the areas covered in this chapter regarding trustee eligibility.

Remember, trustees are not expected to be experts in every topic confronting the board, but they are expected to understand their duties and responsibilities. All trustees should be provided with an introduction, or induction, into their responsibilities as a trustee, covering the essential information needed. Section 20.3 includes a sample induction programme and checklist.

2

Legal structures and charitable status

As a trustee, you take ultimate responsibility for your charity. Chapters 2 and 3 introduce what this means in practice. They cover:

- what a charity is
- the legal structure of your organisation
- the duties of trustees
- trustee liability
- the structure of the trustee board and where it fits into the organisation.

2.1

Charitable status

What is a charity?

The modern concept of charity has evolved from an Elizabethan statute of 1601, which defined 'charitable' as 'the relief of aged, impotent and poor people, the maintenance of schools of learning, the repair of bridges, churches and highways, and the relief or redemption of prisoners or captives', among other things. This definition was developed over the years by the courts. In 2006, a new Charities Act restated the charitable purposes and set out a separate public benefit requirement and a range of other changes.

Charities have exclusively charitable purposes

Today, charities are organisations that are set up with purposes that are exclusively charitable. Charitable purposes are set out in the Charities Act 2011 (an Act that consolidated the 2006 Act with earlier charity legislation). The purposes of a charity will be set out in the 'objects' clause in its governing document and must fall under one or more of the following:

a) the prevention or relief of poverty

b) the advancement of education

c) the advancement of religion

d) the advancement of health or the saving of lives

e) the advancement of citizenship or community development

f) the advancement of the arts, culture, heritage or science

g) the advancement of amateur sport

h) the advancement of human rights, conflict resolution or reconciliation or the promotion of religious or racial harmony or equality and diversity

i) the advancement of environmental protection or improvement

j) the relief of those in need, by reason of youth, age, ill health, disability, financial hardship or other disadvantage

k) the advancement of animal welfare

l) the promotion of the efficiency of the armed forces of the Crown, or of the efficiency of the police, fire and rescue services or ambulance services

m) other purposes currently recognised as charitable and any new charitable purposes which are similar to another charitable purpose.

Charities must benefit the public

All charities must be able to demonstrate how their purposes benefit the public. For a charity to benefit the public it must be able to demonstrate that:

• it provides an identifiable benefit, the benefit being balanced against any detriment or harm and

• the benefits are to the public, or a section of the public

• any private benefit must be incidental to a charity's work. This includes the restrictions over how far trustees can benefit personally from a charity (see section 3.7) and the benefits to members in a membership charity.

The Charity Commission guidance on the Public Benefit Requirement is available on its website. Under the Charities Act 2011 trustees must have regard to this. Trustees must also set out in the trustees' annual report how they have carried out their charitable purposes for the public benefit.

When are organisations required to register with the Charity Commission?

The Charity Commission exists to regulate and support charities. If your organisation's annual income is over £5,000 and you meet the criteria for registration then your organisation is viewed as a charity and must register by applying to the Charity Commission.

In the past, two categories of charity were not required to register: excepted charities (including many individual churches) and exempt charities (including charitable industrial and provident societies, and universities and colleges). Under the Charities Act 2011 some of these now have to register with the Charity Commission and more of the excepted charities will be subject to compulsory registration in the future.

Remember that when an organisation registers as a charity, it is gaining charitable status not a new legal structure. Charitable status and legal structure are different. Except in the case of a CIO, an organisation will first establish itself with a legal structure, such as a company or association structure (see section 2.2) and then, if eligible, register as a charity. This means that it is common for an organisation to be both a charity and, say, a company at the same time. This is sometimes a cause of confusion.

What are the advantages of charitable status and charity registration?

All charities, whether or not they are registered, can get some relief from direct taxes such as income tax, corporation tax, stamp duty and capital gains tax. There are also some limited concessions on VAT.

Charities can claim back any income tax paid on donations made through Gift Aid and can benefit from the payroll giving scheme whereby payments can be made to charities from employees before deduction of tax. They are also entitled to 80% business rate relief on any premises they occupy, and this can be extended to 100% at the discretion of the local authority.

Registration enables a charity to apply for grants from trusts or donors who have a policy of giving only to registered charities.

Registered charities may also benefit from an improved public image because they are regulated and have a charity number.

What are the disadvantages of charitable status – or what should I be aware of?

Charitable status brings with it restrictions and requirements.

- Charities are only permitted to undertake charitable activities or to fund the charitable activities of another organisation, which does not have to be a charity. This places restrictions on:

  – the type of work charities can carry out or fund – all activities must further or support the charity's objects

  – political activities undertaken by the charity (see next page)

  – trading activities undertaken by the charity (see next page).

- Charities must comply with regulatory requirements, including those relating to the preparation of annual accounts and returns (Chapter 7).

- The governing body of the organisation takes on the duties and responsibilities of charity trustees (see Chapter 5). There are restrictions over how far trustees can personally financially benefit from their role (see section 3.7).

Further information
'Setting up a charity' pages on the Charity Commission's website.

Charitable status – political activities
Whether you are trying to save a local community centre from closing or lobbying government, campaigns are created to produce change and make an impact.

Campaigning is 'the mobilising of forces by organisations or individuals to influence others in order to effect an identified and desired social, economic, environmental or political change.' NCVO (2010) Trustee Guide to Campaigning and Influencing. London: NCVO

As a charity trustee, you are responsible for ensuring that your charity complies with the law relating to political activities by charities.

Under English law, charities cannot have political purposes. This means they cannot seek to change a law or government policy either in the UK or abroad as their main purpose, but they can carry out political activity (seek to change a law or policy both in the UK and abroad) that supports the delivery of its charitable purposes. Charities can never engage in party political activities (ie trying to persuade members of the public to vote for or against a candidate or political party).

Charity Commission guidance is set out in Charity Commission (2008) Speaking Out: Guidance on campaigning and political activity by charities. London: Charity Commission. The guidance makes an important distinction between campaigning that is mainly about changing public attitudes and political campaigning, which is about changing law or government policy. It also clarifies that:

- a charity can devote all of its resources to a campaign that seeks to raise awareness, education or behaviour change and can also campaign to change a law or policy provided that this activity does not become the charities' sole or continuing purpose

- a charity can campaign using emotive or controversial material where it is lawful and justifiable in the context of the campaign

- campaigning against a private company and behaviour change of corporations is not a political activity

- special rules apply in the context of an election.

Why do some charities have a separate, non-charitable arm for political activities?
Charity Commission guidance states that: 'political activity can only be a means of supporting or contributing to the achievement of its charitable purposes. It cannot be a charitable purpose in its own right, or the only means by which the charity pursues its objects.'

Some charity trustees decide to set up separate non-charitable companies or associations to carry out their policy work and political activities so that they will not be subject to restraints imposed by charity law.

Charitable status and political activities: what role should I play as a trustee?
You should ensure that you and your fellow trustees take the major decisions about the educational, policy and campaigning work of your charity.

Depending on the size and complexity of your operations, this could involve some or all of the following activities.

- Ensure that staff and volunteers understand the guidelines and restrictions on political activities.

- Put mechanisms in place to review your charity's policy statements and reports to ensure that all political activities comply with charity law (see definition on previous page).

- Discuss the degree to which engaging with political activities would help to achieve your charity's aims – it can be useful to set clear and measurable objectives and have an appropriate campaign strategy from the start.

- Decide how much of your charity's resources it is appropriate to use in this area of work – this may vary depending on internal priorities and the external environment in which your organisation is operating.

- Ensure independence and transparency when working with politicians and political parties.

- Ensure that you have procedures in place to monitor and evaluate political activities.

- Enhance organisational learning and build confidence – campaigning is not always successful, but when it is, the impact on the lives of beneficiaries can be great. This means that it should be acceptable to make a mistake in your campaigning work, but not to keep making the same mistakes.

- Regularly review membership of any campaigning alliances and coalitions to ensure that any involvement in these is part of a coherent campaign strategy and can be expected to further your charity's objectives.

Further information:

See checklist in Charity Commission (2008) *Speaking Out: Guidance on campaigning and political activity by charities.* London: Charity Commission.

Charity Commission guidance on their website – Charities, elections and referendums; and Charities and political donations.

Do charities have the right to trade?
According to HM Revenue and Customs, on its trading and business activities web page, 'trading' describes: *'activities, which involve the provision of goods or services to customers on a commercial basis. When deciding whether a trade exists, it is of no relevance that you do not intend to make a profit or that you intend profits to be used only for charitable purposes.'*

If your organisation is a registered charity, there is no reason why charity and tax law should stop it from engaging in all kinds of trading. However, there are strict rules and you should take thorough legal advice. Don't let the law deter you. Do make sure you understand how it works.

The fact that all profits may be applied to charitable purposes is irrelevant when determining 'trade'. It is the activity, not the outcome that is under scrutiny.

A charity's trading profits are exempt from corporation or income tax if it falls under one of the following categories.

- Carrying out the charity's primary purpose – trading that carries out a primary purpose as stated in the charity's governing rules or constitution (eg a residential care home charging its residents). Where the actual work of trading is carried out by the charity's beneficiaries or where it is undertaken in the course of carrying out the primary purpose (eg a theatre charity selling food and drink to the members of the audience). This is known as ancillary trading.

- Selling donated assets – selling donated goods, land, buildings and investments is not regarded as trading so long as the donations have been given specifically to raise funds for the charity (but significant alterations – eg turning donated fabric into clothing – would render the sale outside allowable activity).

- Small-scale exemption – charities are exempted from income or corporation tax on trading profits where the annual turnover for non-primary purpose trading is below a financial threshold. At present (July 2014) this is £5,000 for charities with a total income under £20,000, 25% of total income for charities between £20,000 to £200,000 and £50,000 for all charities over £200,000.

- Extra-statutory concession – this applies to fundraising events such as car-boot sales, dances, film showings, firework displays or fetes. There are detailed rules that must be followed.

Full details of all these exemptions can be found on the HMRC website.

If your charity intends to trade in a way that does not fit into any of these four categories you will be required to hive off trading activity into an arm's-length trading subsidiary which donates all profits back to the parent charity (see section 2.3).

Further information:
Charity Commission (2007) *Trustees, Trading and Tax: How charities may lawfully trade* (CC35). London: Charity Commission.

Stating charity and company status on documents

The Charities Act 2011 requires certain registered charities to state their charitable status on certain documents. Separate provisions are also in place for companies, laid down in the Companies Act 2006.

These requirements depend on the income level of your charity and apply to a wide range of items including fundraising appeals, letterheads, cheque books and emails. There are also restrictions on what information should be displayed. The rules are too detailed to include here.

What happens if the charity fails to comply?
The trustees and staff of charities or companies who are involved in the issue of any document without the necessary details are committing an offence and can face criminal prosecution.

Further information:
For charity requirements, see: *Charity Commission Charities and Fundraising* (CC20). London: Charity Commission.

For company requirements, see: Companies House Incorporation and Names (GP1).

Checklist

Have you checked the Charity Commission's guidance on public benefit to see how it may affect your charity?

If you are not a registered charity, have you checked the criteria and threshold for charity registration? Do you think you may need to register?

Does your board need to review its campaigning activities to make sure that it complies with charity law?

Does your board need to review the trading activity of your charity to make sure that it complies with charity and tax law?

Have you checked the requirements for stating charity and (if appropriate) company status on documents?

2.2

Legal structures

When an organisation is formally established, it will adopt a governing document or set of rules. The form this takes depends on the legal structure of the organisation.

The document usually sets out the following information.

- The name of the organisation.

- Its purposes or 'objects' – this is a statement of what the organisation is set up to do. It is usually worded in quite formal terms – for example an organisation providing training for young people may have for its object 'the advancement of education of young people'.

- Its powers – how it carries out its purposes. As a trustee, you are responsible for the control and management of the administration of the charity and everything you do must further that. Some activities – appointing staff, managing premises, etc – are not directly related to furthering a charity's objects, so to operate effectively, powers are normally set out in the governing document allowing trustees to carry out indirect tasks and delegate work. Some powers are also set out in law.

- Rules about membership of the organisation, if relevant.

- Rules about who can be a trustee and how they are elected or appointed.

- Procedures for calling general meetings (of members) and trustee board meetings.

- Rules about changing the governing document or closing the organisation.

If the organisation is a charity and meets the criteria to register as a charity (see section 2.1) the governing document must be in a form acceptable to the Charity Commission.

Broadly speaking, there are four main common forms of legal structure for charities, each with its own type of governing document (there are also a number of other, less common legal forms).

- Trust

- Unincorporated association

- Company limited by guarantee

- Charitable incorporated organisation (CIO)

Further information:
Charity Commission (November 2014) *Charity Types: How to choose a structure* (CC22a). London: Charity Commission.

Charity Commission (June 2014) *How to Write Your Governing Document* (CC22b). London: Charity Commission.

NCVO and Bates Wells and Braithwaite, Get Legal: Find the form that fits – an online tool that offers clear guidance and information about legal structures.

Trust

A trust is the traditional structure used for setting up a charity. It establishes a relationship between three groups of people: donors, trustees and beneficiaries.

Many older charities are established as trusts and the structure is typically used today to set up:

- grant-giving trusts

- church restoration or building repair funds

- some smaller service-providing organisations

- organisations not requiring a membership structure.

Advantages
- Relatively cheap to set up and run with no ongoing costs.

- Simple to administer, as minimal formalities are required.

- The board is often self-perpetuating.

Disadvantages
- Trusts are unincorporated bodies, so property cannot be held in the name of the charity; it has to be in the names of the trustees. Contracts are also in the names of the trustees.

- When the trustees resign or new trustees are appointed, trust assets have to be transferred into the names of the new group of trustees, which incurs legal expense (although this can be avoided by appointing a corporate body as custodian trustee, which holds the assets in its name for an indefinite period).

- Unlike trustees of charitable companies, trustees of charitable trusts do not have the protection of limited liability. This means that if the trust has insufficient assets to pay its debts or incurs any other liabilities, for instance arising from negligence or libel or under contract, the trustees will personally have to pay them (see section 3.8).

- A trust does not have a membership, like an association, so it may find it harder to demonstrate accountability to users.

- Unless the trust deed includes a power to remove trustees, it can be difficult to remove an unsuitable trustee, or one who has behaved improperly, if they are not willing to resign.

Governing document

A charitable trust's governing document is usually a declaration of trust or a trust deed. This sets out the:

- names of the first trustees

- initial trust fund (this may be nominal)

- name in which the trust will be administered

- charitable objects

- trustees' powers

- eligibility for trusteeship

- procedures for appointing trustees, holding meetings, voting, etc

- amendment and dissolution procedures.

Trustee appointment

The boards of charitable trusts are normally self-perpetuating although they can be appointed for fixed terms by outside bodies. New trustees are usually appointed by the existing trustees, in accordance with eligibility criteria and procedures laid down in the trust deed.

Closing down

Some trusts, such as a church restoration fund, close down once they have reached their target and the assets have been used. Others stop being financially viable, their purpose becomes out of date or beneficiaries can no longer be found. Some close down because they need to change to a more appropriate legal structure, such as a charitable company limited by guarantee.

If the trust deed does not say what must happen to any remaining assets in the event of the charity closing down, the trustees should approach the Charity Commission to transfer the assets to another charity with similar objects.

Unincorporated association

A charitable unincorporated association is a group of people who come together to pursue a shared aim.

It is a particularly suitable structure for membership organisations, where it is important for the members to have close involvement with the running of the charity. It is typically used by:

- self-help groups

- local societies

- local campaigning organisations.

Advantages

- Simple to set up and inexpensive to run.

- Very flexible, as the constitution can be tailored to suit the needs of the organisation, so control can lie in the hands of either the membership as a whole or a smaller group of trustees (frequently called the management committee) elected by the members.

- The constitution can include a power to alter its terms, usually subject to the approval of a certain percentage of its membership.

Disadvantages

- There is no legal personality, so legal transactions cannot be carried out in the name of the charity. A small group of holding trustees or a custodian trustee (a corporate body such as the Official Custodian for Charities) who do not have any of the responsibilities of trusteeship must be appointed to hold the assets in their names.

- Trustees have unlimited liability, so if the association has insufficient assets to pay its debts, or incurs any other liabilities (eg arising from negligence or libel or under breach of contract) the trustees will personally have to pay them (see section 3.8).

- In exceptional instances the personal liability can extend to the wider membership.

- Relevant law is quite complicated, as there is no statute applicable.

Governing document

An unincorporated association will usually have a constitution, which sets out:

- the name in which the association will be administered

- charitable objects

- trustees' powers

- criteria for membership and voting rights

- procedures for electing trustees, holding meetings, etc

- financial matters

- amendment and dissolution procedures.

Trustee appointment

Trustees will normally be elected from the membership, following procedures set out in the constitution. They are often appointed by outside bodies, such as a local authority, or may be *ex officio*, which means they are automatically trustees because of the office they hold, eg a mayor or a vicar. There is often, a power enabling the board to co-opt a certain number of trustees in addition to the elected and appointed trustees.

Closing down

Some unincorporated associations close down because they have grown considerably and now employ staff and occupy premises, so the limitation of trustees' liability offered by a company limited by guarantee becomes desirable. Others close as members lose interest or when the value of their innovative services is recognised and their provision is taken over by a statutory body such as a local authority.

If the constitution does not say what must happen to any remaining assets if the charity closes down, the trustees should apply to the Charity Commission for guidance to transfer the assets to another charity with similar objects.

Company limited by guarantee

A charitable company is a limited company set up to carry out charitable activities. The trustees of a charitable company enjoy the protection of limited liability.

Advantages

- Has legal status of being incorporated with its own legal personality.

- Property can be owned by the charity, so names on legal documents do not have to be changed every time there is a change of trustees.

- Has membership instead of shareholders, and members all guarantee to pay a nominal sum of usually £1 or £5 if the company becomes insolvent.

- Trustees and members of charitable companies have limited liability (see section 3.8).

Disadvantages

- Extra cost of setting up a company.

- Additional bureaucracy involved in meeting the requirements of company law.

- The register of members is available to the public as are the names of directors. However the directors' private addresses need no longer be available to the public.

Governing document

The document that sets out the purpose of a charitable company and the way in which it will run its affairs is in the memorandum and articles of association.

Under the Companies Act 2006, most of the detail formerly included in the memorandum of association, such as the objects and powers clauses, is now in the articles of association and the memorandum has become a short document mainly for the purpose of incorporation.

The articles of association also give the rules and regulations that govern the internal proceedings of the company. These usually include:

- membership of the company

- the number of trustees, how they are elected, for what period and restrictions on who can become a trustee

- procedures for holding meetings – including annual and extraordinary general meetings and for voting

- financial and auditing procedures

- powers to delegate to staff or committees

- administrative provisions, eg notices, indemnities, standing orders.

Trustee appointment

The articles set out the procedures for the nomination and election of trustees, whether from within or outside the membership, and/or the appointment of trustees by outside bodies.

The articles also set out who can become a member of the company, the procedure for becoming a member and the procedure for expelling a member.

When using the term 'member', it is important to differentiate between those who are in a strict legal sense the members of the charitable company, usually entitled to elect the trustees, and when the term is used more colloquially to mean someone who pays an annual 'membership' subscription or is receiving services from the charity, who may be only 'affiliate' or 'associate' members with no legal status.

Closing down

If a charitable company goes into voluntary liquidation, the surplus assets must be distributed for exclusively charitable purposes. A formal winding-up process must be carried out by a duly appointed liquidator but usually a shorter striking off procedure will be followed.

Charitable incorporated organisation

This is a new legal structure for charities now covered by the Charities Act 2011 and regulations made under the Act. The charitable incorporated organisation (CIO) structure allows charities to have the benefits of incorporation and be regulated solely by the Charity Commission, and not by Companies House. The advantage of this new form of legal structure for charities is that it is designed specifically for charities, so they will no longer need to be regulated by two separate bodies.

A CIO is only created once it is registered with the Charity Commission, and there is a single application for registration. Every CIO must have a two-tier structure with both trustees and members, but there are two forms: the foundation model, where the trustees are the only voting members and the association model, where there is a wider voting membership.

As the CIO is new, it is not yet clear who will use it but it is likely to be more suitable for smaller and medium-sized charities.

Advantages
• Has legal status of being incorporated with its own legal personality.

• The trustees and members of the CIO have limited liability (see section 3.8).

• Only one application is needed for both incorporation and charity registration.

• There is a single regulator.

• The CIO only has to comply with charity law.

• Members have a qualified duty to act in the best interest of the charity.

• The register of members is not open to the public.

• Decision-making may be by consensus.

• There are currently no registration fee and no late filing fees.

• There is more flexibility around members' rights.

• CIOs with an annual income under £250,000 (as at 2014) can choose to prepare accounts on a receipts and payments basis.

Disadvantages
• CIO is a new, untested legal structure, and there are still some questions about how some of the provisions, eg dissolution and insolvency, will work in practice.

• CIOs have the power to borrow, and banks should be prepared to lend for property purchases. However there is no public Register of Charges, so banks and other financial institutions may be unwilling to lend for other purposes, eg overdrafts.

• As registration creates the CIO, the organisation is in limbo during the application process, which may take some time in a complex case. During this time there is no legal personality.

• The Charities Act does not give members the right to call a meeting, vote by proxy, remove trustees or receive accounts, but these can all be included in the constitution.

• Amendments to the constitution require member approval, which must be unanimous if not at a meeting.

Governing document
The governing document is a constitution. The Charity Commission has model constitutions available on its website for the foundation model (where the trustees are the only members) and one for the association model (where there is a wider membership). You can draft your own constitution, but it must cover a number of areas set out in the Charities Act 2011 and Regulations; the Charity Commission advises that registration is likely to be quicker if you follow their model.

The main areas to be covered include:

• name

• purposes

• whether the principal office is in England or Wales

• whether members are liable to make a contribution if wound up and if so how much

• the names of the first charity trustees

• membership provisions, eg who is eligible, how to become a member and how termination of membership works

- procedures for members' meetings

- procedures for decision making

- electronic communication

- appointment, eligibility and retirement of charity trustees

- the extent to which a trustee may benefit subject to the Charities Act 2011

- procedures for trustee meetings

- application of charity's property on dissolution.

Trustee appointment

How trustees will be appointed must be explained in the constitution. If the CIO is using the association model, it is likely that some or all of the trustees will be elected by the voting membership. If the CIO is using the foundation model, appointment of trustees is likely to be closer to that of the trust with a self-perpetuating trusteeship.

Closing down

Every CIO constitution must include a provision which sets out how the property will be applied for charitable purposes on dissolution.

A CIO can be wound up in four different ways:

- a solvent dissolution

- a merger with another CIO

- an insolvent dissolution

- dissolution by the Charity Commission.

The procedures for dissolution are set out in the CIO (Insolvency and Dissolution) Regulations 2012. A solvent dissolution will normally require a resolution passed by members, a declaration by the trustees that all the debts and liabilities have been paid and an application to the Charity Commission. The procedures for an insolvent liquidation are largely taken from the insolvency regime for companies. A CIO can be wound up by the Charity Commission in several circumstances, including where the Commission considers the CIO has ceased to operate or has ceased to be a charity.

Conversion

The Charities Act 2011 provides for conversion to the CIO by both unincorporated and incorporated charities.

Conversion from an unincorporated charity to a CIO involves setting up a new entity and transferring property over either by simple resolution or by more detailed transfer deed with indemnities for liabilities. The procedure is similar to the incorporation of an unincorporated charity to a charitable company.

Conversion from a charitable company to a CIO is not yet possible, but is likely to be introduced by the end of 2014. The conversion procedure will be simpler and will enable the same legal entity to change its identity from a company to a CIO. A new constitution will need to be adopted in place of the memorandum and articles of association. The full details of the process and the procedures to be adopted will be set out in new regulations.

Further information:
'Starting a charity' pages of the Charity Commission website, which includes a number of helpful FAQs).

Industrial and Provident Society (IPS)

An IPS is another form of incorporation. Until the Charities Act 2006 it could not be a registered charity but could have charitable status as an exempt charity. Under the Charities Act 2011 some IPSs retain their exempt status (including housing associations), but others will now be required to register with the Charity Commission. An IPS is defined as a society for the benefit of the community and should carry on a business, industry or trade. This legal framework is commonly used by housing associations.

Further information:
Financial Conduct Authority website.

Drawing up a governing document

To simplify the process of drawing up a governing document, the Charity Commission has approved the use of:

- model governing documents, containing many of the standard provisions suitable for charities

- model governing documents for the branches or affiliated organisations of certain national bodies

- model objects clauses.

Further information:
'Starting a charity' pages of the Charity Commission website.

Amending a governing document

There may be times when a charity finds its original purposes – perhaps agreed many decades ago – no longer fully reflect the environment in which it operates or that its procedures for electing or appointing trustees have become unwieldy. Changes in legislation may also mean that an organisation's procedures for, say, holding general meetings are no longer up to date.

These are all examples of situations where a charity may look to review and, if necessary, amend provisions in its governing document.

Amending your charity's governing document is a significant piece of work, involving the approval of members (if your charity has a membership) and in some cases the prior approval of the Charity Commission.

Where is our amendment clause in our governing document?
Companies limited by guarantee have a statutory power of amendment in the Companies Act 2006. This means that there may not be an amendment clause in your governing document.

Some trust deeds contain a power to vary the deed. Similarly, the constitution of many unincorporated associations will include a power to alter its terms, usually subject to the approval of a certain percentage of the membership. Unincorporated charities that do not have a specific power to amend their governing document may be able to rely on the power to modify powers and procedures under section 280 of the Charities Act 2011. In other cases you will need to apply to the Charity Commission for a scheme.

Is Charity Commission approval required to amend our governing document?
Most charities will require the consent of the Charity Commission to any change to the objects and provisions conferring benefits to the trustees. In the case of charitable companies, this is a statutory requirement.

Do we need to call a general meeting to approve changes?
If your charity has a membership, then members will normally be required to approve any proposed change to the governing document at a general meeting. Usually, the procedures for calling a meeting and the percentage of members present and voting required to approve the amendment are set out in the governing document.

Whom should we notify?
The Charity Commission must be informed of the change and may need to give prior approval.

Companies limited by guarantee must inform Companies House of the change.

> **Further information:**
> Charity Commission (2011) *Changing your Charity's Governing Document* (CC36). London: Charity Commission.

Incorporation

It is quite common for charities to move from an unincorporated association or trust structure to a company limited by guarantee structure. This is because the company structure can be more suitable as an organisation grows in size and complexity. If your organisation is unincorporated but employs staff, occupies property and/or has significant contractual arrangements, you may consider moving to a company structure. In a company, the organisation has its own legal identity, which means that contractual arrangements can be made in the name of the company, not the name of the trustees, and hence provides trustees some (although not comprehensive – see Chapter 3) protection from personal financial liability.

The process of moving to a company structure is called 'incorporation' and involves setting up a new company limited by guarantee, registering it as a charity and then transferring assets and liabilities from the unincorporated organisation to the new company organisation. Because of the complexity of the process, it is recommended you seek professional advice before taking any action.

> **Further information:**
> Becoming a charitable company' or 'CIO' pages of the Charity Commission website (see 'Starting a charity/As your charity grows').

2.3

Checklist

Have all trustees received a copy of the governing document?

Are all trustees familiar with the objects of the organisation?

Do trustees understand the provisions of your governing document?

Have you reviewed your governing document recently to ensure the objects reflect your current and planned work, and the administrative provisions (appointment of trustees, etc) are workable and meet your needs?

Are you confident that your organisation's current legal structure best meets the organisation's needs?

Do you need to consider changing your legal structure?

Branches and subsidiaries

Branches

Many charities have local groups or branches. These may fundraise only, provide services, carry out advice and campaigning work or operate as self-help groups. Some of these may not themselves be charitable – for example social clubs for the benefit of members but which also raise funds for the main charity. The degree of control and autonomy that the branches have varies considerably from charity to charity.

Are trustees responsible for the activities of local groups?

If you are a trustee of the national or 'parent' charity, you need to know what the relationship is to any local groups.

In some instances the local group will be part of the national charity. If this is the case, then the trustees of the national charity will be responsible for all the activities and actions of the local groups or branches.

Other charities, such as Age UK and Mencap, have a structure in which all local groups are separate, autonomous organisations, each registered as a charity. Each local group has its own trustees and the trustees of the national charity are not responsible for the activities of the local groups. Many such organisations have membership agreements between the national charity and local organisations.

If you are not sure about the relationship between the national charity and local branches, check your governing document. If you are still unsure, seek advice from the Charity Commission.

If you are a trustee of a national charity with dependent local groups you should:

- establish an adequate system for overseeing and monitoring local groups

- consider having a written code of conduct for each local group

- ensure that local groups state that they are a registered charity on all their stationery, appeal documents, cheques, invoices and receipts

- provide accounting returns which have to be consolidated into the national accounts

- consider the needs of local groups when allocating reserves.

If you are a trustee of an autonomous local organisation you should:

- have your own governing body and produce your own accounts

- register with the Charity Commission if your organisation has exclusively charitable purposes and meets the minimum requirements for registration

- comply with legislation for PAYE, VAT and other fiscal or legal requirements

- consider having a written agreement between autonomous local groups and the 'parent' charity.

Trustees of autonomous local organisations should be aware that mismanagement of their affairs could result not only in their personal liability, but also in adverse publicity that could be damaging for the national charity.

Checklist

Are you a trustee of a charity with branches?

Are the branches separate legal entities?

If your charity has dependent branches, does your board need to review how it exercises its responsibilities for the activities of the branches and how the branches ensure their accountability to the trustees?

If your charity has branches that are separate legal entities, does your board need to review the relationships between local branches and the national charity – for example membership agreements that may exist between the national charity and local branches?

Subsidiaries

Some charities have a separate, non-charitable subsidiary. This can occur if your charity wishes to benefit from continuous trading activity that is not directly related to its objects or where it wants to isolate the risk. Trustees should get detailed legal advice before setting up a wholly owned trading company. Some charities have separate charitable subsidiaries. For example, a 'parent' charity could establish one or more charitable subsidiaries to deliver a range of specialist or complex services. The charitable subsidiaries would have their own boards of trustees to provide a focus on the subsidiary's work but would also benefit from the support of the parent charity.

For further information
Charity Commission (2009)
*Collaborative Working and Mergers:
An introduction* (CC34). London:
Charity Commission.

Trading

Trustees should obtain detailed legal advice before setting up a wholly owned trading company. In particular, advice should be sought on any deeds of covenant and the circumstances in which a charity can lend money to its trading arm. The charity's governing document will need to include powers for the trustees to invest in the shares of a private company. The consent of HM Revenue and Customs may be required if the charity is not to lose some tax exemptions. Expert advice will be needed on dealing with the financing of the wholly owned trading company.

As a matter of charity law and good practice you should ensure that:

- the financial structures of the charity and any trading subsidiaries are kept separate

- the interests of the charity do not become dominated by those of the trading subsidiary

- any loans made to a trading subsidiary are within the terms of the charity's governing document, are at a commercial rate of interest and are properly secured

- if the charity and the trading subsidiary share premises, equipment or staff, care is taken to apportion costs accurately between them, to avoid any hidden subsidy of the trading company by the charity.

Checklist

Does your charity have a non-charitable trading subsidiary?

Have you carried out a review of your subsidiaries?

Are your non-charitable trading subsidiaries or associates adequately capitalised without putting the funds of your charity at risk?

Would you be able to recover your entire investment if you now disposed of your trading company?

3

Duties and responsibilities of trustees

As a trustee, you must make sure that your organisation:

- pursues its objects or purposes, as set out in its governing document

- uses its assets exclusively to pursue those aims

- acts in the interests of its beneficiaries.

You should also:

- take an active part in the charity

- avoid conflict with your personal interests

- not profit from your role unless it has been authorised.

More guidance on the role of the board and its relationship with staff can be found in Chapter 4.

3.1

Where day-to-day management and operations are delegated to staff or volunteers, your board remains responsible for supervising the chief executive (and sometimes other staff) and ensuring that the organisation is being well managed and operating within agreed policies, the law and its budget.

In order to carry out its role, the board must:

- meet as often as is necessary for the proper administration of the charity

- consider the need for professional and other expert advice where necessary.

Tip: It is a good idea to draw up a role description for a trustee, setting out their duties and responsibilities. A model role description, including role descriptions for trustees with specific roles is available in section 4.1.

Duty to comply with the governing document

Trustees must comply with the provisions of their governing document (see section 2.2). They should be familiar with its provisions, in particular with the stated charitable objects.

Trustees have a duty to act within the objects of the charity and to apply the charity's assets exclusively to pursue those objects. It is a breach of trust to undertake any activities outside the objects. You could be held personally liable to repay to the charity any money spent on activities outside the objects.

In addition to your statutory powers and limitations, you will usually have additional powers to pursue the charity's aims as set out in the governing document. For example, the governing document usually defines the powers that trustees have to delegate work to committees or staff, but this does not mean that they have to delegate. You should make sure that you know your powers to act and do not exceed them.

Some organisations also have written rules or standing orders for internal procedural matters, such as the conduct of board meetings, the composition of the board and other committees, and the election or appointment of new trustees. You will need to be familiar with and follow these rules, which must not contradict or repeal anything contained in the governing document. The standing orders can be amended in accordance with the procedure set out in the governing document.

3.2

Duty of care

The Charity Commission states that trustees must: *'use reasonable care and skill in their work as trustees, using their personal skills and experience as needed to ensure that the charity is well-run and efficient; and consider getting external professional advice on all matters where there may be material risk to the charity, or where the trustees may be in breach of their duties'.*[1]

To 'use reasonable care and skill' means allowing for:

- any special knowledge or experience a person has or says they have; and

- any special knowledge it is reasonable to expect from a business or professional person when acting in either capacity.

The level of competence and proficiency required of a trustee will vary according to the level of expertise the person has.

If you do not seek advice on matters on which you are not an expert, be they legal, financial or managerial, you could be regarded as having acted imprudently and you may be personally liable for the consequences. The Charities Act 2011 requires you to seek professional advice in some instances, for example, in relation to certain land transactions. When you do seek advice, you should keep copies of relevant correspondence and/or notes of conversations.

The Trustee Act 2000 introduced a new statutory duty to create certainty and consistency about the standard expected from a trustee in relation to investment powers (see Chapter 7).

3.3

Duty to comply with the law

Trustees must ensure the organisation complies with laws that may be relevant to its work. Such laws will vary from organisation to organisation depending on size and activities, but often include:

- charity law and the requirements of the Charity Commission (see following page)

- company law and the requirements of Companies House (see following page)

- Industrial and provident society law and the requirements of the Financial Conduct Authority

- employment law (see Chapter 11)

- health and safety legislation (see section 9.3)

- data protection legislation (see section 10.3)

- legislation against discrimination on grounds of race, disability, gender and other factors (see section 12.1)

- any other legislation that may apply to particular organisations, such as that relating to fundraising, the protection of children or vulnerable adults, the provision of health or care services, the provision of financial advice, housing and tenancy law and others.

---

1   Charity Commission publication
    *The Essential Trustee: What you need
    to know* (CC3). Crown Copyright.

As a trustee you are not expected to have detailed knowledge of this legislation. However, you should be aware that legislation exists and, where necessary, you should be satisfied that someone is responsible for making sure that effective compliance systems are in place. The Code of Governance confirms that trustees *'must ensure through appropriate policies, procedures and reporting mechanisms that the organisation understands and complies with all legal and regulatory requirements which apply to the organisation.'*

Charity law

Under charity law, all trustees must be eligible for trusteeship (see section 1.1). You must follow the Charity Commission's disclosure, reporting and accounting requirements, including those included in the Charities Act 2011. Failure to do this is a criminal offence. You must keep within the law on trading, political activities and fundraising.

Company law

Trustees of a charitable company are also company directors and must comply with the legal requirements relating to company directors. You must ensure that your charity keeps up to date with its company returns and record keeping.

You must act in the best interests of the company, even where this conflicts with your private or other interests. You must not continue trading as a company if you know, or should have known, that your company is insolvent.

The Companies Act 2006 sets out the duties of company directors. These are:

• to act within the company's powers

• to promote the success of the company for the benefit of its members as a whole; in the case of a charitable company, this will mean to achieve its charitable purposes including the need to consider the company's actions on the community and environment

• to exercise independent judgment

• to exercise reasonable care, skill and diligence

• to avoid conflicts of interest

• not to accept benefits from third parties

• to declare an interest in proposed transactions and arrangements.

Checklist

If your charity is established as a company, have you made all trustees aware of their statutory duties as company directors?

Does your board need to check that there is someone responsible for ensuring that the charity complies with the law, particularly with the requirements of the Charities Act 2011 and Companies Act 2006?

3.4

Duty to protect the charity's property

Trustees have a duty to protect all the assets belonging to the charity, for example by ensuring that there are adequate financial controls and that any land or buildings the charity owns are well maintained and insured.

Any funds, land, buildings or other assets that form part of the charity's permanent endowment (property that the trustees may not spend as if it were income) cannot usually be expended without the Charity Commission's consent in accordance with provisions of the Charities Act 2011. If they are investment assets they should be invested to produce a good income while protecting the real value of the capital. Section 4 of the Trusts (Capital and Income) Act 2013 amended the Charities Act 2013 to give charities with permanent endowment the power to adopt a total return approach to investment and spend part of the capital gain.

The Charity Commission has produced guidance under the 2013 Act to provide a framework for the exercise of the statutory power. This is a complex area and more detail, including the guidance, can be found on the Charity Commission's website.

Trustees also have a duty to protect the charity's reputation and its intellectual property, such as trademarks and databases.

Further information:
Charity Commission (November 2013) *Total Return Investment for Permanently Endowed Charities.* London: Charity Commission.

3.5

Duty to act in the interests of beneficiaries and avoid conflicts of interest

When you sit down at the board meeting table, all of your other interests have to be left outside or, if they can't, they need to be properly managed.

The law is quite clear – your first duty as a trustee is to the charity's beneficiaries, which means you must act in the interests of the charity as a whole. You must remain independent and not come under the influence of another organisation. Anything that might conflict – or be perceived to conflict – with your duty as a trustee should be managed using a conflicts of interest policy. A good test is to ask if the charity's reputation would be damaged if your connection with a member of staff, a firm of professional advisers or a building company, for example, were made public. Conflicts of interest relate not only to the charity trustee, but also to connected persons (family members or businesses connected to the trustee).

This is a very important issue and the Charity Commission has recently produced detailed new guidance for charity trustees following extensive consultation.

Situations where a conflict of interest may occur

- Where a trustee may benefit personally. Trustees cannot benefit beyond what is allowed by law and permitted in the charity' governing document. This restriction also applies to people connected with the trustee. This situation could include, for example, a trustee:

  - receiving payment for a particular service they provide to the charity

  - also using the charity's services and benefiting personally (eg receiving a grant).

- Where a trustee's loyalties are divided between the charity and another organisation (or perhaps a personal situation). Inevitably, in practice, trustees have a wide range of interests in private, public and professional life, and these interests might, on occasions, conflict. For example, local councillors sometimes sit on the boards of organisations that are funded by the local authority to which they are members.

Dealing with conflicts of interest

Any potential conflict of interest should be carefully considered and managed in the correct way. Your governing document will often include provisions for the management of conflicts of interest. It is also good practice to have an agreed policy and an agreed practice that trustees should follow when considering conflicts of interest. This can include:

- a code of conduct for trustees (see page 46)

- a register of interests disclosing potential personal interests

- a procedure for identifying conflicts and withdrawing from discussion and decision-making and the minuting of this process (this should also extend to the discussion and decisions).

An example conflicts-of-interest procedure

- Any trustee who has a financial interest in a matter under discussion should declare the nature of his or her interest and withdraw from the room, unless he or she has a dispensation to speak.

- If a trustee has any interest in the matter under discussion that creates a real danger of bias, that is, the interest affects him or her, or a member of his or her household, more than the generality affected by the decision, he or she should declare the nature of the interest and withdraw from the room, unless he or she has a dispensation to speak.

- If a trustee has any other interest that does not create a real danger of bias but might reasonably cause others to think it could influence their decision, he or she should declare the nature of the interest, but may remain in the room, participate in the discussion, and vote if he or she wishes.

- If in any doubt about the application of these rules, he or she should consult with the chair.

- It is recommended that trustees' interests are listed in a register.

- If conflicts of interest are so frequent as to limit an individual's usefulness as a trustee, then he or she must stand down from one of the posts.

Conflicts of interest: other issues to consider

The Companies Act 2006 includes provisions for conflicts of interest for company directors. There are duties to avoid conflicts of interest, not to accept benefits from third parties and to declare an interest in proposed transactions. There is also a requirement to disclose the nature and extent of interests in an existing transaction or arrangement. This includes transactions between the company and the directors where there are special rules for charitable companies. There are detailed rules for this and the procedures required for disclosure. It is good practice to include an item for disclosure of any interest on every board meeting agenda.

If the company's articles of association (in its governing document) include provisions for dealing with conflicts of interest, and the directors follow them, they will be protected from breach of their statutory duties.

The articles of association may also include a provision for the directors to authorise a conflict. Again, there are detailed rules for this situation, which are outside the scope of this book.

Further information:
Charity Commission (2014)
Conflicts of Interest: A guide for Charity Trustees (CC29). London: Charity Commission.

Checklist

Do you have a conflicts-of-interest policy for trustees?

If you are a charitable company are you aware of the new provisions under the Companies Act 2006 and do your articles include procedures to deal with conflicts of interest?

3.6

3.7

Duty to act collectively

Trustees are jointly and severally responsible for the activities of the charity and must act together. No trustee acting alone can bind his or her fellow trustees, unless specifically authorised to do so.

Trustee boards operate collectively, and decisions are taken together. The board's decisions do not have to be unanimous. Therefore the majority bind the minority, and you are bound by the decisions of your fellow trustees even if you were absent from a meeting. If you vote against a decision, make sure your vote is recorded in the minutes and if the matter is serious, for example if you think the charity is going to spend resources on something outside its objects (which would be a breach of trust), you should consider resignation (see section 3.8).

Meetings are the formal setting for all trustee decisions. Trustees should meet often enough to carry out their business of governing the charity. Trustees act collectively and they cannot act individually in their role as trustee unless authorised. In practice, trustees are often involved in aspects of a charity's work (eg on committees, as advisers or as volunteers to specific services) and this should be encouraged, but it should also be made clear which role the trustee is in.

There are restrictions over the use of electronic or 'virtual' meetings (see Chapter 21).

Duty not to financially benefit unless authorised

The voluntary principle – that trustees serve primarily to benefit others, rather than for personal gain – is one of the defining principles that distinguish charities from other types of organisation. According to the Charity Commission, the vast majority of trustees in the country carry out this principle by serving on their boards without receiving payment of any kind – perhaps with only their basic out-of-pocket expenses covered.

What does the voluntary principle of trusteeship mean in practice?

According to the Charity Commission, it means that *'trustees must not put themselves in a position where their personal interests conflict with their duty to act in the interests of the charity unless authorised to do so'.*[2]

In practice, the voluntary principle means that there are restrictions over how far trustees can receive benefits from the charity. Restrictions on benefits cover the following situations.

- Payment for serving as a trustee. There is no general power in law to allow this type of payment, and special authority would need to be given by the governing document, the Charity Commission or the courts. Any organisation considering paying their trustees to 'be a trustee' would need to demonstrate that it is 'clearly in the interests of the charity and provides a significant and clear advantage over all other options'. Authority to pay a trustee in this

way is only given in exceptional circumstances, for example where a charity's work is very complex and trusteeship carries a very high burden.

- Where an employee of the charity is also a trustee. It is rare for a trustee also to be an employee and there is no general power to allow this. Authority would need to be given by an express clause in the governing document or by the Charity Commission. There are some types of charity where this situation is more common, for example schools often include the head teacher as a trustee and religious charities often include the spiritual leader as a trustee. There have also been recent cases where the Charity Commission has authorised a chief executive to serve as a trustee in the same organisation. It is important to note that if a trustee resigns in order to take up a paid position in the charity, Charity Commission approval may also be needed (see Charity Commission publication Trustee Expenses and Payments (CC11) (2012)). Approval must also be obtained where a trustee's spouse or partner becomes a paid employee if they have shared finances.

2 Charity Commission (2012) *Trustee Expenses and Payments* (CC11). London: Charity Commission.

• Payment to a trustee for services provided for the charity (eg providing legal advice or electrical services). The Charities Act 2011 allows trustees to be paid for goods or a service they may provide to the charity (not as an employee), provided that the governing document does not expressly prohibit payment and provided that certain conditions are met. These conditions include that the payment is reasonable and in the best interests of the charity, ensuring a written agreement exists over the payment, that the trustee to be paid is not involved in the decision and that only a minority of trustees are paid (there are other conditions and it is recommended you consult Charity Commission publication Trustee Expenses and Payments (CC11) (2012)).

• Payment to 'connected persons' or businesses. Most of the restrictions over payment also apply to family members or businesses connected with a trustee.

• Payment in kind. Payment does not just involve a financial transaction, for example payment could include where a trustee is given free use of office space for their business in return for joining the board or where a trustee is also a service user and receives free use of facilities for which service users normally have to pay.

• Payments that may sometimes be perceived as being expenses. For example payment for loss of earnings or 'honoraria' payments are considered to be payments.

Can I claim back out-of-pocket expenses?

Yes, provided the organisation's governing document does not expressly prohibit this (which is unusual).

Expenses that may be reimbursed are actual costs that a trustee has incurred in their role and can include items such as travel, meals, childcare whilst at trustee meetings, postage and telephone calls. Payments to trustees above actual expenses incurred and those that do not relate to legitimate trustee activities cannot be treated as expenses. Examples of these are travel costs for a spouse or payment of telephone bills unrelated to the charity.

Any payments that are excessive or are not genuine and reasonable out-of-pocket expenses will be treated as income and be subject to tax as with other forms of income. A trustee who receives an unauthorised payment may be required to pay it back to the charity. The Charity Commission provides further guidance on what are permitted expenses in *Trustee Expenses and Payments* (CC11) (2012).

Payments – issues to consider

The Charity Commission recommends that any departure from the voluntary principle of trusteeship should be given very careful consideration, and be carried out with the proper authority. This may involve seeking prior Charity Commission approval.

Drawing up a trustee expenses policy
– good practice guidelines
- Explain which items are legitimate expense claims, for example travel, childcare, accommodation, etc.

- Only reimburse actual costs, and pay against receipts. Extra money may be regarded as taxable income (see above).

- Include an expenses claim form with every agenda. Trustees can always donate their expenses back and if they are a taxpayer the charity can reclaim the tax under Gift Aid.

Checklist for those considering paying a trustee (from the Charity Commission)
- Who will receive the payment – will it be a trustee, or a person or business connected with a trustee?

- What is the payment expected to cover?

- Is the payment clearly in the best interests of the charity?

- Is there a legal authority for it?

- What conditions must be met if the payment is to be made?

- How will any conflict of interest be managed?

Further information
Charity Commission (2012) *Trustee Expenses and Payments* (CC11). London: Charity Commission.

Checklist

Is payment of trustees likely to be an issue for your board?

If so, have you checked your governing document to see what it says about payment of trustees?

If so, have you familiarised yourself with the Charity Commission's guidance and ensured that it is followed?

3.8

Trustee liability

Trustees are often concerned about their personal liability. This section summarises the types of liability that trustees may incur.

Remember... keep it in perspective!
Before describing the different types of liability that trustees may incur, it is important to point out that very few trustees who have acted honestly have suffered financial loss as a result of their trusteeship. There are risks, but they should be kept in proportion. When breaches of trust (see below) have been committed as the result of an honest mistake, or when trustees have been found wanting in the degree of control they exercised over staff, the Charity Commission has rarely required trustees to make good any loss. Insurance will not protect you from liability incurred as a result of a breach of trust knowingly committed.

What are the personal liabilities of trustees?

Trustees of all types of charities can be held personally liable for:

• breach of trust under charity law (this includes spending the charity's money on an activity that is outside the charity's legal objects, carrying out unpermitted political activity, fraud, serious negligence or a trustee receiving personal benefit) (see below)

• acting as charity trustees when disqualified

• failure to comply with relevant statutory requirements in areas such as health and safety, trade descriptions and financial services

• failure to deduct an employee's PAYE.

The degree of risk of personal liability will vary according to the activity of your charity. In general, charities engaged in service provision will face greater risks than those involved in grant making.

Liability for breach of trust

Trustees may be liable for a breach of trust, for example if they distribute assets on causes falling outside the express objects of the charity, or fail prudently to protect the trust property. If trustees are found to be in breach of trust, they may be required by the Charity Commission or the court to make good the losses to the charity which arose as a result of breach of trust.

All trustees, regardless of the charity's legal structure, may be jointly and severally liable for a breach of trust. However, it is important not to get the risk of being found in breach of trust out of proportion; it is unlikely that the trustees of a well-run charity will be found personally liable if they have acted honestly and reasonably. Trustees can apply to the Charity Commission for relief from personal liability if they have acted honestly and reasonably.

The Charity Commission's position is even more robust. In its booklet *The Essential Trustee* (CC3), it states that:

'If trustees act prudently, lawfully and in accordance with the governing document, then any liabilities (ie debts or financial obligations) that they incur as trustees can normally be met out of the charity's resources.'

Steps you can take to minimise the risk of acting in breach of trust include:

- Ensure the organisation acts in accordance with the requirements of its governing document.

- Ensure the organisation is well managed and follows good practice.

- Comply with all relevant legislation.

- Take appropriate legal or other professional advice when you don't have enough information to make a decision.

Liability for the debts and liabilities of the organisation

As well as for breach of trust, trustees may in some circumstances be personally liable for the debts and other liabilities of the charity. The extent to which this is the case depends on whether the charity is a trust, an unincorporated association, a company or a CIO.

Trusts and unincorporated associations

Trusts and unincorporated associations do not have their own independent legal personality. This means that the trust or unincorporated association cannot contract on its own account. If the trustees enter into any contractual or other arrangements they must do so by contracting in their capacity as trustees. As a result of this, they are personally liable to settle any debts or other liabilities that occur as a result of the arrangement entered into. Liabilities of this type might include fees for professional services, repairing covenants or rent under a lease, damages for breach of contract, etc.

If the trustees have acted honestly and reasonably, they will usually be entitled to be indemnified against their liability from the assets of the trust or unincorporated association. However, if the charity does not have sufficient assets to meet the liability, then the trustees will still be jointly and severally liable to any shortfall. If trustees are concerned about any potential liability of this type, for example if the organisation is taking on significant responsibilities such as employees or premises, then one option is to incorporate as a company limited by guarantee or CIO (see following page).

Charitable companies

Charitable companies have their own legal personality, so that contracts and other legal relationships can be entered into by the company. Charitable companies also afford trustees limited liability. This is because the members of the company (who may or may not also be trustees/company directors) will typically guarantee that, in the event of the winding up of the company, they will contribute a nominal amount, usually £1 or £5, towards its assets.

This means that, unlike with an unincorporated association or a trust, the trustees of a charitable company cannot be personally liable for the debts of the company, or liable in contract or tort (a legal term covering civil wrongs such as negligence or liability).

However, the benefits of becoming an incorporated charity and limiting liability are not as comprehensive as is sometimes thought. Trustees of a charitable company can still be personally liable for the activities of the organisation in certain circumstances, as this section explains, and can be held liable for certain breaches relating to their duties as company directors, including:

- breach of their fiduciary and statutory duties as company directors (for example using the charitable company's assets to procure an unauthorised benefit for the trustees)

- wrongful trading under the Insolvency Act 1986 (ie continuing to trade when you know, or ought to have known, that there was no reasonable prospect of avoiding going into insolvent liquidation) (this has never yet happened to trustees of a charitable company)

- fraudulent trading – where a trustee deliberately seeks to defraud a creditor when the company is insolvent or about to become insolvent

- acting as a company director when disqualified

- other breaches listed in the section 'What are the personal liabilities of trustees?' (see page 42).

Charitable incorporated organisations

Trustees of CIOs have similar protection from liability to that of directors of charitable companies.

Provisions of the Insolvency Act have been applied to CIOs by regulation, so liability for wrongful and fraudulent trading will also apply.

How does liability relate to trustees' terms of office?

The Charity Commission normally expects new trustees to assume responsibility for decisions made by the board of trustees in the past. However, new trustees do not have to assume responsibility for past breaches of the charity's trusts. If new trustees discover, when they start, that the charity is currently acting in breach of trust, they must take steps to remedy the situation or else they too will become liable for the breach.

Trustees do not stop being liable for their actions in breach of trust when they retire or resign; they will remain liable for any breaches of trust committed during their term of office. This means that if the Charity Commission instigates an enquiry into the activities of a charity during 2005 and decided that, for example, the trustees had spent some of the charity's assets on activities outside their charitable objects, then they could require the people who were trustees in 2005 to repay to the charity the amount that was misspent.

What should trustees do if a bank asks for a personal guarantee?

If your charity approaches a bank or other lender for a loan, the trustees may be asked for personal guarantees as well as any agreement with the charity. If the charity subsequently gets into financial difficulty, the trustee can be left with a personal liability. You should always take legal advice before agreeing to provide a personal guarantee.

What steps can trustees take to protect themselves?

There are a number of ways in which trustees can limit the risk of personal liability.

- Good management practice: this, in particular financial management and clear procedures, is the starting point for risk limitation.

- Clear roles and responsibilities: job descriptions and induction procedures for trustees are important, as are clear lines of responsibility, budgetary guidelines and good communication.

- Records of decisions taken: you should make your own notes of the board's decisions and check them against the minutes before agreeing them. The minutes are the legal record of the board's decisions.

- Provisions in your governing document: you can have express provisions put in the governing documents that exempt trustees from personal liability to the charity if they act reasonably and make an honest mistake that results in loss to the charity.

- Insurance: trustees may take out trustee liability insurance. They may pay the premiums themselves or, under the Charities Act 2011, in most circumstances (unless prohibited by the governing document) the costs can be met by the charity (see section 9.2).

- Incorporation: becoming a company limited by guarantee can offer protection to trustees against liability for debts incurred by the charity.

- Contingency funds: these can be built up so that there are sufficient reserves to meet potential liabilities such as premature termination of leases or staff redundancy costs.

- Professional advice: this should be obtained by the board if there is any doubt about the correct course of action to be taken.

- Board development: your board should consider having a continuous programme of board development – trustee training and governance reviews – to keep up to date with changes in law and practice.

Can trustees limit their liability by distancing themselves from decisions? If you disagree with your board over an issue and are concerned about your liability, you should withdraw from the decision and ensure that your disagreement is minuted. However, trustees are judged to act jointly so it could be argued that your continued membership of the board will not remove your liability.

Further information
Governance Hub (2006) *Reducing the Risks: A Guide to trustee liabilities*. London: NCVO.

Charity Commission (2012) *The Essential Trustee: What you need to know* (CC3). London: Charity Commission.

Checklist

Are all trustees aware of their roles and responsibilities?

Do you have trustee role descriptions?

Do you have an induction process for new trustees?

Have you conducted a risk assessment of the personal liability of your board of trustees?

Are you confident that your management practices and board practices limit this risk as far as is reasonably possible?

Does your board seek expert advice when faced with a complicated legal or technical issue that it is not confident to deal with?

Do trustees understand their personal liabilities?

Have you considered taking out trustee liability insurance?

Does your trustee board have a development programme that includes a regular review of its role and effectiveness?

Does your board need to consider incorporation (unincorporated charities only)?

A code of conduct for trustees

A trustee code of conduct is an agreement between the charity and individual trustees that spells out the standards of behaviour expected from trustees. Trustees sign up to the code when they join the board. When they do so, they are pledging to uphold its standards.

The governing board, with input from other parts of the charity, writes the code to establish a set of organisational values, for example integrity, honesty and transparency. It also asks for specific behaviours from trustees designed to put these principles into practice.

NCVO recommends that every charity introduces a trustee code of conduct. A well-formulated and properly implemented trustee code of conduct can be a powerful way to improve the quality of trustee board governance.

• The very act of writing a code can have a good effect on the board by bringing concerns into the open and inspiring debate.

• Codes of conduct provide basic protection for the organisation by defining inappropriate behaviour on the part of its trustees.

• Codes can be used to improve trustee recruitment, induction, assessment, training and development.

NCVO's model codes are intended to offer a place for boards to begin the vital process of policy-making. They are not intended as templates for policy for all organisations. A policy written by anyone other than the board (even by NCVO) and adopted without discussion won't necessarily suit the organisation. It is the board's responsibility to know about its organisation's special needs and tailor policy to fit.

Fostering trustee ownership
For the code of conduct to be effective, the board must feel that it comes from them, reflecting their concerns and expressing their wishes. This sense of ownership comes from the writing process when the board formulates the code. Once a code has been created, this ownership has to be kept alive. New trustees have to buy into existing codes of conduct and serving trustees need to keep them in mind.

A model trustee code of conduct

Organisational values
As a trustee of [organisation] I promise to abide by the fundamental values
that underpin all the activity of this organisation. These are:

Accountability
Everything [organisation] does will be able to stand the test of scrutiny by
the public, the media, charity regulators, members, stakeholders, funders,
parliament and the courts.

Integrity and honesty
These will be the hallmarks of all conduct when dealing with colleagues within
[organisation] and equally when dealing with individuals and institutions
outside it.

Transparency
[Organisation] strives to maintain an atmosphere of openness throughout
the organisation to promote confidence of the public, stakeholders, staff,
charity regulators and parliament.

Additionally, I agree to the following points:

Law, mission, policies
I will not break the law or go against charity regulations in any aspect
of my role of trustee.

I will support the mission and consider myself its guardian.

I will abide by organisational policies.

Conflicts of interest
I will always strive to act in the best interests of the organisation.

I will declare any conflict of interest, or any circumstance that might
be viewed by others as a conflict of interest, as soon as it arises.

I will submit to the judgment of the board and do as it requires regarding
potential conflicts of interest.

Person to person
I will not break the law, go against charity regulations or act in disregard
of organisational policies in my relationships with fellow trustees, staff,
volunteers, members, service recipients, contractors or anyone I come
into contact with in my role as trustee.

I will strive to establish respectful, collegial and courteous relationships
with all I come into contact with in my role as trustee.

Protecting the organisation's reputation

I will not speak as a trustee of this organisation to the media or in a public forum without the prior knowledge and approval of the chief executive or chair.

When prior consent has not been obtained, I will inform the chair or chief executive at once when I have spoken as a trustee of this organisation to the media or in a public forum.

When I am speaking as a trustee of this organisation, my comments will reflect current organisational policy even when these do not agree with my personal views.

When speaking as a private citizen I will strive to uphold the reputation of the organisation and those who work in it.

I will respect organisational, board and individual confidentiality.

I will take an active interest in the organisation's public image, noting news articles, books, television programmes and the like about the organisation, about similar organisations or about important issues for the organisation.

Personal gain

I will not personally gain materially or financially from my role as trustee, nor will I permit others to do so as a result of my actions or negligence.

I will document expenses and seek reimbursement according to procedure.

I will not accept gifts or hospitality without prior consent of the chair.

I will use organisational resources responsibly, when authorised, in accordance with procedure.

In the boardroom

I will strive to embody the principles of leadership in all my actions and live up to the trust placed in me by [organisation].

I will abide by board governance procedures and practices.

I will strive to attend all board meetings, giving apologies ahead of time to the chair if unable to attend.

I will study the agenda and other information sent me in good time prior to the meeting and be prepared to debate and vote on agenda items during the meeting.

I will honour the authority of the chair and respect his or her role as meeting leader.

I will engage in debate and voting in meetings according to procedure, maintaining a respectful attitude towards the opinions of others while making my voice heard.

I will accept a majority board vote on an issue as decisive and final.

I will maintain confidentiality about what goes on in the boardroom unless authorised by the chair or board to speak of it.

Enhancing governance

I will participate in induction, training and development activities for trustees.

I will continually seek ways to improve board governance practice.

I will strive to identify good candidates for trusteeship and appoint new trustees on the basis of merit.

I will support the chair in his or her efforts to improve his or her leadership skills.

I will support the chief executive in his or her executive role and, with my fellow board members, seek development opportunities for him or her.

Leaving the board

I understand that substantial breach of any part of this code may result in my removal from the trustee board.

Should I resign from the board I will inform the chair in advance in writing, stating my reasons for resigning. Additionally, I will participate in an exit interview.

4

Board and committee structures

This chapter looks at the make-up of the board and how the trustees and committees fit in. Like the rest of Part One, it concentrates on defining the role. After reading this chapter you can visit Part Three for information about practical ways of enhancing the effectiveness of meetings and committees.

4.1

Who's who in the boardroom

Who they are	What they do	Special features
Board members (may be called the trustee board, committee, the board of directors, the executive committee, the board of governors etc)	• Work as a team to make the most important decisions for their charity • Take overall responsibility for everything the charity does and how it does it	• Receive no 'benefit' unless authorised • Team of equals • Unique form of group leadership
The chair (also called the chairman, chairwoman or chairperson of the board)	• Board member chosen to chair meetings and to provide leadership to the board and make sure it works effectively • Usually provides a link between the board and staff by working closely with the chief executive	• Important role that requires tact and diplomacy • Oversees board meetings • Helps all board members' opinions be heard • Recognises the difference between 'chairing' and 'facilitating' and understands when each is appropriate
The chief executive or head of staff (if one is appointed) (may be called chief executive, chief executive officer, director, co-ordinator, manager, director general, executive, etc)	• Responsible for the day-to-day running of the charity • Puts the board's decisions into practice	• Gets paid • Rarely a board member • Hired (and may be fired) by the board • Held to account by the board • Reports to the board
Board committee	• Small group assigned by the board to focus on a particular task or area (such as finance, remuneration, nominations, governance, etc) • Committees can be a permanent part of the charity's governance ('standing committees') or set up to fulfil a time-limited task (working group)	• Can include non-board members • Can't make decisions unless authorised • Reports to the board • Can add value to governance
Advisory Group	• Group of non-board members that advises the board	• No official role • No voting power • Can provide valuable information and expertise

Board meetings

Meetings are the formal setting for all trustee decisions. The quality of your decisions will depend on planning, preparation, efficient running and chairing of board meetings and the time you devote to team building. Trustees should attend all board meetings. If you are unable to attend you should send your views and comments to the chair before the meeting.

Many charities will have a quorum (the minimum number of people who must be present for the meeting to take place) laid down in their governing document. Some governing documents contain clauses requiring trustees to resign if they have been absent without sufficient reason from a specified number of meetings.

Procedures in your governing document about calling meetings must be followed. You may also have procedures governing the conduct of meetings (see Chapter 21 for information on effective meetings).

On the board

Honorary officers
Many boards find it useful to have a number of trustees who take on specific roles. Trustees with specific roles may:

- deal with matters needing attention between meetings of the full board

- take a lead in preparing issues in readiness for board meetings.

In charities that employ staff, they sometimes:

- act as an effective link between the staff and the board of trustees

- share with the chief executive the task of representing the charity

- sit on recruitment panels for senior staff appointments

- sit on disciplinary panels

- act as a final court of appeal for serious disciplinary matters.

Trustees with specific roles are often called 'honorary officers'. Honorary officers can only carry out aspects of the charity's business if they are authorised to do so. Honorary officers commonly comprise a chair, vice-chair, secretary and treasurer. The roles of chair and treasurer are particularly common.

The board should draw up a role description for each honorary officer, setting out their duties and powers (where they exist). The role descriptions should capture any specific roles, functions and responsibilities that are set out in the charity's governing document, standing orders, etc (model role descriptions are available on pages 53–57).

The honorary officers are sometimes elected by the members of the board of trustees or by the charity's membership. Unless the board has explicitly delegated decision-making powers to honorary officers, they should act in an advisory capacity and must report their activities fully to the board to prevent the other trustees feeling excluded by an inner group. This is particularly important if honorary officers meet as a group in between board meetings.

The chair
The chair's role is essentially one of leadership and to make sure that the board fulfils its duties and responsibilities. The chair will oversee the meetings of the board of trustees but will also take on a number of other, wider roles. Where staff are employed, the chair may work closely with the head of staff, chief executive or manager to support him or her in achieving the aims of the charity and acting as the channel of communication between the trustees and staff. The chair may act as a figurehead of the charity and represent it at functions, meetings and in the press and broadcasting media. Other tasks may include authorising action to be taken between meetings of the full board, signing cheques for amounts above those for which authority has been delegated to staff and signing legal documents.

The vice-chair

The vice-chair may be a chair designate (ie a person in waiting to be chair) or somebody who will deputise for the chair.

The vice-chair as deputy chair

The vice-chair acts for the chair when the chair is not available and undertakes assignments at the request of the chair. To ensure continuity, every charity should ensure that key people have a deputy who can assume their responsibility and are familiar with their work should a sudden absence occur. The vice-chair fulfils this role for the chair. The charity should also consider other key roles that require deputies, for example the chief executive.

Senior independent trustee

As a result of governance developments in other sectors, some charities have created a role for a senior independent trustee. This role is seen as providing a 'safety valve' for the board and in particular involves leading the appraisal/evaluation of the chair's performance and taking responsibility for an orderly succession process for the chair. In difficult times the senior independent trustee could become the focal point for board members if they had any concerns regarding the chair or the relationship between the chair and the senior staff member.

To ensure that the senior independent trustee role works as effectively as possible and is not seen as divisive, boards need to consider carefully the skills, abilities and qualities of the person to be recruited, including someone who has no ambitions to become the chair.

The secretary

In charities with staff, most of the secretarial duties involved in running the board – sending out agendas and board papers, taking minutes, checking that a quorum is present, booking the meeting room, etc are commonly undertaken by staff. The role of the secretary is confined to taking minutes of meetings from which all staff are excluded, being consulted by the chair in between meetings and undertaking other duties delegated to the honorary officers or at the request of the chair.

Where there are no paid staff, the honorary secretary has to undertake all the secretarial duties to support the board. Taking accurate minutes of meetings is a particularly important task, as these form the legal record of the board's decisions (see Chapter 21).

Under the provisions of the Companies Act 2006, charitable companies are no longer required to have a company secretary unless articles of association specifically provide for one. If they do have a company secretary their duties are to ensure that the charity complies with the requirements of company law, including keeping the register of members, register of directors and register of charges up to date and notifying Companies House of any changes in trustees, preparing and filing the annual return and making sure that the company documents are kept safely. In charities with staff, the role of company secretary is not normally assigned to the honorary secretary but is delegated to a member of staff.

The treasurer

The treasurer takes the lead in overseeing the financial affairs of the charity. The treasurer will help other trustees perform their financial duties by interpreting and explaining accounting requirements, ensuring that the board receives reports containing the information trustees need in an 'easy to understand' format, and helping trustees guide any other professional advisers they have appointed.

The precise tasks of a treasurer will depend on the size of the charity, the governing document and/or the remit given to the treasurer by the trustee board. In most charities, the treasurer's duties are likely to include:

• presenting financial reports to the board in an understandable format

• keeping the board aware of its financial responsibilities

• ensuring that the charity's accounts are prepared in a suitable format

• ensuring that the accounts and financial systems are independently examined or audited if required

• liaising with the auditors/independent examiners.

In smaller charities, the treasurer may personally maintain the financial records and prepare budgets and financial reports. The treasurer should have sufficient technical expertise to guide the financial affairs of the charity. For example, if the charity has large investments, the treasurer should have sufficient knowledge to ensure that they are earning the best possible return. The treasurer should also be willing and able to give authoritative advice that protects a charity's financial position but may conflict with the aspirations of the board to expand the charity's work.

Other roles

Apart from the honorary officers, many charities recruit or appoint volunteers to be patrons or presidents of their organisation. What is expected of volunteers recruited to these roles will largely depend on the charity's history, culture and stage of development, but the following general descriptions of the roles may be useful.

Patrons (these are not trustees)

Patrons are people who give credibility or support to the cause of a charity or voluntary organisation. They are not involved in its management nor do they have any legal responsibilities. Patrons can be helpful in fundraising and public relations, for example they may be prepared to be named on letterheads or in annual reports, and can help to gain media coverage if they are willing to attend events.

Presidents (they are not usually trustees)

The role of president or vice-president is usually a figurehead role distinct from that of a trustee. A president or vice-president may be formally elected or appointed or may be informally chosen as a figurehead in a similar way to a patron. Presidents sometimes have specific duties such as chairing the annual general meeting.

Presidents or vice-presidents are not usually trustees and have a separate role to that of trustees, unless the governing document states otherwise (eg the term 'president' is used in some countries to refer to the chair of the board).

Whatever functions are carried out by patrons and presidents, it is best practice to make sure that everyone is clear about what the role entails, and this should include a written agreement or role description.

Checklist

Does your charity have written role descriptions for trustees and its honorary officers?

Does your board need to review the honorary officers' role descriptions in the light of the needs and legal duties of your charity?

If your charity has patrons or presidents, does your board review the benefits and purposes of keeping these roles?

Does your board need to review the written agreement or role descriptions it has with its patrons and/or presidents in light of the needs and legal duties of your charity?

Model role descriptions

Model job description for a trustee
The following specimen trustee role descriptions and person specifications
can be adapted to meet your charity's particular needs.

Role descriptions include the roles, responsibilities and tasks that trustees
are expected to carry out.

Person specifications include the skills, experience and qualities that are
expected from trustees. Again, these will vary depending on what you are
looking for – they could include technical skills or experience of the
community you work with or of a particular culture. These may have come
from a board review or skills audit. However, all trustees should be able to
demonstrate basic qualities of commitment and integrity, which are needed
to be a trustee.

Trustee role description

Title: Trustee of _____

The duties of a trustee are:
- To ensure the organisation pursues its stated objects (purposes), as
  defined in its governing document, by developing and agreeing a long
  term strategy.

- To ensure that the organisation complies with its governing document (ie
  its trust deed, constitution or memorandum and articles of association),
  charity law, company law and any other relevant legislation or regulations.

- To ensure that the organisation applies its resources exclusively in
  pursuance of its charitable objects (ie the charity must not spend money
  on activities that are not included in its own objects, however worthwhile
  or charitable those activities are) for the benefit of the public.

- To ensure the organisation defines its goals and evaluates performance
  against agreed targets.

- To safeguard the good name and values of the organisation.

- To ensure the effective and efficient administration of the organisation
  including having appropriate policies and procedures in place.

- To ensure the financial stability of the organisation.

- To protect and manage the property of the charity and to ensure
  the proper investment of the charity's funds.

- If the charity employs staff, to follow proper and formal arrangements for the appointment, supervision, support, appraisal and remuneration of the chief executive.

- In addition to the above statutory duties, each trustee should use any specific skills, knowledge or experience they have to help the board of trustees reach sound decisions. This may involve scrutinising board papers, leading discussions, focusing on key issues, providing advice and guidance on new initiatives, or other issues in which the trustee has special expertise.

Trustee person specification
- A commitment to the organisation

- A willingness to devote the necessary time and effort

- Strategic vision

- Good, independent judgement

- An ability to think creatively

- A willingness to speak their mind

- An understanding and acceptance of the legal duties, responsibilities and liabilities of trusteeship

- An ability to work effectively as a member of a team

- Nolan's seven principles of public life: selflessness, integrity, objectivity, accountability, openness, honesty and leadership.

Role description for a chair

Title: Chair of _____

In addition to the general responsibilities of a trustee, duties of the chair include the following (the list below contains examples – see section 4.1).

- Providing leadership to the organisation and the board by ensuring that everyone remains focused on the delivery of its charitable purposes in order to provide greater public benefit

- Chairing and facilitating board meetings

- Giving direction to board policy-making

- Checking that decisions taken at meetings are implemented

- Representing the organisation at functions and meetings, and acting as a spokesperson as appropriate

- Bringing impartiality and objectivity to decision-making

- With the chief executive:

  – Planning the annual cycle of board meetings and other general meetings where required, for example the annual general meeting

  – Setting agendas for board and other general meetings

  – developing the board of trustees including induction, training, appraisal and succession planning

  – addressing conflict within the board and within the organisation, and liaising with the chief executive (if staff are employed) to achieve this.

- Where staff are employed:

  – Liaising with the chief executive to keep an overview of the organisation's affairs and to provide support as appropriate

  – Leading the process of supporting and appraising the performance of the chief executive

  – Sitting on appointment and disciplinary panels.

- The vice-chair acts for the chair when the chair is not available and undertakes assignments at the request of the chair.

Person specification
In addition to the person specification for a trustee, the chair should have the following qualities.

- Leadership skills

- Experience of committee work

- Tact and diplomacy

- Good communication and interpersonal skills

- Impartiality, fairness and the ability to respect confidences.

In most circumstances, it would also be desirable for the chair/vice-chair to have knowledge of the type of work undertaken by the organisation and a wider involvement with the voluntary sector and other networks.

Role description for a secretary

Title: Secretary of _____

The role of the secretary is to support the chair by ensuring the board functions smoothly. The secretary may carry out their duties directly or delegate them to a member of staff and ensure that they have been carried out. In addition to the general responsibilities of a trustee, duties of the secretary are as follows.

- Preparing agendas in consultation with the chair and chief executive and circulating them and any supporting papers in good time

- Making all the arrangements for meetings (booking the room, arranging for equipment and refreshments, organising facilities for those with special needs, etc)

- Receiving agenda items from other trustees/staff

- Checking that a quorum is present

- Taking minutes (or being responsible for them being taken) and circulating draft minutes to all trustees

- Ensuring that the minutes are signed by the chair once they have been approved

- Checking that trustees and staff have carried out actions agreed at a previous meeting

- Circulating agendas and minutes of the annual general meeting and any special or extraordinary general meetings (where required)

- In organisations that are companies, fulfilling the functions of a company secretary if these responsibilities have not been delegated to a member of staff

- Sitting on appraisal, recruitment and disciplinary panels as required

Person specification
In addition to the person specification for a trustee, the secretary should have the following qualities.

- Organisational ability

- Knowledge or experience of business and committee procedures

- Minute-taking experience, if this is not being delegated to staff.

Role description for a treasurer

Title: Treasurer of _____

The overall role of a treasurer is to maintain an overview of the organisation's affairs, ensure its financial viability and ensure that proper financial records and procedures are maintained. In small charities without paid staff, the treasurer may take a greater role in the day-to-day finances of the organisation.

In addition to the general responsibilities of a trustee, duties of the treasurer include the following.

- Overseeing, approving and presenting budgets, accounts and financial statements

- Being assured that the financial resources of the organisation meet its present and future needs

- Ensuring that the charity has an appropriate reserves policy

- Preparing and presenting financial reports to the board

- Ensuring that appropriate accounting procedures and controls are in place

- Liaising with any paid staff and volunteers about financial matters

- Advising on the financial implications of the organisation's strategic plans

- Ensuring that the charity has an appropriate investment policy

- Ensuring that there is no conflict between any investment held and the aims and objects of the charity

- Monitoring the organisation's investment activity and ensuring it is consistent with the organisation's policies and legal responsibilities

- Ensuring that the accounts are prepared and disclosed in the form required by funders and the relevant statutory bodies, for example the Charity Commission and/or the Registrar of Companies

- If external scrutiny of accounts is required, ensuring that the accounts are scrutinised in the manner required (independent examination or audit) and any recommendations are implemented

- Keeping the board informed about its financial duties and responsibilities

- Contributing to the fundraising strategy of the organisation

- Making a formal presentation of the accounts at the annual general meeting and drawing attention to important points in a coherent and easily understandable way

- Sitting on appraisal, recruitment and disciplinary panels as required

Person specification
In addition to the person specification for a trustee, the treasurer should have the following qualities.

- Financial qualifications and experience

- Some experience of charity finance, fundraising and pension schemes

- The skills to analyse proposals and examine their financial consequences

- Being prepared to make unpopular recommendations to the board

- A willingness to be available to staff for advice and enquiries on an ad hoc basis

Checklist

Do all trustees have a copy of their role description and person specification?

Are all prospective trustees sent copies of a trustee role description?

4.2

Delegation

Trustees are required to act in person and any decisions affecting the charity must be made by the trustees acting together. In general terms, trustees are able to delegate administrative functions and the implementation of any decisions they have taken to others but not their power of decision-making unless this is expressly allowed by statute or the governing document. In practice, all but the smallest charities will delegate day-to-day matters to:

- individual trustees, for example delegating the role of financial oversight to the treasurer

- committees, for example to investigate a particular issue in more detail

- staff or volunteers, for example the day-to-day running of the charity.

What matters should be reserved for the trustee board?

It is recommended that some tasks should not be delegated from the trustee board but instead be the subject of a board decision. All boards should therefore seek to draw up a policy which includes a list of matters that are reserved to the board and, on the understanding that no list can ever provide definitive guidance, set the boundaries within which senior staff can operate.

Committees

Can trustees delegate to committees?

Trustees are required to act in person and any decisions affecting the charity must be made by the trustees acting together. If your governing document gives you the power to do so, you may delegate authority to a committee of your board for a particular aspect of the charity's work or delegate authority to a task group or committee whose members need not necessarily all be trustees.

On the whole, any decisions made by such groups remain the responsibility of the board of trustees. The terms of reference and reporting back procedures of any committees, working groups or task groups should be put in writing and agreed by the board of trustees.

For many charities, monthly, bimonthly or quarterly meetings of the board of trustees are sufficient to carry out its work. As organisations however become larger, take on more staff and expand into new areas or activities, boards sometimes establish committees or working groups, which can allow more time to be spent on certain issues and involve people from outside the trustee board.

Committees – good practice

- Boards must have a power in their governing document to delegate decision-making.

- Boards can delegate decision-making to committees, but the board remains ultimately accountable for decisions taken.

- The role and accountability of the committee should be clear to all members of the committee and the board.

- Committees and their terms of reference should be regularly reviewed to ensure they are effective.

Do you have the power to set up committees?

Check your governing document to see what it says about board and committee structure. Is there a clause giving the board of trustees power to establish committees? Does the power allow the delegation of decision-making? Are there rules governing the membership of committees (eg committees with decision-making power may require a majority of trustees as members or may restrict the decision-making to trustees only)?

Trustees who serve on a committee should be able to distinguish between their role as board member and their role as a committee member.

For more guidance on good practice in the use of committees see Chapter 4.

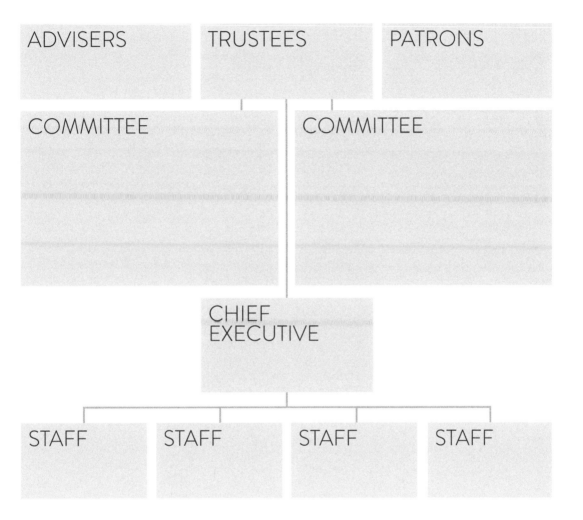

ADVISERS

TRUSTEES

PATRONS

COMMITTEE

COMMITTEE

CHIEF EXECUTIVE

STAFF

STAFF

STAFF

STAFF

Boards of trustees and committees compared

Board of trustees	Committee
Ultimate responsibility for the charity.	May specialise in certain areas of the board's work – for example, finance, fundraising, staff remuneration or board recruitment.
Can delegate decision-making and ratify recommendations of committees if it has the power to do so.	The remit and any decision-making power is set by the board of trustees and the governing document in its terms of reference.
May invite non-voting observer members to meetings who are not trustees.	Depending on its terms of reference it can have a mix of trustees, staff, volunteers and external advisers.

Checklist

Does your governing document include a power to establish committees?

Do all your committees and working parties have written terms of reference?

When trustees join committees, are they fully briefed about their role?

Staff and volunteers

What can trustees delegate to staff and volunteers?

Charities have a power to employ agents. All trustees can delegate implementation of their decisions, but a power is required to delegate decision-making powers.

While staff, particularly in large charities, will have wide-ranging responsibilities and a significant amount of discretion in the way they fulfil their role, they do not have the authority to make the strategic decisions that are reserved for the board.

In all but the very smallest of charities the day-to-day management of the charity and all its operations will be delegated to employed staff and/or volunteers. The scope of delegated authority should be put in writing, and decisions made by staff and/or volunteers on important matters must be reported to the board of trustees as soon as possible. The board remains legally responsible for all activities of the charity, including matters delegated to staff and/or volunteers and it is recommended that some duties are never delegated to others. What is appropriate to delegate to staff and/or volunteers will vary with the size of the charity. For example, the trustees of a small grant-giving trust might be expected personally to examine all grant applications, but this would be impractical for the trustees of a charity whose grants run to many millions of pounds.

The trustees of such charities should produce written guidelines explaining their grant-giving policy and then delegate to staff and/or volunteers the authority to make grants within those policy guidelines up to a specified amount. The trustees should be given a report of any grants made. Similarly, the boards of trustees should make major policy decisions.

Trustees of a charitable company running charity shops may decide whether properties should be purchased or rented but will delegate decisions about shop location and layout to local staff and/or volunteers.

Can trustees take on other roles?

Trustees sometimes have several roles in their charity. As well as their volunteer role as a member of the governing body, they may act as volunteers in other ways, for example, running fundraising events, doing the accounts or delivering the service provided by the charity.

If you have a number of different roles, it is important to be aware of when you are acting in a particular role. In your role as a trustee, you are responsible for setting objectives for the chief executive's work plan, but if you are in another volunteer role, you must be prepared to take direction from the person with responsibility for supervising that area of the charity's work. For example, if your charity runs a community centre that has a paid manager, when you are in your role as a trustee the manager will be accountable to you, but when you work as a volunteer helping to run the community centre's crèche, you will be accountable to the centre's manager.

Tip: If you are a trustee and take on other roles in the charity, for example volunteering in the office or organising events, think of yourself as having different 'hats' – in this case, a trustee hat and a volunteer hat.

Checklist

Do trustees delegate day-to-day running to others?

Have you agreed the scope of delegated authority in writing (eg in job descriptions or policies)?

When were these last reviewed?

Part Two:

Good governance

5

What is governance?

Your charity's success depends on how it meets the needs of its beneficiaries, its vitality, its standing in the voluntary sector and its ability to manage change. Achieving this success largely depends on whether you and your fellow trustees govern effectively.

It is essential for your board to be able to stand back and take the wider view of your charity. Are you clear about why your charity should exist? Do you know where the organisation is going in the future? Is the charity meeting its objects in the most effective way?

Perspective and leadership are vital, whatever the management structure of your organisation. If your organisation does not employ staff, you will be involved in the day-to-day management of its work, so stepping back helps to give trustees the 'big picture'. Where staff are employed, your responsibility will be to ensure that the charity is well managed – rather than being actively involved in running it – and well monitored.

Trustees take overall responsibility for everything the charity does and they act collectively to govern the organisation. The term often used to describe this role is 'governance'.

5.1

Defining governance

Chris Cornforth describes governance as

'the systems and processes concerned with ensuring the overall direction, effectiveness, supervision and accountability of an organisation'.[3]

Sandy Adirondack defines governance as

'the process by which a governing body ensures that an organisation is effectively and properly run… Governance is not necessarily about doing; it is about ensuring things are done'.[4]

Principles of good governance

The 12 essential responsibilities of trustees set out in Chapter 1 are underpinned by six principles of good governance, as set out in: NCVO (2010) *Good Governance: A code for the voluntary and community sector.* London: NCVO (the Code). The Code was originally drawn up in 2005 by a number of different voluntary and community sector support and membership bodies. Following a sector-wide consultation exercise, a second edition of the Code was published in 2010, and it sets out a statement of best practice in governance. The six principles for a board are as follows.

1. Understanding their role

Members of the board will understand their role and responsibilities collectively and individually in relation to:

- their legal duties

- their stewardship of assets

- the provisions of the governing document

- the external environment

- the total structure of the organisation

and in terms of:

- setting and safeguarding the vision, values and reputation of the organisation

- overseeing the work of the organisation

- managing and supporting staff and volunteers, where applicable.

2. Ensuring delivery of organisational purpose

The board will ensure that the organisation delivers its stated purposes or aims by:

- ensuring organisational purposes remain relevant and valid

- developing and agreeing a long-term strategy

- agreeing operational plans and budgets

- monitoring progress and spending against plan and budget

- evaluating results and assessing outcomes and impact

- reviewing and/or amending the plan and budget as appropriate

3 Routledge (2003) *The Governance of Public and Non-profit Organisations: what do boards do?* London: Routledge.

4 NCVO (2002) *The Good Governance Action Plan for Voluntary Organisations.* London: NCVO.

3. Working effectively both as individuals and a team

The board will have a range of appropriate policies and procedures, knowledge, attitudes and behaviours to enable both individuals and the board to work effectively. These will include:

- finding and recruiting new board members to meet the organisation's changing needs in relation to skills, experience and diversity

- providing suitable induction for new board members

- providing all board members with opportunities for training and development according to their needs

- periodically reviewing their performance both as individuals and as a team.

4. Exercising effective control

As the accountable body, the board will ensure that:

- the organisation understands and complies with all legal and regulatory requirements that apply to it

- the organisation continues to have good internal financial and management controls

- it regularly identifies and reviews the major risks to which the organisation is exposed and has systems to manage those risks

- delegation to committees, staff and volunteers (as applicable) works effectively and the use of delegated authority is properly supervised.

5. Behaving with integrity

The board will:

- safeguard and promote the organisation's reputation

- act according to high ethical standards

- identify, understand and manage conflicts of interest and loyalty

- maintain independence of decision making

- deliver impact that best meets the needs of beneficiaries.

5.2

6. Being open and accountable

The board will lead the organisation in being open and accountable, both internally and externally. This will include:

- open communication that informs people about the organisation and its work

- appropriate consultation on significant changes to the organisation's services or policies

- listening and responding to the views of supporters, funders, beneficiaries, service users and others with an interest in the organisation's work

- handling complaints constructively, impartially and effectively

- considering the organisation's responsibilities to the wider community, for example its environmental impact.

Further information:
NCVO (2010) *Good Governance: A code for the voluntary and community sector.* London: NCVO.

Hallmarks of an effective charity

The Charity Commission's *Hallmarks of an Effective Charity* set out 'the standards that will help trustees to improve the effectiveness of their charity, and the principles that our regulatory framework exists to support'.[5]

Governance is concerned with leadership and direction. It is about ensuring your charity has a clear, shared vision of its purpose, what it is aiming to achieve and how in broad terms it will go about doing it and that it maintains a sense of urgency about its work.

As trustees, you must set clear aims and objectives, establish priorities, safeguard the charity's assets (money, property – including intellectual property – equipment and human resources) and use them effectively and exclusively for the benefit of those the charity exists to help.

Trustees take ultimate responsibility for the governance of their organisation. However, governance is not a role for trustees alone; it is the way trustees work with chief executives and staff (where appointed), volunteers, service users, members and other stakeholders to ensure their organisation is effectively and properly run and meets the needs for which the organisation was set up.

This Guide shows you how you can use various approaches – such as clarifying board–staff relations, planning trustee recruitment and induction, organising board development and conducting board reviews – to energise and enhance the effectiveness of the way your board works. Many of these draw on the Code as a set of principles.

Further information:
Charity Commission (2008) *Hallmarks of an Effective Charity* (CC10). London: Charity Commission.

5 Charity Commission (2008) *Hallmarks of an Effective Charity* (CC10). London: Charity Commission.

6

Strategic planning

A key responsibility of your board is to ensure that your charity makes a difference while working within its objects as laid out in its governing document.

This means agreeing (usually every three to five years):

- the ideal state your charity wants to see (the vision)

- the role it will play to work towards the vision (the mission)

- the changes it hopes to bring about (the outcomes)

- how it will act (the values)

- what it actually plans to do (the activities and outputs).

6.1

Objects and mission

What is your mission?
Your mission should sum up in clear, non-legal language the medium-term goals of your charity. It should be consistent with your objects as defined in your charity's governing document (see section 2.2), but may refine them and outline how they will be met in the coming years.

It should be short – just one or two sentences – and set out:

- the purpose of the charity – what changes do we want to bring about?

- the beneficiaries or cause – who or what are we here for?

- how and where the charity will work – how do we do it?

For example:

The Worcestershire Association of Carers exists to relieve the stresses experienced by informal carers and those they care for in the county of Worcestershire, through the provision of information and support services and the promotion of the needs of carers.

6.2

What is strategic planning?

Strategic planning involves:

- clarifying your charity's purpose

- reviewing your charity's situation

- opening up options and choices

- making decisions

- making sure the right people know what has been decided and what it means for them.

Strategic planning may not always seem relevant to a small association or grant-giving trust. However, the trustees of even the smallest groups will benefit from standing back and questioning whether their charity should carry on doing what it has always done or make changes. In fact, the smallest charities may have the most to gain: strategic planning can help them to keep nimble and make the most of new opportunities.

1	Get ready	Prepare: decide on the process and timescale you want your strategic planning to follow and form a group to take the lead and to share tasks
2	Clarify your organisation's purpose	Consider your vision, mission and values: what your organisation is going to be like and how it's going to act
		Define the outcomes and changes your organisation exists to make
		Analyse and build your knowledge of your user group
		Consider the views of relevant stakeholders (eg service users, staff, volunteers and funders) on what they hope the organisation will achieve
3	Open up options and choices	Look internally: consider the organisation's strengths, weaknesses, competencies and capacity
		Look out: consider how external trends and issues will influence how and to what extent the organisation can deliver its mission in the future
4	Make decisions	Refine options for the future and discuss them with stakeholders
		Develop detailed priorities
5	Communicate, implement and review	Communicate your strategy internally and externally
		Weave strategy into team and individual work plans
		Track the progress of the strategy and judge its success in strengthening your organisation

6.3

Case study

A community-based forum on sustainability issues wanted a new strategy. It was keen to take advantage of the emergence of environmental issues on the mainstream political agenda, but it had very limited resources.

The charity's trustees led the strategic planning process and began with a special informal meeting to explore the charity's mission, vision and values, as well as members' needs. After this review, the trustees planned to propose amendments to their vision and mission at the next annual general meeting. They also organised a stakeholder consultation meeting to generate ideas for new projects, which they later explored and refined.

The forum has now become more focused on its identity as a delivery agent rather than an advocacy body, and collaborative working is a priority to enable it to punch above its weight.

The forum has been particularly effective in communicating its strategy to stakeholders, who are now much more aware of its role and its openness to partnership working.

The strategic plan

A strategic plan sets out how your charity will move from the present position to the one it aspires to reach by the end of the identified period. The format of your plan will depend on your charity's needs and to whom you are communicating the plan. There are no hard and fast rules about what a strategic plan should look like or what it should contain. It should be as long or as short, as detailed or as basic, as it needs to be.

Types of plan
Here are five suggestions of what a strategic plan could look like.

1. Story: A plan that tells a powerful and convincing narrative about where your charity has come from and provides an exciting vision for the future.

2. Roadmap: A technical plan that gives your charity a route to a destination, highlighting landmarks you will pass, potential hazards you may encounter on the way and resources you'll need.

3. Logbook: A framework that sets out what your charity wants to be and how it will act, but gives the space for the charity to record and capture the pattern of strategic choices it makes in the coming years.

4. Flyer: A short, snappy plan that is designed to promote your charity's successes and future intent to an external audience.

5. Library: More of a store that pulls together plans, budgets and information about the charity's environment for staff to draw on than a single plan.

6.4

You might also want to consider creative ways of communicating your plan. For example, some charities have found events, posters, visual diagrams and even 3D models of their strategy effective.

If you find it helpful to have a written plan in a single document, consider including the following elements.

- A clear statement of the charity's vision and mission and the specific changes it wants to deliver.

- A summary of its performance so far and reasons for this.

- An analysis of potential opportunities and challenges in the future.

- Priorities and aims for the coming years.

- Plans for how the whole organisation will change to deliver these priorities.

- An outline of how the organisation will track the progress of this strategy, including milestones and indicators of success.

Keeping the strategy alive

Strategic planning is an ongoing process. Even once a plan has been agreed, you and your fellow trustees should review it at regular intervals to:

- monitor progress against targets

- check that any assumptions made are still valid

- see if the plan should be modified.

You will also need to communicate the plan in different ways to reinforce the ideas behind it and ensure that all your stakeholders not only understand your direction, but also support your goals and help you to achieve them. Updates on progress are equally important.

Your strategic plan should form the basis of all your charity's operational planning. Operational planning translates your high-level strategic plan into a more detailed description of who will do what and when. Operational plans usually relate to the short to medium term – maybe one to three years – and may apply to your whole charity or a particular project or area of work. Business plans, annual plans, project plans, action plans and individual work plans are all different types of operational plan. Don't worry too much about these terms; the important thing is to develop plans that will help you to deliver your work and keep on track.

The board's role in strategic planning

- The board should lead the strategic planning process with the chief executive (if you employ one). This is a crucial part of your remit: making sure the charity has clear goals and is achieving the most for its beneficiaries or cause.

- You are removed from the day-to-day 'fire-fighting' and can take a holistic approach to your organisation and offer perspective.

- It is the trustees' role to assess regularly how the charity meets its purposes – including a review of how far its purposes reflect the current operating environment and whether they need to change (see section 2.2).

- You can help to draw together the views of different stakeholders.

- The board should ensure that stakeholders such as staff, volunteers and users have the opportunity to feed into the strategic planning process. This will produce richer ideas and improve the links between your board's strategic level work and day-to-day operations, making a plan really robust.

How strategic planning can help the board improve its own work

- It provides the overall framework for the board to assess the charity's progress.

- It provides an opportunity for your board to review its own role and performance.

- It can help to identify board priorities.

- It can provide opportunities for board meetings, committees and working parties to be remodelled around strategic priorities.

- The experience can help identify board member interests and expertise and form the basis of board recruitment (around particular skills, experience, etc needed to fulfil the plan).

- The process can help to strengthen the relationship between your board and chief executive.

Further information:
NCVO (2012) *Tools for Tomorrow.*
London: NCVO.

Checklist

Does your charity have an up-to-date vision and mission?

Does your charity have a strategic plan?

Is the strategic plan reviewed at regular intervals?

Has the strategic plan been communicated to the right stakeholders in the right way?

Does your board need to review its strategic planning process?

7

7.1

Resources

Financial responsibilities

What financial responsibilities do trustees have?
Trustees are legally responsible for the financial resources entrusted to the charity.

Charity accounting changed in the 1990s with the official recognition that charity operations were very different from commercial companies. Since then, the Charities Acts and regulations along with a framework for charity accounting – the Statement of Recommended Practice (SORP) – have brought in clearer guidance and requirements to ensure trustees are able to discharge their responsibilities effectively.

Charitable companies are also subject to company law and trustees must ensure that the accounting procedures set out in the Companies Acts are followed.

Key financial responsibilities of trustees include:

- ensuring that the charity's assets and income are used exclusively to pursue its objects (purposes)

- safeguarding the charity's assets, funds and resources and making sure they are correctly applied

- ensuring proper accounting records are kept and policies adopted

- ensuring annual reports and accounts are produced, and where appropriate independently examined or audited, in a form that satisfies the requirements of regulators and the charity's governing document, and are filed with regulators as required

- making decisions on financial policy (for example, in relation to investments and reserves)

- ensuring that proper control is exercised over both income and expenditure, in particular monitoring continued solvency

- monitoring fundraising policy and activities

- overseeing any trading activities and ensuring that the tax affairs of the charity are managed effectively

- ensuring that, where a charity has financial assets to invest, it:

  - does so in accordance with the charity's powers of investment as set out in its governing document

  - adopts an appropriate investment policy (see Further information below) including the aims and objectives, the risks and any ethical or responsible investment criteria

  - takes advice where necessary

  - earns the best possible financial return for the level of risk that you consider acceptable.

Note: charities can make 'social investments', which seek to achieve financial and social outcomes, but these are generally considered under a different framework (see section 7.1) ensuring that reasonable steps are taken to prevent and detect fraud and other irregularities. If your charity is large enough to warrant having internal audit staff, these staff should report directly to your board.

Further information

Charity Finance Group and Charity Investors Group (undated) *Guide to Investment Policy.* London: Charity Investors Group. www.charityinvestorsgroup.org.uk

I am new to finance. What role should I play as a trustee?
Financial information can seem daunting to the inexperienced or the non-financial expert: don't let it. As a trustee you have a duty to ask questions and take advice when you need to.

All trustees should either have, or be prepared to develop, basic skills in financial management. In particular, trustees should know how to:

- read budgets and accounts so they know if the annual accounts properly summarise their charity's activities and state of affairs

- interpret financial reports and advise on appropriate action in response

- guide professional advisers entrusted with property and financial reserves

- assist and monitor fundraising activities

- recognise actual or pending insolvency.

Some trustees will not have previous experience of dealing with a charity's finances. They should be given support by the honorary treasurer or the charity's finance officer or in another way. This chapter gives trustees basic information about their financial responsibilities.

Trustees can be personally liable for the misuse of charity funds or the liabilities of an insolvent charity so you should make sure you and your board members understand your wide-ranging financial responsibilities.

Getting meaningful information

Trustees should ask for financial information to be presented in a form that they can understand (eg tables, charts and graphs) and the information should be accompanied by a written commentary. Some charities give new trustees a glossary of the terms used in their accounts.

Key questions to ask

- Are we running a gain or a loss?
- Are key expenses under control?
- Do we have sufficient reserves?
- Do we have an investment policy (if appropriate)
- Is cash flow adequate?
- Where are we compared to budget?
- Is our financial plan consistent with our strategic plan?
- Are the staff satisfied and productive?
- Are we filing reports on a timely basis?
- Are we fulfilling our legal obligations?

Can financial responsibilities be delegated to an honorary treasurer, financial advisers, staff or volunteers? Your charity may have an honorary treasurer, financial advisers or a committee that co-ordinates its financial management. You may appoint staff, volunteers or an outside agency to undertake day-to-day financial duties (such as bookkeeping or payroll). All trustees, however, should take an active interest in the financial affairs of the charity and exercise care when appointing or supervising anyone to manage its finances. You cannot escape your financial responsibilities by delegating control and supervision of the finances to someone else; you remain responsible for the financial affairs of the charity and would share liability for any financial wrongdoing.

How will the financial management exercised by trustees be judged?

You have two principal duties when fulfilling your financial responsibilities.

'Proper care and diligence'

A trustee will not, for example, be held personally liable for wrongdoing by any financial agents if the board of trustees has given proper attention to the appointment, duties and supervision of the agents.

'Prudence of ordinary men and women of business in the management of their own affairs'

This requires trustees to satisfy themselves that the financial affairs of the charity are being properly handled in the same way that they would manage their own finances or those of someone else for whom they were morally responsible. Ignorance of what is happening, or the absence of dishonesty on the part of a trustee, is not accepted as prudent behaviour. As a trustee, it is your responsibility to find out all relevant information.

Charities that are established as companies have detailed general duties of directors that must also be observed (see Chapter 2 of the Companies Act 2006).

The requirements of charity accounting are too detailed to include in this book. This chapter only briefly outlines these requirements – for more detailed guidance see the Charity Commission's website/helpline or: NCVO (2014) *The Good Guide to Financial Management*. London: NCVO.

Checklist

Examine your governing document. Does it give you powers to delegate financial matters?

Do you know the terms on which individuals or committees have been delegated financial responsibility by the board of trustees?

Are you satisfied that the charity's financial agents are properly supervised and accountable to the board?

Have you made sure that you know who is responsible for each aspect of your charity's financial management?

Have you made sure that reporting requirements have been agreed and maintained?

Does your board need to organise any training to strengthen the financial skills of the trustees?

Does your charity give all trustees a guide to its accounts that covers items such as designated or restricted funds, and gives any necessary explanations, for example clarifying if amounts raised at fundraising events are shown at gross or net value?

Does your charity give all trustees a list of any significant assets, and any obligations attached to them?

Accounting records

Charity trustees must ensure proper accounting records are kept of all the charity's transactions (including, in particular, all monies received and paid and all assets and liabilities).

The accounting records should disclose with reasonable accuracy at any time the financial position of the charity.

Trustees are not required to keep the records personally, but can delegate this task to staff, volunteers or an agency.

Internal accounting records must be kept for at least six years.

Gift Aid records must be kept for at least six years in line with guidance from HMRC.

Your charity's choice of accounting system should be proportionate to the needs of your charity. For example, a very simple bookkeeping system, perhaps operated by the treasurer or volunteer bookkeeper, should suffice for a small community group with a few thousand pounds of income each year.

On the other hand, a large charity with significant income and expenditure, several projects or services and large numbers of monthly transactions is likely to require a complex system, which could include online billing and invoicing systems, with day-to-day financial management delegated to staff.

In both examples, however, the treasurer has an important role in presenting financial information to trustees, ensuring they understand the financial picture of the charity and can make informed decisions. The mere fact a charity has a treasurer does not lessen responsibilities on trustees collectively for the financial management of the charity.

Budgeting

The board of trustees is responsible for ensuring that the income and expenditure, and assets and liabilities, of the charity are managed in an efficient and effective manner. As a trustee, therefore, you are responsible for taking financial decisions and exercising financial controls. You will need to ensure that the financial management information you work with is accurate, up to date and sufficiently detailed.

Introduction to budgeting

Trustees are responsible for scrutinising and approving a charity's budget. Budgets are simply estimates of future income and expenditure over a period of time (often a financial year). They perform three central roles:

1. controlling activities involving income and expenditure relating to both capital and revenue items

2. monitoring financial performance

3. planning future operations.

Budgets must be more than guesswork. They should be based on the agreed operational plan for the year and be realistic about expected income. You and your fellow trustees should be given details of any assumptions made, such as the rate of inflation, and details of any underlying calculations should be available if you want to investigate any particular item. Trustees should also be made aware of any major risks relating to the budget and how they will be managed.

The budget should build on the accounts for the previous year and include estimates for all significant items of income and expenditure, and an estimate of the surplus or deficit that is expected at the end of the budget period. If the expected income is very uncertain, for example if it depends on the success of several fundraising events, two or three budgets may have to be drawn up prioritising the work your charity will be able to do at different levels of income.

Budget monitoring and reporting

Totals for income and expenditure in the budget should be monitored on a regular basis. A comparison should be made between budgeted income and expenditure and actual income and expenditure.

Trustees should receive reports showing this comparison and explaining the reasons for any material difference between actual and budget figures and giving up-to-date forecasts of income and expenditure for the rest of the financial year. The reports, which should be made at least every three months, should also advise trustees of any action that may be required to bring income or expenditure into line with the budget or forecast. These reports are sometimes called management accounts.

Although management accounts will vary in complexity depending on the size of a charity, all trustees should expect to be able to quickly identify key financial issues from a board financial report – you shouldn't have to wade through pages of figures. You may find that a summary narrative report drawing out key points can help interpret the figures. The treasurer has an important role here to help the board interpret reports and on the bigger picture.

On the basis of these reports, you should authorise appropriate management action and, if necessary, agree changes to the main budget itself. Exception reporting – reports that highlight the items on which there has been a significant overspend or underspend or a significant excess or deficit in income – can help trustees concentrate their attention on areas where action may be needed.

Should individual activity budgets be monitored?

If your charity has several different activities, you should consider having separate income and expenditure budgets for each activity. Reports should also be prepared for each budget on the same basis as that described for a single budget. Trustees will then be able to compare the financial performance of different activities and will be alerted to any financial problems resulting from a particular activity. Individual activity monitoring can help trustees to make informed decisions and can also help identify where the costs of activities are not being fully covered. Charities are encouraged to adopt a 'full cost recovery' method for budgeting individual activities wherever possible (see box).

Full cost recovery

This is a method of understanding the full costs of a particular project, activity or service (the word project is used in this box for clarity), including the proportion of overheads used by that project.

Why use a full cost recovery approach? This method can help charities to be more sustainable by ensuring project budgets cover both direct costs and a fair overhead contribution.

Full cost recovery can also help to monitor overhead costs and ensure the best use of a charity's resources, for example by identifying disproportionately high overhead costs.

Full cost recovery also makes common sense. How can you make rational decisions and future plans without knowing the true cost of a project or service and how it impacts on overhead costs or reserves? For example, understanding the full costs of an activity can help trustees identify where a particular activity is not fully funded. If trustees are to decide to run a project or activity at less than full cost – for example as a pilot, loss leader or for raising profile – they need to do so knowingly. In some cases, it might be inappropriate to subsidise a service from charitable funds, for example where a government body is required by statute to provide the service.

The full cost recovery method involves:

- identifying the overhead costs of the charity, sometimes called 'core costs', which are the costs that cannot be directly attributable to a service or activity, for example the costs of a finance officer or the rent of a general office

- identifying the direct costs associated with a particular activity or service, for example the salary costs of a project worker

- allocating overhead costs to specific projects – rather than, say, allocating a percentage of all overheads to each project, a 'full cost recovery' method can enable you to apportion costs in a sophisticated way that can help better reflect the true cost of a service.

A straightforward example of apportioning overhead costs is to divide the rental costs of a general office between projects based on the floor space used by each project.

A more complex example is the apportioning of governance and strategic costs between projects in a large organisation. The first step involves identifying the governance and strategic costs themselves, including the proportion of the chief executive's time (and hence salary and proportion of their own overhead costs) spent on this activity, along with activities like the cost of organising trustee board meetings. The second step is to allocate the governance and strategic costs between projects, for example by the relative size of each project.

Useful tools exist to help charities adopt full cost recovery. A detailed analysis of the approach is outside the scope of this book; further information is listed in the resources section.

Cash flow

What are cashflow forecasts?
A cash-flow forecast – usually repeated on a monthly basis – analyses money coming into and out of an organisation over a period of time. Cash-flow forecasts and reports are important in helping trustees ensure the charity always has sufficient cash funds to continue operating and to pay bills as they fall due. For example, it might be known that a payment from a contract will be made after the work is completed (in arrears). A cash-flow forecast will warn the board of trustees of any cash shortage that might occur as a result of the timing of payments and enable you to plan accordingly, for example by negotiating a temporary overdraft with your charity's bankers.

Financial controls

Trustees are responsible for establishing, maintaining and regularly reviewing the internal financial controls of their charity. The Charity Commission says trustees should review the effectiveness of their internal financial controls 'at least annually'.

What are internal financial controls? Financial controls are written procedures governing the management of a charity's finances. They help the board ensure finances are safeguarded and used effectively, responsibly and legally, and that everyone is clear about their roles and responsibilities. It is important that the controls are appropriate to the size of your charity and they should not be unduly bureaucratic. If you use an independent examiner or auditor, they may be able to help you decide what measures are suitable for your charity.

In general, trustees should ensure that internal financial controls include:

- details of responsibility for maintaining financial records and preparing reports

- the basis on which trustees delegate responsibilities for financial matters to paid staff, volunteers, committees or financial agents

- procedures for preparing and approving financial plans and budgets

- the charity's banking arrangements

- the payment of staff and other agents of the charity

- policies and procedures for purchasing goods and services

- procedures for authorising expenditure on behalf of the charity

- procedures for controlling, opening, listing and distributing incoming post, including monies received

- procedures for authorising and controlling activities concerned with raising or generating funds by or on behalf of the charity.

The board should review these regulations from time to time to ensure that they are in keeping with the changing needs of the charity.

Further information:
Charity Commission (2012) *Internal Financial Controls for Charities* (CC8). London: Charity Commission.

Charity Commission (2012) *Internal Financial Controls for Charities Checklist* (CC8). London: Charity Commission.

Checklist

Do you have a copy of your charity's budget for the current financial year?

As a trustee do you know how well the charity is performing against its budget?

How regularly do you receive financial monitoring reports and how old are the reports when you get them? (For example, every month/every three months/less frequently than every three months?)

Have you taken appropriate action to deal with any budget deficiencies?

Does your board need to review the financial reports you receive to ensure that they provide sufficient details of the financial performance of individual activities undertaken by your charity?

Do the budget monitoring reports you receive include:

• a comparison of actual and budgeted income and expenditure?

• an explanation of any differences between the actual and budget figures?

• revised forecasts of income and expenditure?

• recommended action (including revisions to the budget) to address any divergence from the budget?

Do you adopt a full cost recovery approach to project budgeting?

Does your board need to check that your charity's financial regulations are comprehensive and relevant to the needs of the charity?

If required, do you ask your independent examiner or auditor to comment on the charity's financial controls?

Annual reporting and accounting

A trustees' annual report and accounts is:

• a crucial document for public accountability (see Chapter 14)

• a good opportunity to review your charity's purposes and progress (or lack of progress) towards them.

What are the minimum regulatory requirements?

All charities must maintain accounting records and prepare accounts covering each financial year. All registered charities (for exempt and excepted charities see page 85) must prepare an annual report, but it is also seen as good practice for excepted and exempt charities to produce an annual report even if it is not legally required.

Who should receive copies of the trustees' annual report and accounts?

All charities must make the accounts and annual report (where they are required to prepare one) available to the public on request. A reasonable charge may be made. Registered charities with a gross income of over £25,000 per year must file the report and accounts with the Charity Commission within 10 months of the financial year end (although early filing is encouraged).

Charities with a formal membership are likely to have requirements in their governing document regarding the circulation of annual reports and accounts to members.

A funder may require a copy of the annual report and accounts.

Charitable companies are subject to company law and must submit a directors' report, including the charity's annual accounts, to Companies House within nine months of the end of the charity's financial year. Company law also requires that the annual reports and accounts are circulated to members.

It should be noted that the information in this section mainly covers the minimum regulatory requirements on charities to produce of annual reports and accounts, but in practice, trustees may wish to go beyond these requirements. For example, trustees often want to ensure that their annual report and accounts are circulated as widely as possible to all those with an interest in the charity, not just to those required by the law and governing document. Trustees also often produce a shorter and more accessible 'annual review' to help with this process (see following page). Note that trustees also need to ensure their 'annual return' is made to the Charity Commission and, where appropriate, to Companies House.

What information should be contained in the annual report and accounts?

The trustees' annual report and accounts consist of two sections:

1. the annual report, summarising the charity's achievements over the financial year

2. the annual accounts, summarising the charity's financial position over the financial year.

The SORP

The accounting and reporting requirements for charities are contained in the Charities Act 2011, The Charities (Accounts and Reports) Regulations 2008 and the Statement of Recommended Practice: Accounting and Reporting by Charities 2005 (SORP). The SORP provides recommended guidance on charity accounting and is a mechanism to help charities comply with the charity accounting regulations.

Although the SORP is described as 'recommended', it is based on the charity accounting and reporting regulations and, therefore, charities are expected to follow the guidance in it. However, the extent to which an individual charity is expected to follow the SORP depends on the charity's size, legal structure and status (some charities such as universities or registered social landlords have a specialist SORP that must be followed instead).

For example, a charity with an annual income of over £100,000 is expected to prepare accounts in accordance with the SORP, whereas a small unincorporated charity with an annual income of under £10,000 is only expected to follow the SORP for the simplified requirements around the content of the annual report and may instead prepare accounts on a receipts and payments basis (see below).

All charitable companies are expected to prepare accounts and an annual report in accordance with the SORP and in accordance with the requirements of company law to prepare a directors' annual report and accounts. In practice, charitable companies often prepare a modified directors' annual report and accounts that is in accordance with the SORP.

A new SORP was published in July 2014, with it becoming effective for all accounting periods beginning on or after 1 January 2015. The extent of the impact of the new SORP on your charity will depend on its legal structure and size.

Excepted, exempt and voluntarily registered charities

The accounting and reporting requirements for excepted and exempt charities are slightly different, and trustees of these charities should consult: Charity Commission (2013) *Charity Reporting and Accounting: The essentials* (CC15b). London: Charity Commission.

Charities registered voluntarily must meet the same requirements as those of registered charities.

Trustees' annual report

The annual report is an opportunity to reflect on the charity's progress over the year, celebrate achievements and explore challenges.

Some of the content of the trustees' annual report is mandatory. The specific requirements for charity annual reports are contained in the Statement of Recommended Practice (SORP) on Accounting by Charities which places an emphasis on the formal narrative section of the annual report and accounts as well as on the format of financial information.

A summary list of the SORP requirements that must be included in a trustees' annual report is included in section H of: Charity Commission (2013) *Charity Reporting and Accounting: The essentials* (CC15b). London: Charity Commission. The requirements vary depending on the size of a charity.

Charitable companies must comply both with the regulations for charity annual reporting and with the regulations under the Companies Acts to produce a directors' report. However, rather than produce two annual reports, many charitable companies produce a directors' report that is modified to contain information that complies with the requirements of charity law.

However, the Charity Commission encourages organisations to go beyond the mandatory list and ensure that the report accurately reflects the charity's achievements during the year.

The annual report does not need to be long, but it should set out the purposes of the charity and how it has gone about achieving those purposes over the year. The Charity Commission, in *Charity Reporting and Accounting: The essentials* (CC15b), says a good annual report will 'bring the charity to life'. It is also a good opportunity to reflect on the progress, achievements and challenges over the year and to highlight the public benefit of the charity's activities.

Our charity publishes an annual review. Is this the trustees' annual report?

Not necessarily. Some organisations produce a trustees' annual report and accounts that satisfy regulatory requirements and a separate 'annual review'. Such a review may be in a 'glossy' format that provides information about a charity's work for supporters, donors, potential funders and beneficiaries. The SORP includes guidance on what needs to be included and the general principles that should be followed in any 'summary financial information and statements' that you may produce.

The annual accounts

The required format of a charity's accounts varies depending on the charity's annual income, level of assets, legal structure, status (ie registered, excepted or exempt) and provisions in its governing document. The circumstances of each charity will determine:

- the type of accounting method that must be used in the preparation of the annual accounts

- how far the charity should prepare accounts in accordance with the SORP

- the level of external scrutiny required of the annual accounts

- what needs to be sent to the Charity Commission and Companies House.

A summary of the requirements for registered charities is set out here. However, it is strongly recommended that trustees check the Charity Commission's clear and helpful guidance to pinpoint their charity's exact requirements: Charity Commission (2013) *Charity Reporting and Accounting: The essentials* (CC15b). London: Charity Commission.

Accounting thresholds

The current accounting and reporting requirements for charities are outlined in Charity Commission (2013) *Charity Reporting and Accounting: The essentials* (CC15b). The following table contains a summary of the current requirements.

Charities that are not companies (including CIOs)

Income per annum	Type of accounting method	Requirements for external scrutiny of accounts	Accounts prepared in accordance with SORP?	What to send annually to the Charity Commission
Gross income does not exceed £25,000	Can be receipts and payments or accruals method	None unless required by governing document	Not if receipts and payments method used	Annual return form if income is £10,000 or more*
				Annual update if income is less than £10,000
Gross income is over £25,000 but less than £250,000	Can be receipts and payments or accruals method	Independent examination or audit unless governing document requires one or the other	Not if receipts and payments method used	Annual return, report (may be simplified) and accounts
Gross income over £250,000 but not more than £500,000 and total assets not more than £3.26m	Accruals method	Independent examination or audit by a registered auditor. If income more than £250,000 then independent examiner must be a member of a body specified under the Charities Act 2011	Yes	Annual return (plus Summary Information return if income over £1m), report and accounts

Gross income over £500,000 (or total assets over £3.26m and income over £250,000)	Accruals method	Audit by a registered auditor	Yes	Annual return report (full) and accounts
CIOs	Can be receipts and payments or accruals method if gross income is less than £250,000 If gross income exceeds £250,000 must be accruals	Must have an audit if either of the following are met in a financial year: • gross income exceeds £500,000 • gross assets exceed £3.26m and gross income exceeds £250,000 Independent examination required if gross income exceeds £25,000. If gross income exceeds £250,000 the independent examiner must be a member of a body specified under the Charities Act 2011	Not if receipts and payments method used	Annual return, report and accounts

* Although very small charities are not obliged to submit an annual information update, by doing so the trustees will meet their charity's legal obligation to keep the Charity Commission informed of changes to the charity.

Charitable companies

Income per annum	Type of accounting method	Minimum statutory requirements for external scrutiny of accounts	Accounts prepared in accordance with SORP?	What to send annually to the Charity Commission	What to send to Companies House **
Gross income does not exceed £25,000	Accruals method	None unless required by governing document	Yes	Annual return, report and accounts	Annual return (in addition to the charity annual return), report and accounts
Gross income is over £25,000 but does not exceed £500,000 and where gross income exceeds £250,000 and gross assets do not exceed £3.2m	Accruals method	Independent examination or audit by a registered auditor unless articles of association require an audit	Yes	Annual return, report and accounts	Annual return (in addition to the charity annual return), report and accounts
Gross income is over £500,000 (or total assets over £3.26m and income over £250,000)	Accruals method	Audit by a registered auditor	Yes	Annual return report (full) and accounts	Annual return (in addition to the charity annual return), report and accounts

** Charitable companies are required to comply with a number of company law reporting requirements, including the filing of an annual return (this is separate from the Charity Commission's annual return), report and accounts and registering changes to the directors, company secretary and the company's registered office as they occur. Please refer to Companies House guidance for further information.

Format of accounts

Accounts must be prepared either on a receipts and payments basis or an accruals basis.

Receipts and payments accounts are a simpler form of accounts, summarising income and expenditure during the year along with a statement of assets and liabilities.

Accruals accounts must be prepared in accordance with the SORP and the 2000 regulations and are designed to show a 'true and fair view' of the accounts. They consist of a balance sheet (see page 91), a statement of financial activities during the year (see page 90) and explanatory notes.

Charitable companies must prepare accruals accounts in accordance with company law and the SORP. By following the SORP, most but not all company law reporting requirements will normally be met.

The Charity Commission produces template accounting packs to help non-company charities follow the receipts and payments or accruals methods. Because of the extra requirements placed on charitable companies, these are only suitable for non-company charities.

Scrutiny of accounts

Independent examination

The 'independent examination' is designed to give small-to medium-sized charities a way of having their accounts reviewed by an independent examiner without the formality or cost of having a professional audit. The regulations have specific requirements over who can carry out an independent examination and the type of report. If a charity's income exceeds £250,000, the independent examiner must be a member of a body specified under the Charities Act 2011.

Professional audit

A professional audit (rather than an 'informal' audit) as required by the Charities Act 2011 involves the accounts being scrutinised by a registered auditor.

Your charity's own requirements

Your charity's own governing document may differ from statutory requirements and may set a higher standard than legislation or the SORP. As trustees, you must comply with your governing document (although you may want to consider amending the governing document to bring your charity into line with the above requirements. You may also want to consider amending your governing document if it just refers to an 'audit' because this may not make it clear what type of audit is required.

A full professional audit may also be a requirement of a funding agreement. If this is the case, it must be followed regardless of the legislative requirements.

The Charity Commission may require an audit in exceptional circumstances, even where one is not a statutory requirement.

Group accounts

Charities with subsidiaries (charitable or non-charitable) must prepare group accounts where the group's annual income – after eliminating intra-group transactions and consolidation adjustments – is over £500,000. For more information, see: Charity Commission (2013) *Charity Reporting and Accounting: The essentials* (CC15b). London: Charity Commission.

Statement of Financial Activities (SOFA)

The SOFA is an annual statement of financial activities and is prepared in accordance with the SORP for organisations preparing accruals accounts. The SOFA is a development from the traditional income and expenditure account and recognises the distinct reporting needs and requirements of charities. It recognises that charities do not usually have one indicator of performance comparable to the bottom line for commercial businesses. The SOFA shows, in summary form, the charity's funds and how they have been used:

- all its funds
- all its incoming resources
- all its revenue expenditure
- all transfers between funds
- all recognised and unrecognised gains and losses on investments
- how the fund balances have changed since the last balance sheet date.

Income and expenditure in the SOFA is in a column format that separates unrestricted funds, restricted funds, permanent endowments and total funds. Income and expenditure is classified under standard SORP headings (although smaller charities are not required to use these headings) including, for incoming resources:

- voluntary income
- activities for generating funds
- investment income
- incoming resources from charitable activities
- other incoming resources

and for outgoing resources (resources expended):

- cost of generating funds (broken down between generating voluntary income, cost of goods sold, investment management costs etc)
- charitable activities
- governance costs (this might not appear under the new SORP).

The balance sheet

The balance sheet is a 'snapshot' of assets (what the charity owns), creditors (what the charity owes) and funds (what resources the charity has available to use to meet its charitable objects) at a particular date. A specimen balance sheet is shown on page 92.

Charities that are required to prepare their accounts in accordance with the SORP must prepare their balance sheet according to SORP guidelines.

Charities preparing accounts on a receipts and payments basis may prepare a statement of assets and liabilities. This is not the same as a balance sheet, because there is no requirement to balance.

What do trustees need to look out for in a balance sheet?

If you think your charity may be in financial difficulty you should apply the following simple balance sheet test for insolvency.

Are your assets less than your total liabilities?

Bear in mind that the fixed assets are not generally available to provide short-term funds, and balance sheet figures are not an indication of what might be obtained for the assets in a forced sale.

If 'provisions' are included in your accounts, it is important that you determine whether or not these provisions are realistic and relevant to the accounts in which they are made. For example, if there is a legal case pending against the charity, your lawyers may estimate that the costs and damages payable will add up to £1,000. If the case were to be settled you could reduce or eliminate the provision.

Trustees should look at the net current asset position, because it gives some indication of the charity's ability to meet its short-term financing needs. But remember that a balance sheet shows the charity's position at one point in time. It should not be relied upon in isolation to assess a charity's ability to fund its current and future activities. This must be done by proper cash flow forecasting and budgeting, which should use the balance sheet as its starting point.

The distinction between restricted and unrestricted funds is crucial. Misapplying restricted funds amounts to a breach of trust and could result in the trustees having personally to make good the misspent funds. It is recommended that assets and liabilities representing the funds are analysed between restricted and general funds to ensure that each fund is separately represented by adequate and appropriate assets. Such an analysis would normally be disclosed in the notes to the accounts. Solvency is vitally important, so advice should be taken if there are doubts.

Checklist

Does your board need to review whether your charity is keeping records of accounts in a form that will satisfy your legal obligations?

Are you sure that the most recent accounts and trustees' report were properly authorised by the whole board and that your charity has a procedure for authorising future reports and accounts?

Does your board need to review its procedures for ensuring that an annual return and trustees' report and accounts (if required) are submitted to the Charity Commission?

If your organisation is a charitable company, does your board need to review its procedures for ensuring that an annual return and trustees' report and accounts are submitted to Companies House?

Does your charity need to have its accounts scrutinised? If so, has your charity appointed an independent examiner or auditor to carry out this work for the current year's accounts?

If you already have an independent examiner or auditor, are you sure you have taken due care in their selection and made sure that they have the skill, knowledge and experience required?

If you appoint an auditor, has your board agreed proper terms of engagement with the auditor?

Does your board regularly review the guidance in the SORP?

Specimen balance sheet

Key to terms used:

Accruals – expenses listed in a report that have been incurred but which remain unpaid at the date of the report.

Debtors – money owed to the charity.

Deferred income – income listed in a report which has been received but relate to a period following the date of the report.

Liabilities or creditors – money owed by the charity, either short term – expected to be paid within a year (eg debts to pay) – or long term (eg loans).

Provisions – charges listed in a balance sheet for costs or expenditure which cannot be precisely calculated.

Statement of financial activities – example

Care Home Trust Limited

Consolidated statement of financial activities (including an income and expenditure account) for the year ended March 2013

Consolidated balance sheets as at 31 March 2013

	Notes	Group 2013 £'000	Group 2012 £'000
Fixed assets			
Tangible assets	10	830	850
Investments	4	137	129
		967	979
Current assets			
Stocks	11	217	213
Debtors	12	290	287
Cash at bank and in hand	423	423	319
		930	819
Creditors: amounts falling due within one year	13	242	195
Net current assets		688	624
Total assets less current liabilities		1,655	1,603
Creditors: amounts falling due after more than one year	15	46	56
		1,609	1,547
Funds			
Unrestricted funds			
General	16	1,430	1,363
Designated	16	167	167
Restricted funds	17	12	17
		1,609	1,547

Approved by the board on 13 June 2013 and signed on its behalf by:

S.A. Bloggs, Chairman

Investments

Once a charity has more money than it needs to operate in the forthcoming year, it should start to develop plans as to how that money could be used to further its charitable purposes.

There are a number of ways in which a charity can invest, and different considerations and legal duties will apply to each one. The following guidance is available: Charity Commission (2011) *Charities and Investment Matters: A guide for trustees* (CC14). London: Charity Commission. This mainly concentrates on two types of investment: financial (increasing capital or generating income) and programme related (furthering charitable purposes) – the latter is often referred to as 'social investment'. It also includes information on 'mixed motive' investment, where an investment is made for both financial and programme-related reasons.

The rest of the information in this section relates to financial investment by trustees.

What are trustees' main responsibilities with regard to investment?

Trustees have overall responsibility for the investment of a charity's funds. They may delegate the management of investments to a third party, but they remain responsible for making the strategic decisions in respect of the stewardship of the charity's assets.

Trustees have a general duty of care when making investment decisions. This means that they must use reasonable skill and care when carrying out their duties and use their personal knowledge and experience as required (see section 3.2).

Trustees have a responsibility to get the best possible financial return on a charity's financial investments for the level of risk that is appropriate for the charity. The Charity Commission guidance highlights the legal obligations with regards to investments, summarising that trustees should:

- know, and act within, their charity's powers to invest (legal requirement)

- exercise care and skill when making investment decisions (legal requirement)

- select investments that are right for their charity. This means taking account of:

  – how suitable any investment is for the charity

  – the need to diversify investments (legal requirement)

- take advice from someone experienced in investment matters unless they have good reason for not doing so (legal requirement)

- follow certain legal requirements if they are going to use someone to manage investments on their behalf (legal requirement)

- review investments from time to time (legal requirement)

- explain their investment policy (if they have one) in the trustees' annual report (legal requirement).

In considering the charity's investment policy or criteria, and monitoring the implementation of that policy, trustees may need to seek professional advice. In part this depends on the legal structure of the charity and whether or not the Trustee Act 2000 applies to the charity. Trustees, even those with some financial expertise, tend to seek advice in these circumstances, given their duty to act with reasonable skill and care or prudently. Generally the trustees need to consider:

- diversification to reduce the risk – a diversified portfolio of investments is one in which investment funds are spread across a number of different investments, which reduces the risk attached to any single investment

- asset allocation strategy to best meet the investment objective - the type of investment class (eg equities, bonds or property) and the particular investments within that class (eg direct investment or through pooled funds)

- the long-term future of the charity by considering the effects of inflation.

Trustees should take advice from someone experienced in investment matters where they consider they need it. Where trustees take advice, they should ensure that the person they approach is suitably qualified and has adequate experience of investment matters; this could be an accountant, bank manager, investment manager, member of the charity's staff or one of the trustees. Trustees who give investment advice should consider the extent of any potential professional negligence liability that they may incur by doing so and the charity should consider its ability to rely on such advice.

What are the investment powers of trustees?
All charities can make financial investments, but each charity's specific powers will depend on its legal form (eg incorporated or unincorporated) and any conditions or limitations placed on its powers by its governing document.

Unincorporated charities

If the trust deed or constitution of your unincorporated charity does not specifically restrict your power of investment or if a trust deed or constitution refers to the Trustee Investments Act 1961, the Trustee Act 2000 will apply. The Trustee Act 2000 was introduced to replace the limited powers granted in the Trustee Investments Act 1961 giving trustees wider powers of investment.

Trustees are now able to make the kind of investments that an absolute owner would have the power to do. A range of new powers to appoint agents, nominees and custodians, to insure trust property and to pay professional trustees supports the wider powers of investment.

The powers provided by the Trustee Act 2000 are default powers designed to facilitate trustees governed by old or poorly drafted trust instruments. Some trust instruments may contain wider powers of investment than those conferred by the Trustee Act 2000, in which case these powers would apply.

Charitable companies

The Trustee Act 2000 does not apply to charitable companies in respect of the company's property. A company's charitable powers are derived from and governed by the provisions of the company's governing documents.

Trustees of charitable companies face similar obligations to those listed in the Trustee Act 2000, even though the Act does not apply to them expressly. They must act to promote the purpose of the company and not in their own interest. As a result, when making investments in respect of a charitable company, subject to any specific requirements about investments in the company's governing documents, trustees must act prudently within their power to maximise the return on the invested assets and in the best interest of the company.

The Trustee Act 2000 may apply to other funds held on charitable trust for which the company acts as trustee. For example, a charitable company could administer trusts set up by donors for charitable purposes and the Act would apply to these if the trust deed did not state specific restrictions or give a wide power of investment.

Unincorporated charities

Common law and statutory duty of care

The Trustee Act 2000 introduced a new statutory duty to create certainty and consistency to the standard expected from a trustee in relation to investment powers. The statutory duty applies to trustees of both existing and new trusts. However, the duty can be excluded or amended by the trust instrument (see section 3.2 for more information on the general duty of care for trustees).

The Trustee Act 2000 says that a trustee:

'must exercise such care and skill as is reasonable in the circumstances, having regard in particular:

1 to any special knowledge or experience that s/he has or holds herself/himself out as having, and

2 if s/he acts as trustee in the course of business or profession, to any special knowledge or experience that it is reasonable to expect of a person acting in the course of that kind of business or profession.'

There are two parts to this test.

First, what is reasonable in the circumstances given the knowledge and experience the trustee has or holds themselves out as having? The greater your experience and knowledge, the higher the standard of conduct expected. Second, if you are acting in the course of business, ie as a professional trustee, your conduct would be assessed with the skills normally possessed by such a person.

Exercising your investment powers

Trustees of unincorporated trusts exercising their power of investment, whether under the Trustee Act 2000 or the trust's constitution, have a duty to consider the 'standard investment criteria' and a duty to take advice. The standard investment criteria require trustees to consider:

• the suitability of the general investments of the trust and of particular investments

• the need for diversification, both in terms of risk and to balance income and capital growth.

These duties cannot be excluded or limited by the trust instrument. You must demonstrate that you have considered these criteria and you must review the investments held by the trust from time to time.

Before exercising any power of investment or making a review of investments held by a trust, you must obtain 'proper advice', unless you reasonably conclude that, in all the circumstances, it is unnecessary or inappropriate to do so. The person who gives this advice must be, in the reasonable opinion of the trustees, someone qualified to give it by his or her ability and practical experience of financial and other matters relating to the proposed investment.

Delegation of investment powers
Under the Trustee Act 2000, an agent can be appointed by the trustees to exercise his or her investment powers. Such an agent would be subject to the duty to consider the standard investment criteria.

If the agent is someone who would be a person deemed to give proper advice, she or he is not obliged to obtain and consider proper advice.

Where trustees delegate asset management powers, the agency contract must be in writing and must require the agent to comply with a policy statement. The policy statement sets out the objective of the trust to guide the agent and must ensure that the investment function will be exercised in the best interest of the trust.

There is a duty to review the arrangement of the delegation, and as a matter of good practice, this should take place every 12 months; in some cases a more frequent review may be necessary.

Are ethical/responsible investment policies permitted?
Yes, provided guidelines are followed. An ethical/responsible approach can help ensure that a charity's investment policy is consistent with its charitable objects.

Trustees should normally exercise financial investment powers to provide the greatest financial benefit for the charity with an appropriate level of risk. An ethical/responsible investment approach can be entirely consistent with this duty.

The Charity Commission states that:

'Ethical investment means investing in a way that reflects a charity's values and ethos and does not run counter to its aims. However, charity's trustees must be able to justify why it is in the charity's best interests to invest in this way'.[6]

The guidance goes on to say that the law permits the following reasons for an ethical/responsible investment:

• a particular investment conflicts with the aims of the charity

• the charity might lose supporters or beneficiaries if it does not invest ethically

• there is no significant financial detriment.

What is involved in socially responsible investment?
An ethical/responsible approach may involve one or more of the following behaviours.

1 Screening: drawing up criteria (both positive and negative) governing the selection of investments, for example, companies with good environmental policies (positive) or companies involved in tobacco (negative).

2 Preference: identifying environmental, ethical or social guidelines that trustees would like companies to follow.

3 Engagement: encouraging companies, for example through 'stakeholder activism', to make improvements in their environmental, ethical or social performance.

6 Charity Commission (2011) *Charities and Investment Matters: A guide for trustees* (CC14). London: Charity Commission.

In developing an ethical/responsible investment policy, trustees should make decisions in the interests of the charity and not based on their own personal ethical concerns. However, given that an ethical/responsible investment policy should satisfy the charity's stakeholders, it is important to debate the ethical views of trustees and stakeholders as part of the development of a policy.

Ethical/responsible investment is a complex topic and if trustees are in any doubt they should seek professional advice.

Further information:
Charity Commission (2011) *Charities and Investment Matters: A guide for trustees (CC14)*. London: Charity Commission.

Charity Commission (2013) *Charities and Social Investment* (RS30). London: Charity Commission.

NCVO (2014) *The Good Guide to Financial Management*. London: NCVO.

Other investment issues
How should assets be treated?
Trustees have a general duty to ensure that the assets of a charity (eg property owned by the charity) are managed efficiently and held securely and that income is used in pursuit of the charity's objects. You should be provided with details of the assets owned by the charity and given information on any special, restricted categories of funds, such as permanent endowments or appeal funds, which may not be used for the general purposes of the charity and details of the safeguards in place to protect them.

See section 3.4 for guidance on investment of assets that form part of the charity's permanent endowment.

Are there any investment funds designed specifically for charities?
Common investment funds and common deposit funds for charities have been approved by of the Charity Commission. They are similar to unit trusts but take advantage of charities' tax position. They allow charities to pool their funds so that they can be invested in a wide spread of investments by specialist investment managers, thus spreading the management costs and risks.

Tax issues
Charities can benefit from tax exemptions on investment income when the income is used to further their charitable objects. Trustees however need to be clear about the type of investments that HMRC might consider to be 'non-charitable expenditure', as this could lead to restrictions on the charity's tax reliefs. For example, there may be tax implications for loans to or investments in a trading subsidiary that is connected to the charity. Advice should be sought.

Can trustees be held personally liable for investment decisions?
The Charity Commission's guidance states that:

'If trustees can demonstrate that they have considered the relevant issues, taken advice where appropriate and reached a reasonable decision, they are unlikely to be criticised for their decisions, or for adopting a particular policy.'[7]

Should trustees agree an investment policy?
It is strongly recommended by the Charity Commission that trustees agree an investment policy in writing and keep it under regular review. Such a policy is a legal requirement if investment is delegated to an investment manager. An investment policy can help trustees ensure they are fulfilling their duty to make good use of a charity's funds.

7 Charity Commission (2011) *Charities and Investment Matters: A guide for trustees* (CC14). London: Charity Commission.

A written investment policy should include the following.

1 Investment objectives: What the charity is trying to achieve by investing its funds, eg to maximise income and/or to preserve or grow the capital.

2 Risks: What are the key risks relevant to the investment assets (eg inflation, reputational, cash flow) and how are these risks minimised.

3 Other considerations: Liquidity requirements, time horizon, ethical or responsible policies and the management and monitoring arrangements.

See Chapter 8 for guidance on the policy-making role of trustees.

Checklist

Does your board need to satisfy itself that the charity's governing document contains all of the appropriate investments powers that may be needed?

Do trustees understand their duties and responsibilities in respect of investments?

Does your charity have a written investment policy that effectively links to the strategic plan?

Does your policy refer to ethical or responsible considerations?

• If so, have you got a copy? And

• Is it reviewed and updated when required?

Does your board need to check the terms on which advisers or investment managers have been appointed?

Are you satisfied that any investment managers employed by your charity are properly supervised and holdings appropriately safeguarded?

Do you have up-to-date records of your charity's assets and restricted funds?

Social investment

Unlike financial investments, the primary purpose of 'social investments' or 'programme-related investments' is to further an organisation's charitable objects or purposes rather than purely for financial gain. The Charity Commission considers that with social investment there is an expectation that there will be a financial return. With social/programme-related investments, the trustees' legal duties are different to those for financial investments.

What is social/programme-related investment?

Social/programme-related investment uses charitable resources to finance other organisations and individuals in a way that:

- furthers the charity's charitable objects/purposes

- is for public rather than private benefit

- is expected to produce some financial return (although not the primary purpose).

Further information:
Charity Commission (2011) *Charities and Investment Matters: A guide for trustees* (CC14). London: Charity Commission.

Charity Finance Group and Charity Investors Group (undated) Guide to Investment Policy. London: Charity Investors Group – www.charityinvestorsgroup.org.uk/ Charity_Investors_Group/ Initiatives_files/Investment%20 Policy%20Statement%20Final.pdf

Reserves

What are reserves?

Reserves are defined by the Charity Commission as: 'that part of a charity's unrestricted funds that is freely available to spend on any of the charity's purposes'. This definition excludes funds where use is restricted or funds that have been designated for a particular purpose.

What are trustees' responsibilities with regard to reserves?

Trustees have a duty to spend the income of the charity within a reasonable time unless they have a power to do otherwise. This power may be explicit in the governing document or, more often, trustees will need to rely on an implied power to hold reserves. The Charity Commission states: in its publication Charities and Reserves (CC19):

'The holding of reserves will be authorised either by using an express or implied power to hold reserves. Trustee are justified in exercising their power to hold income reserves, whether express or implied only if, in their considered view, it is necessary in the charity's best interests... If the power is used without justification then the holding of income in reserve might amount to a breach of trust.'[8]

Trustees should therefore explain and justify the level of reserves their charity holds and, to fulfil this duty, should agree a reserves policy.

Why have reserves?

All charities require a minimum level of reserves to cover contingencies and to provide a level of working capital. Reserves can ensure the charity has, for example sufficient funds to provide its service, pay its staff and creditors, allow for possible maternity, sickness or redundancy payments, keep its property in good repair, pay for insurance and replace equipment and, if necessary, close down in a controlled way.

Indeed, the existence of reserves is a sign of good financial management. You could be judged to be acting negligently if you do not ensure that your charity has adequate reserves.

However, allowing reserves to build up without good reason could lead to bad publicity, funders being unwilling to grant further funding and, ultimately, could amount to a breach of trust or trigger tax liabilities.

8 Charity Commission (2010) *Charities and Reserves* (CC19). London: Charity Commission.

What should a reserves policy cover?

A reserves policy should cover:

- why the charity needs reserves

- the level of reserves believed to be required

- how the reserves will be maintained at the agreed level

- arrangements for monitoring and reviewing the reserves policy.

Drawing up a reserves policy involves:

- conducting an analysis of existing funds, income streams, expenditure and cash flow

- analysing the need for reserves

- calculating the reserves level

- formulating the reserves policy

- deciding how the reserves policy should be presented.

The reserves policy should be based on the assessment of:

- the level, reliability and source of future income streams

- a forecast of future, planned expenditure

- an identification of future circumstances, for example needs, opportunities, contingencies and risks, that are unlikely to be met out of income

- identifying the likelihood of each future circumstance and the consequences of the charity in not being able to meet them.

The reserves policy should be in writing and agreed by the trustees. In the unlikely event that trustees decide that their charity does not need to hold money in reserves, they will still need a reserves policy in order to explain and justify their position.

What must trustees do?

Charity trustees are required by SORP to make a statement in their annual report about the level of reserves held and the reasons for holding them.

Further information:
Charity Commission (2010)
Charities and Reserves (CC19).
London: Charity Commission.

Checklist

Does your charity have a policy on the level of reserves it holds or is seeking to hold and why it needs reserves?

Is the reserves policy reviewed each year?

Are new trustees given a copy of the reserves policy? Does it meet regulatory requirements?

Insolvency and wrongful trading

If your charity is unincorporated, the rules explained here will not apply. Because an unincorporated charity has no separate legal personality from that of its trustees/members, the trustees/members of such charities could face unlimited personal liability for the debts and obligations of the charity if it cannot meet those debts from its own assets. Trustees of unincorporated charities that employ staff, occupy property and/or have significant contractual arrangements should consider incorporation.

What is the law concerning insolvency and wrongful trading?

Wrongful trading is defined in the Insolvency Act 1986 and applies to charities established as companies or CIOs. It takes place if a company continues to operate when the company directors know, or ought to know, that there is no reasonable prospect of the company avoiding going into insolvent liquidation, which is the equivalent for a company of becoming bankrupt. The only defence to the claim is that the company directors took every reasonable step to minimise potential losses to the charity's creditors.

The directors of a charitable company are the charity trustees and, when wrongful trading occurs, the term 'director' can include shadow directors, ie the people 'in accordance with whose directions or instructions the directors of the charitable company are accustomed to act'. The intention is to cover those who 'pull the strings' of a company but who are not formally on the board. Therefore, in some instances, staff, such as the chief executive or finance director, could also share responsibility.

Charitable companies do sometimes get into financial difficulties. It can be tempting to continue the charity's activities in the hope that the financial situation will improve. However, where the charity is in danger of going into insolvent liquidation, the trustees of charitable companies must put the needs of the company's creditors first and always take positive steps to minimise their potential loss. An essential part of this is ensuring the trustees have up-to-date financial information and act on it. This may mean meeting more often than usual.

Assessing whether the charity can survive – for example where the trustees consider a grant application or a tender for a contract is reasonably likely to be successful – and balancing this against the risk of becoming insolvent can be a difficult decision and advice may be required. In some cases, stopping all activities immediately may not be in the interests of creditors either, for example closing a shop may prevent further sales and reduce funds available for creditors.

If found guilty of wrongful trading, you and your fellow trustees could be held personally liable by the court to make a contribution to the assets of the charity for the purposes of enabling payment to creditors. In practice, this is very rare, especially in the context of unpaid charity trustees. If your charitable company becomes insolvent you could be disqualified (for 2–15 years) from being a company director.

What is the law concerning fraudulent trading?

Fraudulent trading is judged to have happened if, in the course of winding up a charitable company, it appears that any business of the charity has been carried on with the intent to defraud the charity's creditors or for any fraudulent purpose. An example is where trustees incur a debt knowing there is little prospect of it ever being repaid.

It should be noted that employees as well as trustees could find themselves liable for fraudulent trading if it is proven.

Fraudulent trading is both a criminal and civil offence and applies where there has been actual dishonesty in the running of the charity. Apart from any penalties a court may impose, trustees may be required to make good the creditors' losses.

Insolvency is a complex legal area, a full consideration of which is outside the scope of this guide. If your charity finds itself in any financial doubt or difficulty, then the best action is to take advice.

If your charity is in financial difficulties, you need to take advice from your solicitor or from an insolvency practitioner about your ability (or otherwise) to trade through the difficulties or alternative insolvency procedures that might be pursued by or against you.

Checklist

Are trustees aware of their responsibilities in respect of insolvency and wrongful trading?

Are trustees aware of the importance of taking advice when necessary?

Are trustees clear about whether they need the protection of incorporation as a company?

Taxation and rating

It is widely believed that charities are in some way exempt from paying taxes or VAT. This is not true, but they can and do benefit from specific tax exemptions and relief.

Trustees therefore need to understand how taxation may affect their charity for two main reasons:

- an unexpected tax bill or unclaimed tax relief could have a significant effect on the organisation's financial position

- failure to manage the organisation's tax affairs properly may expose trustees to personal financial liability for its tax bills.

Who is responsible for paying the charity's tax?

An unincorporated charity has no separate legal identity from its trustees and members. This means that you can be held personally liable for taxes arising from your charity's activities. In practice, this is not a problem when the organisation has the necessary funds to pay, but personal liabilities can arise if it becomes insolvent.

Trustees of a charitable company are not liable for the charity's taxes except where personal liability arises as a result of poor administration.

What are trustees' responsibilities with regard to tax and rates?

Trustees are responsible for ensuring that the tax affairs of their charity are properly handled in a way which gives rise to the minimum tax. This involves payment of any tax liabilities, including PAYE, income tax (unincorporated charities), capital gains, VAT and corporation tax, structuring the charity to minimise these liabilities, including for example establishing a trading subsidiary for any non 'primary purpose' or charitable trade, and promptly claiming all tax reliefs available to the charity. Trustees should ensure that the charity reclaims income tax paid on donations made under Gift Aid, payroll giving or other tax-effective giving schemes (see page 113). They should also ensure that the charity has obtained the 80% mandatory business rate relief on any premises occupied by the charity. This relief does not apply to the premises of wholly owned trading companies. Some local authorities allow charities up to 100% business rate relief, so trustees should ensure that applications for additional relief have been made.

Trustees should ensure their charity is not involved in a scheme designed to reduce a landlord's exposure to business rates, which are under increasing scrutiny from local authorities and the Charity Commission.

Obtaining advice

The taxation of charities can be a complex matter and professional advice may be necessary. If you fail to organise your charity's affairs in a way that minimises the tax liability, you could be judged to be acting imprudently and be personally liable to make good any resulting loss. Keep notes of any professional advice you receive. You will remain responsible for any decisions you make regarding your charity's tax and rating provision, but having sought professional advice will be a protection if problems arise.

Checklist

Are you confident that your organisation complies with its tax obligations?

Have you kept copies of any professional advice you may have received on this subject?

Internal audit

Internal audit is a practice that has spread across government and business, its value being dependent on the need for it to provide an independent and objective assessment. Although mainly associated with finance, it can also give assurance of compliance and performance, proper recording and honesty. Internal audit may be the responsibility of an audit committee or staff advisors, or a separate group who report direct to the board.

Should charities have an audit committee?

The Code states that the board, as the accountable body, needs to:

'maintain and regularly review the systems of financial controls, internal controls, performance reporting, policies and procedures with the board periodically taking steps to assure itself of their effectiveness and relevance to the activities the organisation undertakes and the risks it faces.'[9]

One way in which trustees could demonstrate that they are fulfilling this responsibility would be by establishing an internal audit function or committee with a remit to review, monitor and assure adherence to the law, standards, policy etc and to share its findings.

Some larger charities have done this by setting up a small internal audit committee, appointed at the highest level, to fulfil that role. Those involved in internal audit are committed to act as 'protectors of the conscience' of the charity – to be guarantors of the proper stewardship of resources and the charity's integrity. The board lays down its remit and it reports directly to the board.

A small charity is unlikely to need a separate internal audit committee, as the scale of the charity's operations will mean that it will be possible for the whole board to keep in touch with all the organisation's activities.

An audit committee is likely to work best through a small group of high-calibre members chosen for their experience, maturity and independence of mind, drawn from varied backgrounds. A typical audit committee will have about four members and will meet about four times a year.

What are the terms of reference of an audit committee?

Audit committees assist the board by ensuring that appropriate accounting and financial policies and controls are in place. Internal audit is the process of checking that such policies are actually followed.

The audit committee will consider the reports of external auditors and the responses of staff to them, ensuring that external and internal control processes are properly co-ordinated and working effectively. In some circumstances, the committee should be prepared to oversee special one-off inquiries.

Should the work of the audit committee be reviewed?

The work of an audit committee can be worthwhile, providing it concentrates on essentials, avoids being 'a rubber stamp' and earns respect within and outside the charity. It is appropriate for the committee itself to be reviewed and assessed for effectiveness.

A developing role for audit committees

Audit committees are coming to be seen as a hallmark of a healthy and responsible organisation. However, even when at their best, there is a limit to the protection they can offer against serious misjudgements or the ill-advised use of resources.

Public pressures are in the direction of greater accountability, which is reflected in the development of social and environmental audits; trustees need to be aware account of this.

These ideas have been brought together in the concept of the triple bottom line – adding a social and environmental bottom line to the traditional financial bottom line.

9 NCVO (2010) *Good Governance: A code for the voluntary and community sector.* London: NCVO.

7.2

Checklist

Have trustees reviewed the need for an audit committee?

If an audit committee is in place, does it have clear terms of reference?

Is the role of the audit committee periodically reviewed?

Is an internal audit process appropriate as a separate function and if so to whom should it report?

Land, property and intellectual property

Responsibilities for acquiring, managing and disposing of land and property

Trustees have a duty to protect all the charity's assets, for example by ensuring that there are adequate financial controls and that any land or buildings the charity owns are well maintained and insured (see section 3.4). Particular responsibilities arise in relation to land and property, which means that decisions about its acquisition, use and disposal should be taken by the whole trustee board and not delegated to an individual or committee. Caution is required when borrowing money and using charitable assets as security. Given the complexity and potential risks involved, trustees should consider the need to seek professional advice in relation to these matters.

What do trustees need to do before acquiring land or property?

Trustees have a duty of care when acquiring land and property (see section 3.2 for more information on duty of care), but they also have specific duties that the Charity Commission expects them to consider.

The Charity Commission states that:

Trustees need to take all reasonable steps to ensure that:

- they have the necessary power or authority to purchase the land

- the property is suitable for its intended use and, in particular, is not subject to any legal or planning restrictions or conditions which might conflict with that use, or with which it may be difficult for the trustees to comply

- any necessary planning permission is obtained

- the price or rent to be paid is a fair one compared with similar properties on the market

- the charity can afford the purchase – in particular that if a property is being bought with a mortgage, the mortgage can be financed out of the resources of the charity which are available for the purpose and that any potential rises in interest rates have been budgeted for

- when acquiring a lease, they understand the obligations to which they will be subject under the lease, and that the terms of the lease are fair and reasonable

- on specialised matters, appropriate professional advisers (a solicitor or a qualified surveyor, for instance) should be consulted. The cost of taking professional advice can be met by the charity

- if trustees are buying land with the aid of a loan, it is their duty to secure the best borrowing terms reasonably obtainable by comparing interest rates and other terms between various lenders.[10]

10 Charity Commission (2001) *Acquiring Land* (CC33). London: Charity Commission.

Does the charity, or do the trustees, own the land or property?
Charitable companies, as incorporated organisations, have a legal personality. It is therefore possible for charitable companies to own land and property legally as well as beneficially.

Unincorporated charities (ie trusts and associations) have no independent legal existence, so they cannot legally own land or property. Land and property must be held on behalf of the charity by named individuals. As trustees change, a formal deed transferring trust land or property to the new trustees or the remaining trustees is essential. The details registered at HM Land Registry will also need to be amended. These procedures can be time consuming and costly, particularly if there are a large number of trustees or their turnover is high. Many trusts and associations therefore appoint holding trustees or a custodian trustee. However, as a trustee you could still be personally liable, for example, if fundraising fails and there is not enough money to pay the rent. If you have behaved reasonably and honestly you may be entitled to an indemnity from the charity's assets, but you would remain personally liable if the assets were insufficient to meet the debts.

Unincorporated charities

What are holding trustees?
Holding trustees, or custodian trustees, are individuals appointed by an unincorporated charity to hold land or property on that charity's behalf. The holding or custodian trustees take no active part in the management of the charity; they merely carry out the instructions of the trustees. Sometimes it is difficult to find people willing to act as holding trustees and it may be preferable to appoint a corporate body to be a custodian trustee, such as a parish council or the Official Custodian – an official of the Charity Commission whose function is to hold land on behalf of charity trustees. However, before carrying out the trustees' instructions, the Official Custodian will check that these are in accordance with the terms of the trust and any necessary consents have been obtained.

> **Further information:**
> Charity Commission (2004)
> *The Official Custodian for Charities' Land Holding Service* (CC13).
> London: Charity Commission.

What are trustees' responsibilities for managing property and land?
Trustees have a duty to protect the charity's land and property and should make sure that any land or property owned by the charity, or held on the charity's behalf, is kept in a good state of repair and is adequately insured. Sufficient funds should be set aside for routine maintenance, interior and exterior redecorating and longer-term repairs, such as re-roofing.

If any property is a permanent endowment (given in perpetuity so that the capital may not be spent) you must make sure that it is used by the charity for its purposes or earns an income for the charity to maximise the income you can earn from it without reducing its capital value (see section 3.4 for more information on permanent endowment).

What are trustees' responsibilities for disposing of land or property?
If you want to sell or lease any of your charity's land or buildings, even for a short period on an informal tenancy, the Charities Act 2011 requires you in most instances to obtain and consider a report from a qualified surveyor, who must act exclusively for the charity (ie the surveyor must not act for any other party involved in this transaction). In some instances, as advised by the surveyor, the disposal must be advertised. Any agreement must be concluded on terms which are the best that the charity could reasonably obtain in the circumstances. The surveyor's report must be in writing if the disposal is a sale or a lease for more than seven years.

If the property or land being sold or leased is subject to trusts requiring it to be used for a specific purpose of the charity (eg an orphanage or museum), you must check if you have the power to sell the property before you put it on the market. You must then advertise what you are planning to do to give the public the opportunity to raise any objections.

If you are unable to follow this procedure, or if you wish to sell the land to a person connected with the charity or its trustees (the definition of a connected person for the purpose of disposing of charity land is set out in the Charities Act 2011), you must seek the consent of the Charity Commission.

You are allowed to accept less than the full market price if you are disposing of land or property to another charity whose charitable objects come within the objects of your charity.

You may raise a mortgage on the charity's property provided you obtain written advice from someone experienced in financial matters who has no personal interest in the proposed loan. The person giving advice can be a trustee or an employee of the charity. The advice must include whether the loan is necessary, whether the terms are reasonable and whether the charity can repay the loan.

Further information:
Charity Commission (2011) *Sales, Leases, Transfers or Mortgages: What trustees need to know about disposing of charity land* (CC28). London: Charity Commission.

Checklist

Do you need to appoint holding or custodian trustees?

If your board is acquiring or disposing of land or property, are you following the correct procedures?

Are you confident that you have set aside sufficient funds to meet the cost of repairs and maintenance?

If your responsibilities towards a property are significant, have you considered incorporating as a company limited by guarantee?

Intellectual property and brands

Charities are often unaware of the value of the rights they have in so-called 'intellectual property'. This can include a wide range of things that are produced by a charity, including:

- trademarks, for example to protect the charity's name and logo
- copyright, such as copyrights in marketing and promotional materials and in computer software specially commissioned for the charity (eg a specially written database application)
- database rights, for example in donor and fundraising databases
- design rights, in artistic and other designs
- patents, for example in pharmaceutical products or a piece of equipment that might help a charity fulfil its objectives, such as a water pump.

These rights can be a valuable asset to a charity, and as a result the trustees have a duty to preserve their value and prevent them being wrongfully used or damaged by third parties.

7.3

Your charity should take steps to ensure that it:

- knows what intellectual property it owns

- properly identifies intellectual property when it is created

- secures and preserves all intellectual property.

When a charity commissions any intellectual property, it should ensure that it owns the intellectual property and has free access to all other materials necessary to use it properly. If anyone other than an employee creates intellectual property (eg a consultant), the intellectual property will generally belong to the person creating it rather than the charity in the absence of an agreement to the contrary.

If third parties are using intellectual property without authorisation, trustees should consider taking steps to stop that use to prevent the charity losing any rights it has over that intellectual property.

If a charity has a valuable piece of intellectual property that it wishes to preserve and protect, it is often worth getting appropriate legal advice about the best way to do so. It is usually easier to achieve the charity's objectives if this advice is sought before the relevant piece of intellectual property is acquired or created.

Checklist

Does your organisation know what intellectual property it holds?

If so, have you taken adequate steps to secure and protect intellectual property?

Financial sustainability

Trustees should seek to ensure that the charity remains solvent and has sufficient resources to pursue its charitable purposes – a duty that will require you to take an active interest in the funding base of the organisation.

We use the term 'funding base' as opposed to 'fundraising' because increasingly charities are working beyond traditional 'fundraising' to help them ensure their charity has a financially sustainable future. This involves diversifying their income streams and developing 'a mixed economy of funding' that incorporates grants and donations, contracts and service level agreements but also unrestricted income from trading goods and services.

The income spectrum
There are many different sources of funding and financing available to help cover the costs of charitable activities. One way of understanding these sources of income is by using the 'income spectrum' a tool developed by NCVO.

From asking to earning – the income spectrum

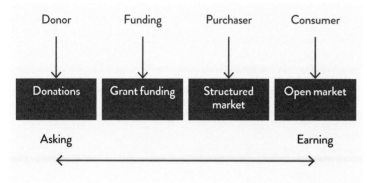

What are trustees' duties and responsibilities for financial sustainability?

The trustees must ensure that the charity:

• is and will remain solvent

• uses charitable funds and assets reasonably and only in furtherance of the charity's objects

• avoids undertaking activities that might place the charity's endowment, funds, assets or reputation at undue risk

• takes special care when investing the charity's funds or borrowing funds for it to use.

Trustees must also:

• comply with the law and the charity's governing document

• act in the best interests of the charity's beneficiaries now and in the future

• comply with the trustees' 'duty of care' (see section 3.2).

These duties have implications for all of the charity's income-generating activities. Trustees should therefore ensure that the risks, benefits and consequences of any income-generating activities are assessed and managed where appropriate.

Examples do exist of trustees committing a charity to new income streams that turn out to be strategic or commercial mistakes. Inevitably, not all new initiatives will succeed, but it is important for trustees to keep the risks in perspective and not become risk averse. Successful organisations understand the nature of the risks they are taking and make sure they are proportionate and appropriate within the context in which they are operating.

Developing a strategy

The trustees, working closely with staff and volunteers, should aim to develop and oversee a strategy or plan for raising funds that is sustainable over the longer term. Every charity will have a different mix of income sources and a different level of experience and knowledge of accessing those sources of funding. It is not suggested that every charity diversifies its income across the whole 'spectrum'.

Trustees should look to ensure that their strategy for raising funds:

• is in the best interests of the charity

• is in line with the charity's values and purposes

• is not subject to excessive risk

• meets all legal and constitutional requirements.

Further information:
NCVO (2012) *Sustainable Funding: A guide for trustees*. London: NCVO.

Trustees' responsibilities for fundraising

Fundraising from members of the public is a significant source of income for many charities and it can take a number of forms: major gifts and legacies; competitions, raffles and lotteries; organised events and activities; small-scale giving for example street collections etc.

Trustees are responsible for ensuring that the fundraising activity of their charity is properly controlled and accounts are kept. This involves proper budgeting, controlling professional fundraisers and observing relevant legislation and regulation.

Trustees must also ensure that fundraising activity embodies its values and does not contradict the objects and purposes of the charity. Trustees need to recognise the value of the charity's reputation and brand and ensure that fundraising methods do not devalue it. Trustees should be aware of any potential issues and risk factors, including ethical considerations, before agreeing to a particular fundraising approach.

Where funds are raised for a specific purpose as understood by the funder/donor, trustees must make sure that the funds are treated as restricted funds as required by the charity accounting and reporting regulations (set out in the SORP, see page 84).

In addition to the legal requirements, trustees should also:

- be familiar with the relevant voluntary codes of practice and self-regulation that exists, including the Institute of Fundraising's Code of Fundraising Practice

- approve fundraising approaches that are to be adopted and agree the key messages that will be used to promote any fundraising appeal to the public

- be open and honest about the costs of fundraising initiatives

- report on the income raised and the costs of generating those funds in the trustees' annual report and accounts.

You may delegate some of the tasks to a fundraising committee if your governing document provides you with the power to do so. However, it must be emphasised that this does not absolve you of your legal responsibilities. Trustees must continue to exercise control over the committee and it is good practice to draw up terms of reference that define the committee's objectives, the authority it has been given and the reporting back that will be required by the board.

Fundraising budgets

Fundraising budgets will help you ensure that fundraising activity is organised in an efficient and effective way. Many charities also make a policy decision on the target ratio of fundraising expenditure to income as an additional control. Trustees should take into account the relative cost-to-income ratios of alternative methods of fundraising. As with other budgets, a fundraising budget should include targets for income and expenditure. Regular reports should be made that compare actual figures with budget figures and identify any appropriate action that needs to be taken to bring the funds raised back on target.

Fundraising from members of the public

A wide range of laws, regulations, standards and codes of practice cover different types of public fundraising. Legislation not specifically related to fundraising might also be relevant for example, data protection in relation to holding information about donors. If trustees are in any doubt about what laws, regulations and codes apply to any particular fundraising initiative, they should seek advice in order to ensure that the charity is able to comply with what is required.

Trustees also need to be aware of any tax and trading implications that may arise from particular types of fundraising. Advice should be sought if trustees are unclear about the detailed rules that must be followed.

Further information:
Charity Commission (2011)
Charities and Fundraising (CC20).
London: Charity Commission.

Employing professional fundraisers

'Professional fundraisers' are people carrying on a fundraising business or someone paid to solicit funds or property for charities (not including the charity itself, its staff and trustees and, for most purposes, its associated companies).

Specific legal requirements govern professional fundraisers and trustees should take appropriate guidance and advice.

Fundraising from commercial organisations

Relationships between commercial organisations and charities can be mutually beneficial and extremely successful. Many charities report that as well as the financial rewards they have received, they have also benefited from increased public awareness and non-financial support including secondments and other benefits in kind.

However, there are also inherent risks in any partnership arrangement and trustees need to make sure that the risks have been identified and appropriately addressed before entering into any agreement with a commercial partner.

Income from commercial organisations takes a variety of forms including:

- sponsorship, where a company pays to have its name associated with a charity's programme or activities and expects commercial benefits as a result

- cause-related marketing (CRM), where a charity endorses a product or company, with a benefit in return

- payroll giving, where employees of a company give directly to a charity from their payroll

- corporate philanthropy, where companies give cash or in-kind donations; this is often linked to the corporate social responsibility agenda of commercial organisations.

Companies deal with charitable support in many different ways. For example, the directors or owners of some companies might make all charity support decisions, whereas others might have a staffed philanthropy or corporate social responsibility department.

Corporate support only accounts for a very small proportion of the charity sector's total income.

What do trustees need to consider when working with commercial partners?
The Charity Commission states:

'In our experience, charities that enter into commercial partnerships without giving due regard to ethical issues are in danger of putting their name and reputation at risk, in addition to causing a possible breach of trust. Overall responsibility rests with the trustees to ensure that they act responsibly and with a sufficient level of care when considering any ethical questions that may be attached to a proposed commercial partnership.'[11]

The following issues should also be considered.

• Corporate support can be a significant source of funding, as many companies prefer to work with charities over a prolonged period. However, corporate relationships take time to develop and any partnership must be governed by a written agreement – frameworks for agreements are available from the Institute of Fundraising but need to be adapted to reflect the desired arrangements.

• Significant corporate sponsorship or support almost always depends on a discernible fit between the company's aims and activities and those of the charity. Trustees must make sure that any arrangement with a company (eg endorsing a product) is compatible with the charity's objects, purposes and values. How the charity can exit such an arrangement should also be considered.

• If a corporate partner is classed as a 'commercial participator', the charity must comply with specific legal requirements, including a written agreement. Arrangements with corporate organisations might also have tax, VAT and trading implications.

Further information:
Charity Commission (2011) *Charities and Fundraising* (CC20). London: Charity Commission.

Fundraising and the SORP

The Statement of Recommended Practice (SORP) on Accounting by Charities (see page 84), recommends ways that fundraising proceeds and costs should be treated in in the trustees' annual report and accounts . In general, voluntary income and capital funds raised by the charity or its agents should be reported in the accounts as a gross figure and the costs of raising it, including agents' costs, accounted for as fundraising expenditure, which should be deducted from the relevant fund to show the net amount raised.

11 Charity Commission (2002) *Charities and Commercial Partners* (RS2). London: Charity Commission.

Fundraising standards, codes and self-regulation

For charities, fundraising as an activity is predominantly a matter of self-regulation with the ultimate responsibility for ensuring compliance with legislation and best practice falling on the trustees. Information, advice, guidance and voluntary codes of practice are available to charities and their trustees to help them to meet their responsibilities.

Three organisations that are instrumental in the fundraising self-regulation framework.

• The Institute of Fundraising (IoF) is a professional body that represents fundraising in the UK and has developed the Code of Fundraising Practice.

• The Fundraising Standards Board (FRSB) aims to be a mark of reassurance about fundraising for the public. The FRSB handles complaints from donors about fundraising issues and breaches of the IoF's Code.

• The Public Fundraising Regulatory Association (PFRA) works with local authorities and others to promote and implement the IoF's Face-to-Face Activity Code. It also co-ordinates street collections with local licensing bodies.

It is not yet known whether fundraising self-regulation can effectively eradicate poor practice and increase public trust and confidence in the work of charities. Ultimately, if self-regulation by charities is deemed to be ineffective, statutory regulations to control fundraising could be introduced.

Tax-effective giving

Should trustees promote tax-effective giving?
Yes. This is a key responsibility. A number of schemes allow charities to reclaim the tax already paid by UK taxpayers on money that is donated to charity. These include Gift Aid, share giving and payroll giving.

NCVO states that:

'In 2012/13 64,000 organisations reclaimed Gift Aid, suggesting that over one-third (46%) of all UK voluntary organisations reclaim Gift Aid. In 2012/13 the value of Gift Aid claims (which now include covenants) amounted to £1.1 bn; the value of donations was estimated at £4.1 bn (net) and £5.2 bn (gross)'[12]

Charities must register with HMRC and fulfil certain criteria in order to benefit from Gift Aid donations.

12 NCVO (2014) *The UK Civil Society Almanac 2014.* London: NCVO.

Trustees sometimes establish subsidiary companies to undertake non-charitable trading or, in some instances, 'risky' activities. Where a charity has one or more trading subsidiaries, trustees must use tax-effective giving in order to reduce the overall tax liabilities and comply with their duties to minimise tax (see page 103). Trustees need to consider the benefits of a trading subsidiary and the basis on which they intend to invest in it and ensure the charity does not inadvertently subsidise its activities. Trustees must avoid situations where there is a conflict of interest between the charity and its trustees, and the subsidiary and its directors. From the charity trustees' perspective, the charity's interests must prevail. Usually the relationship is managed through an agreement dealing with governance and cost recovery.

Further information:
Institute of Fundraising

HM Revenue and Customs

Loan finance

Loan finance is playing an increasingly important part of the 'mix' of funding and financing sources available for charities. This is not an income stream, but it should be seen as a financial tool or enabler. Loans might be an option, for example, where investment is needed to buy a building, provide new equipment, start a trading activity or cover periods of low cash flow and when the charity has a reasonably assured prospect of repaying the loan but does not have funds of its own to invest.

Loans are not suitable for all charities, but trustees should be aware of what loan finance can offer and be able to weigh up the alternatives before deciding either way. However, loans require repayment, usually with interest, arrangement fees may apply and security might be required in the form of a charge on the charity's assets.

What are the advantages of taking a loan over applying for a grant?
Loans can be faster to arrange than grants. Applying for a loan is not competitive, unlike increasingly over-subscribed grant programmes. Loans are often more flexible, not being restricted to particular funder interests, often involve less reporting and monitoring and are paid in advance.

What should trustees consider when determining whether to apply for a loan?
The following considerations are a good starting point to determine whether a loan may be suitable for a particular project, within a particular organisation and at a particular point of its lifecycle.

Financial risks
Trustees must ensure that the loan is in the best interest of the charity and will not put its assets at risk. There should be a clear plan setting out how the charity plans to repay the loan. Trustees must understand the degree of risk arising from a loan agreement, in particular any covenants, payment dates and amounts that must be complied with and compared against expected cash-flow forecasts.

Governing document
Trustees must ensure they have the power to take out a loan in the charity's governing document and, if necessary, pledge assets as security. If the governing document does not contain such powers, trustees should consider the alternative routes available to acquire the power to borrow money.

Type of loan
There are an increasing number of options for raising finance from 'social lenders' rather than traditional banks. Such social lenders often have more flexibility in designing loan terms and repayments and often have programmes tailored to particular sectors, for example community organisations or organisations seeking to deliver public service contracts.

Checklist

Do trustees have sufficient powers in the governing document to take out a loan and, if necessary, pledge assets as security?

What will the money be used for? For example, bridging grant and fundraising income cycles or investing in organisational growth?

Have trustees considered other options for raising the money that the charity needs?

Is a loan in the best interests of the charity?

Does the charity have the ability to repay the loan and interest charges?

Do sufficient structures and systems exist to manage the loan including planning, financial and cash management skills and support and understanding from staff?

Are the potential risks of a loan understood, particularly if the charity defaults on the loan?

Do the trustees want/need to seek professional advice in terms of reviewing the loan documents and checking if the terms of the loan are reasonable?

If we decide a loan would be in the best interests of our charity what information will a provider require?

Before approaching a bank or other provider, the organisation should produce a finance proposal that sets out the aims of the financing, in particular:

• what is to be achieved

• at what cost

• with what return

• in what timescale.

Once this information is prepared, a formal proposal can be made to a provider. The proposal should be accompanied by a business plan.

Further information:
NCVO (2014) *The Good Guide to Financial Management*. London: NCVO.

Trading

Charities can and do trade. However, if the trading activity is significant and is not related to the charity's primary purpose, there are charity and tax law implications that might mean trustees need to seek specialist advice. Section 2.1 identifies the restrictions on charity trading.

Trading is an increasingly important source of income for charities of all sizes and there is a huge diversity in the type and scale of trading undertaken. Trading is a tool; how you use it is up to you. It can be used to further your charitable objects or to generate income or profit which, in turn, is applied to the charity's objectives, however the different trades give rise to different considerations from a charity and tax law perspective.

What issues do trustees need to consider when considering trading activity?
Charity law and tax implications
The form of trading must be correctly classified to ensure compliance with restrictions over charity trading and tax laws and must be permitted by the organisation's governing document. A trading subsidiary might be required and charities must ensure they follow regulations in the SORP regarding the declaration of income, expenditure and profits arising from trading activity. VAT implications must also be considered.

Financial risk

Trading carries a risk because it usually involves the investment of charitable funds in a venture that is expected to bring a return. Trustees must be satisfied that any investment of charitable funds is in the interests of the charity and does not subject the charity to excessive risk. Trustees should also be satisfied that the charity will have sufficient cash flow to sustain the activity until income is generated.

Skills and capacity

Does the charity have the skills, staff time and resources to establish what might be new commercial activities? Where will the skills be found if any gaps are identified – what training needs to be provided and do new staff, volunteers or trustees need to be recruited?

What is meant by social enterprise?

Earned income is sometimes referred to as trading or 'social enterprise', meaning a business activity that has a social aims. Social enterprise is also a term used to describe various types of organisation, primarily differentiated by the aim of creating a benefit for the community through running a self-sustaining trade or service. The term has no defined legal meaning and social enterprises can take on various forms of management and legal structures, depending on the organisation's purpose.

Similar to traditional charities, they are usually organisations that have been created for the sole purpose of tackling social or environmental needs. Any surpluses the organisations acquire are generally reinvested back into business or community. Profit-making for shareholders and owners is generally limited.

Most social enterprises have some form of restriction on the distribution of profit to members, directors or staff: sometimes it is a voluntary 'not for profit' clause; for others it is a regulated obligation such as those for community interest companies or charities.

Further information:
NCVO (2009) *Good Guide to Trading: Getting ready for enterprise.* London: NCVO.

NCVO and BWB's web portal Get Legal: find the form that fits.

Checklist

Have you explored the possibility of income generation in your organisation?

Does your board take proactive steps to identify emerging grant-funding opportunities across all potential income sources?

Does your board need to review the fundraising activity of your charity to ensure that it complies with legal requirements?

Does your charity have a budget for fundraising and does your board receive regular monitoring reports?

If your charity has a fundraising committee, does it have clear terms of reference for its activities?

Has your board considered whether trustees require training in the role and techniques of fundraising?

Is there more your charity could do to ensure the tax effectiveness of its fundraising?

Is your legal structure suitable for the type of fundraising and income generation you need to carry out?

Has your board reviewed the role that loan finance could play in your organisation's funding mix?

Has your board considered signing up to the fundraising Codes of Practice and the Fundraising Standards Board?

7.4

Public service delivery and contracting

Public service delivery
Why is there a focus on charities and public service delivery?
Charities have delivered public services for many years, particularly in the health and social care field. In recent years, however, the government has talked about its commitment to transforming public services, and one of the ways it believes this can be achieved is through increasing the involvement of charities and, more widely, the 'third sector' in the design and delivery of services.

It is felt that charities bring an important perspective to public services, for example, many charities have close links with their community or client groups, involving users of services in their governance arrangements and engaging with hard-to-reach groups.

What do we mean by 'public services'?
Public services are services that are funded with public money and are delivered by the state or on behalf of the state, for example by a charity or private sector company. Not all public services are provided under a legal duty, some are discretionary.

The public sector consists of a number of national and local statutory bodies, including local authorities, central government and the health service.

How can charities be involved in public services?
The design and delivery of public services can broadly involve two processes.

- **Commissioning:** Where a public sector organisation plans the provision of services based on an assessment of need.

- **Procurement:** The purchase of goods and services from an external agency.

Charities have an opportunity to be involved in both processes by delivering public services and helping to identify needs and designing services. The Charity Commission warns charities and their trustees that when they are providing advice on the design and delivery of services they should consider whether they are:

- providing free 'consultancy'

- giving away intellectual property

- being appropriately rewarded or funded for their input.[13]

Some public services are delivered under contract; some public service funding arrangements are less clear and can consist of service level agreements or grants. It is very important that trustees clarify the status of any funding arrangement because of the legal, financial or tax implications that may arise (see page 119 for guidance on contracting).

What should trustees consider in relation to public service delivery?
Whether to engage in public service delivery is up to each charity to decide for itself based on how trustees feel the charity can best meet its purposes via the services and activities it provides. The Charity Commission suggests three guiding principles for trustees in deciding whether or not to deliver public services:

- stick to your mission – ensure that any decision to deliver public services furthers the charity's objects and meets the needs of beneficiaries

- guard your independence – trustees must, as at all other times, act solely in the interests of the charity

- know your worth – in setting a price or budgeting for a public service activity, trustees should understand the full cost of the service and the charity's scope to deliver the service.[14]

Trustees should consider the risks involved to the charity's financial position, governance arrangements (such as conflicts of interest), service delivery (such as contractual issues and quality) and reputation.

The Charity Commission also provides a reminder of the general legal responsibilities of trustees that are relevant in relation to public service delivery:

- Charities must only undertake activities that are within their objects and powers.

- Charities must be independent of government and other funders.

- Trustees must act only in the interests of the charity and its beneficiaries.

- Trustees must make decisions in line with their duty of care and duty to act prudently.

13 Charity Commission (2012) *Charities and Public Service Delivery: An introduction and overview* (CC37). London: Charity Commission.

14 Ibid.

The Compact

An important duty of a trustee is to safeguard the position of their charity in any public service funding agreement or contract. One of the tools that charities and the wider voluntary and community sector can use in negotiations is the Compact.

The Compact is an agreement between the government and the voluntary and community sector in England. Established in November 1998 and renewed in 2010, it aims to improve the working relationship between the two sectors for mutual advantage. All local authority areas in England are covered by a local or regional variation of the national Compact and have been developed by local partners.

The Compact recognises shared values, principles and commitments and sets out guidelines for how both parties should work together. It also considers areas such as involvement in policy design and consultation, funding arrangements (including grants and contracts), promoting equality, ensuring better involvement in service design and delivery, and strengthening independence.

Although the Compact is not legally binding and is built on trust and mutual goodwill, its authority is derived from its endorsement by government and by the voluntary and community sector itself through its consultation process. Failure to meet the Compact's commitments can form part of judicial review cases, particularly where there is a 'legitimate expectation' for these to be met and funding to continue.

Further information:
Compact Voice:
www.compactvoice.org.uk

Checklist

Do trustees have an understanding of the public service delivery agenda and how it might affect the charity?

If trustees are considering delivering public services, have they ensured that:

- they are following their legal duties and responsibilities to act in the interests of the charity?

- all current and planned services are within the charity's objects and powers?

- the cost of the service is fully understood?

- risks have been assessed?

Contracting

Contracting has become a significant source of income for charities, mainly due to the increasing trend for public sector bodies to fund services via contract rather than through grants.

Traditionally, local authorities, health authorities and other agencies gave grants to voluntary organisations to undertake a wide range of activities. Grants did not attract VAT. Many of these grants have been replaced by contracts, which in many cases will be subject to VAT. Changing government policy has also led to voluntary and private sector organisations being invited to tender for contracts to provide many of the services formerly provided by the statutory sector. Contractual agreements allow local authorities to exercise greater control over how their money is spent and to set out and monitor quality standards in service provision. There can be differences in the legal remedies available to the parties under a grant or a contract.

The agreement between the charity and a public sector organisation might be called various names, such as a service level agreement. Regardless of the name, it may or may not be a contract for tax and/or VAT purposes, depending on its content. Trustees and senior staff need to be very clear about the nature of the grant/agreement/contract that they are entering into because of the different accounting, tax and procurement rules that will apply.

If your charity has signed or is considering signing contracts to deliver services, it is important that trustees understand the responsibilities involved and – particularly if your charity has traditionally received grants – the differences between contracts and grants.

What is a contract?
A contract is a legally enforceable agreement between two or more parties. For a contract to exist:

- the parties to the contract have to offer something, and accept what the other, or others, offer

- there has to be an exchange of consideration; 'consideration' means anything of value, such as goods, services or money, for example a funder may provide money to an organisation in exchange for the organisation providing a service

- there must be an intention to create a legally binding relationship.

If these three factors exist, then the agreement is a legally binding agreement. It does not have to be called a 'contract'. Contracts between funders and charities are sometimes referred to as service level agreements, although not all service level agreements are legally binding contracts. Seek clarity at the start of any discussion about an agreement as to whether it is intended to legally bind the parties.

Do charities need a power to contract?
In order to enter into a contract, your governing document must give you the power to do what is necessary to carry out the work. These powers could be contained in your governing document in the form of a general power to undertake activities in furtherance of the charity's mission.

What issues need to be considered before entering into a contract?
Trustees should consider how the work proposed under the contract fits in with the charity's legal objects and its present and future plans and priorities. In order to survive in a difficult funding environment, it can be tempting to offer to provide a new service for which funding is available. However, the service must fall within the charity's objects or else the trustees will be acting in breach of trust. It may be possible to modify the objects to allow the work to be undertaken or to run the contract through a separate trading subsidiary.

Trustees should consider the wider impact on the rest of the charity's work of providing the service, and question the degree to which undertaking particular activities will contribute towards the achievement of the charity's mission. They also need to consider whether the charity has the skills and resources, such as equipment and staffing, to fulfil the contract.

If volunteers are to be used, you should be clear what their role is and make sure their expenses, recruitment and training are funded. You may wish to consider inserting a clause in the contract stating that if volunteers are not forthcoming, the level of service may need to be reduced. Cost estimates should include administration, start-up or closure costs and training.

Trustees will also need to consider the general implications of contracting, for example is there a service provision change and, as such, does TUPE apply. If TUPE applies, how many people may transfer and on what terms and conditions? What are the charity's obligations in respect of pensions?

What legal liabilities should be considered?

Before entering into a contract, you should give serious consideration to all the terms and conditions and proceed only if you are certain that your charity can fulfil them.

Unincorporated charities (ie trusts and associations) have no distinct legal identity and therefore cannot enter into contracts in their own name. The contract will be a legal agreement between the trustees and the other contracting party or parties. Where individuals sign contracts, they should state that they are doing so on behalf of the charity, or they alone could be liable (see section 3.8 for guidance on personal liability). The trustees can be personally sued if the terms of the contract are not complied with. To protect yourself, you should include a clause in the contract that limits your financial liability to the assets of the charity. You may also wish to consider changing the charity's legal structure to become a charitable company or CIO in order to limit your potential financial liability (see section 2.2).

Charitable companies or CIOs do have legal status and it is the company or CIO that is party to the contract, not the trustees.

Will a separate trading company be necessary?

There are restrictions on the trading activities that charities are permitted to carry out (see section 2.1). However, if the service being provided under the contract is fulfilling the main objects of the charity (ie primary purpose trading), or arrives from work carried out by beneficiaries, this can be done by the charity and it will not be necessary to set up a separate trading company. If in doubt, trustees should always seek advice.

An example of primary purpose trading might be an art gallery charity selling limited-edition prints, whereas an example of non-primary purpose trading might be the same charity hiring out rooms for functions. It is important for each charity that has trading activities to seek legal advice or agree with HM Revenue and Customs (HMRC) what is primary and non-primary purpose before considering setting up a trading company.

The HMRC threshold for the annual turnover from non-primary purpose trading is a maximum of £50,000 for all charities with a total income over £200,000 (for charities with an income less than £200,000 see section 2.1). A charity generating more non-primary purpose trading net income than this will have to pay corporation tax on the net income over this amount unless a trading company is set up. Other exemptions and extra statutory concessions cover a range of fundraising and ancillary trading activities. There may also be VAT advantages to having a trading company, but this depends on the specific circumstances of each charity and trustees should take professional advice.

What is the liability for VAT?

Services provided under contract will usually be liable for VAT if your turnover is sufficiently high. You may therefore need to be registered for VAT. Prices included in any tenders or contracts should clearly state whether they are inclusive or exclusive of VAT. If the purchaser is a local authority, it will be able to reclaim in full the VAT charged on the provision of the service. The issues surrounding VAT are often complicated and detailed advice should be obtained from your local HMRC office or your professional advisers.

What is the situation when a trustee of the providing charity is an employee of the purchaser?

Local authorities and other purchasers sometimes have the right to nominate members of their staff as trustees of charities they fund. If a trustee of the charity providing or considering providing a service under contract is an employee of the purchasing organisation, a potential conflict of interest arises; appropriate procedures to manage this conflict of interest must be followed. When purchasers are entering into contracts with charities, it may
be more appropriate for a representative of the purchaser to attend the charity's board meetings in an advisory capacity than to act as a trustee. See section 21.7 for more guidance on the appointment of trustees by external organisations.

What should a contract include?

If possible, contracts need to be negotiated. If you are asked to tender, this may be difficult. You should keep control over how the work is managed to ensure that your charity's own policies, ways of working, priorities and standards are safeguarded. Contracts should include:

- names of the parties to the contract

- whether it is intended that third parties such as users can enforce the contract

- start date and duration of the contract

- how risk will be allocated under indemnity and other provisions

- who will insure

- equal opportunities policies of the contracting parties

- service specification, ie what service will be provided, to whom, where and when

- quality, ie what standards must be achieved, how they will be measured and by whom

- monitoring, ie how the work will be monitored by the funder

- finance, ie the amount to be paid and the method and timing of payment

- costs, indicating whether they are inclusive or exclusive of VAT

- applicability of TUPE, other staffing arrangements and rights to sub-contract

- arrangements for reviewing, renewing, varying and terminating the contract

- arrangements for liaison between the funder and the providing charity

- arrangements for settling disputes, with provision for an independent, mutually acceptable mediator to be brought in if necessary

- provisions regarding intellectual property rights, data protection and confidentiality.

Checklist

Trustees should exercise great care when preparing to sign contracts. Use this checklist to help ensure you have considered the implications for your charity.

Has legal and professional advice been sought and considered where appropriate?

Is the charity legally empowered to enter into the contract?

Will the contract maintain the charity's independence and purpose?

Have the implications of the contract for the charity's trading position been considered (eg, in relation to the need for a trading subsidiary)?

Have the risks placed on the charity by the contract been assessed and are they reasonable?

Is the contract commercially fair to the charity?

Is the charity aware of all of the costs, including potential TUPE and pension costs involved in delivering the contract?

Are all of the contract terms fully understood by trustees and senior staff?

Do trustees and senior staff fully understand any contract terms relating to underperformance or failure to deliver?

Have the VAT implications been considered?

Does the charity have the skills and resources to deliver the contract?

Have the implications for governance been considered (eg if a trustee has a relationship with the contractor)

Have all of the risks to the charity and trustees been considered (eg in relation to unincorporated charities)?

8

Policy

Regardless of the size of a charity, trustee boards will nearly always delegate some activities to others – to individual trustees, staff, volunteers or advisors. One of the most important ways a trustee board can manage its delegation is to use written policies and procedures explaining how the charity should be run.

What policies should there be?

The number of policies will vary depending on the size and type of a charity. Trustees working with staff (where they exist) should make sure that they have all of the policies and procedures they require to fulfil their duties, ensure the organisation complies with all of the laws and regulations that apply to it and ensure the organisation runs consistently, fairly and smoothly.

All charities will need policies, and the 'policy hierarchy' (see page 124) illustrates how policies fit into the organisation's structure, governance and operations.

Trustees might want to establish a working party or ask staff to carry out an audit of what policies the organisation has in place and to identify any risks and gaps that may exist.

What is the role of trustees in making and reviewing policies? In organisations with staff, the policies will be written by them or by the relevant board committee or working party that has been set up for that purpose. The board's ultimate role is to approve the policies and determine which ones are important enough to be 'board policies', which they will review at regular intervals.

Policies and procedures are only effective if they are kept up to date and trustees, staff and volunteers know they exist and how to follow them. It is important for trustees to ensure their organisation:

- has mechanisms in place for updating policies and procedures when laws or regulations change or when best practice advice evolves

- provides training (if required) when a new policy is created

- provides updates when existing policies are changed

- has an induction programme in place for all new trustees, staff and volunteers, which includes sufficient information on policies and procedures.

Policy hierarchy

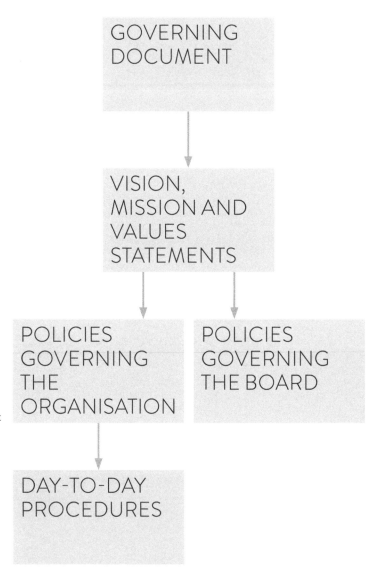

8.1

Policies governing the organisation

Essential or 'do or die' policies cover the essentials required for a charity to operate effectively.

- **Human resources policies** (if staff are employed): These can cover a wide range of areas, from working hours to discipline and grievance. They should include procedures relating to supervision and support members of staff who report directly to the board, commonly the chief executive (see section 11.1)

- **Volunteer management policies** (if volunteers are involved in the charity's work): These can cover a range of areas, from role descriptions to expenses (see section 11.2).

- **Financial management policies**: These should include internal financial controls, authorisation of contracts, procedures for the board's role in monitoring finance and policies around reserves and (if applicable) investments.

- **Risk-management policies**: These should set out the board's overall intention to manage risk and the procedure involved (see Chapter 9).

Other key policies include the following.

- Equal opportunities and diversity

- Bullying and harassment

- Whistleblowing

- Health and safety (see section 9.3)

- Protection of children and vulnerable adults

- Complaints procedures

- Codes of conduct for staff, volunteers and service users

Operational policies include the following.

- Data retention and protection (see section 10.3)

- Information technology (see section 10.1)

- Complaints (see section 14.2)

- Other specialist operational policies, for example for charities whose work places them at some legal risk or those operating abroad

- Fundraising, including working with corporates, if applicable

- Campaigning and political activities (see section 2.1)

8.2

Policies governing the board

The trustee board should also agree policies that set out how it will operate. These policies can be useful to:

- ensure trustees understand their duties and can carry them out effectively

- clarify 'grey' areas of board responsibility

- help new board members get up to speed with basic procedures and working practices

- help identify during a review whether the board is meeting its responsibilities.

Essential board policies include the following.

- Role descriptions for trustees – all trustees should have a written statement of their responsibilities (see page 55 for examples)

- Role descriptions for honorary officers (see page 52)

- A conflicts of interest policy and register of interests (see section 3.5)

- Terms of reference for committees, working parties etc (see section 21.8)

8.3

• A code of conduct for trustees, setting out the conduct and behaviour expected of trustees; these can be developed further by agreeing policies governing specific areas of trustee responsibility

Other key board policies include the following.

• Trustee expenses policy (see page 41).

• Delineating board/staff responsibility (see section 11.3): This lies at the heart of effective governance. The agreement can set out which issues should be dealt with at board level and which at staff level, and where boundaries overlap.

• Design of the board (see Part Three): It may be helpful to agree a policy covering the size of the board, membership, recruitment and selection/election procedures and terms of office (some of this may already be covered in your governing document, so you should ensure your policy is consistent).

• Training and development (see Chapter 18): A code setting out the skills audit, induction training and development of board members can explain to new trustees what support they can receive.

• Board review or 'appraisal' (see Chapter 22): The board can agree a procedure governing how it is going to review its own effectiveness.

• You may decide to agree other specific board policies. One example is a media/social media policy, clarifying the role of individual trustees in acting as a spokesperson for the charity (see Chapter 14).

• Board cycle or annual calendar of key activities.

Creating policy

Use the policy-making flowchart opposite to identify how the issue you are considering should be addressed. Many support organisations produce example, template or 'model' policies. These can be useful in giving you a starting point for a new policy or comparing the practices of your organisation with another.

Be careful not to copy exactly another organisation's policy – their size and circumstances may not fit yours, and you may find the policy does not work for your organisation.

Checklist

Has your board reviewed its lists of policies?

Are policies up to date?

Are new policies required?

Policy-making flowchart

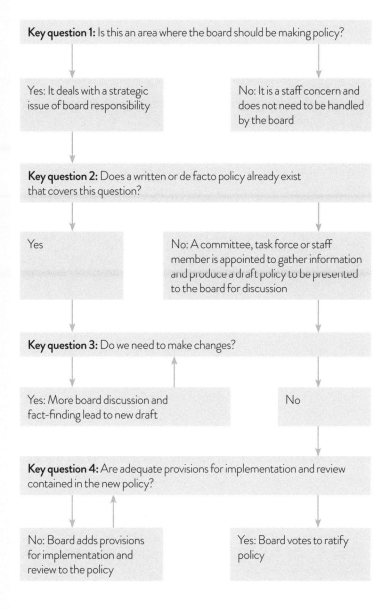

Key question 1: Is this an area where the board should be making policy?

Yes: It deals with a strategic issue of board responsibility

No: It is a staff concern and does not need to be handled by the board

Key question 2: Does a written or de facto policy already exist that covers this question?

Yes

No: A committee, task force or staff member is appointed to gather information and produce a draft policy to be presented to the board for discussion

Key question 3: Do we need to make changes?

Yes: More board discussion and fact-finding lead to new draft

No

Key question 4: Are adequate provisions for implementation and review contained in the new policy?

No: Board adds provisions for implementation and review to the policy

Yes: Board votes to ratify policy

9

Risk and safety

9.1

Risk management

What does the Charity Commission say?
The Charity Commission recommends that all charities carry out a proportionate annual risk assessment and commit to publishing the findings.

Risk management is a requirement for some charities. For charities subject to statutory audit, the trustees' annual report is required to contain:

'A statement confirming that the major risks to which the charity is exposed, as identified by the trustees, have been reviewed and systems or procedures have been established to manage those risks.'[15]

This means identifying risks and describing the procedures or plans you have put in place to safeguard against or reduce likely problems, as well as showing how you monitor the risks and contingencies you have in place. The complexity and extent of your risk review will depend on the size and nature of your charity's operations.

15 Charity Commission (2013) *Charity Reporting and Accounting: The essentials* (CC15b). London: Charity Commission.

What is the role of the trustees?

Trustees are ultimately responsible for the charity and should take the lead in ensuring that risk management is approached comprehensively and considered in all aspects of the charity's operations.

Risk management can be done in participation with staff, volunteers and users; this is likely to create a better analysis and stronger ownership of the results than a 'top-down' approach.

It is a common mistake for risk management to be thought of as a list of processes and risk registers. While it is important that trustees ensure that there are measures or processes in place to manage risks, their role is also about making sure that risks are effectively managed. To manage risk effectively it is important that risk management is not part of an isolated process. It should be built into the strategic thinking for the charity so that the strategy balances opportunities and rewards with potential and related risks.

It is important that trustees understand the main risks to the charity and its risk appetite and ensure that there are controls to manage these risks and risk management is embedded into the organisation's culture.

What is risk?

Risk is often described as the danger of something going wrong, but this is only half the story. Most risk-management experts now consider risks to be potentially good as well as potentially bad. All organisations face uncertainty on a daily basis: the outcomes of events can be either positive or negative and, to varying degrees, are usually a mix of both. There will be a range of implications for your charity, whatever the outcome. You need to plan for the risks of success as well as for possible problems.

For example, if a charity considers one of the largest risks that it faces to be a reduction in committed giving, this might be an opportunity to consider diversification of funding sources.

Another example is where the biggest risk to achieving a charities' campaigning strategy is that they might not have the profile or influence that they need to enable them to achieve their strategy. They might then decide to take the opportunity to partner with another charity that shares the same objectives and has a better profile and access to politicians. In these examples, the risk is high in terms of the potential for negative impact but it provides an opportunity to do things differently.

The word 'risk' is used to mean different things but in this context it is important to be clear and specific about what a 'risk' is and the difference between a risk, an incident and a consequence, as they are often confused.

- A risk is something that might happen (positive or negative), such as the risk of losing a contract with your local authority that makes up 70% of your total income.

- An incident is something that has actually happened, such as where you have already lost the contract with the local authority.

- A consequence (or potential consequence) is the result of the risk happening, such as no longer being sustainable and having to close down, having to stop providing the services, potential reputation damage if you are not providing a useful service etc.

Charities often see reputational risk as a big risk that they seek to mitigate. However, it is more likely that reputational damage is the consequence of another risk happening (a failure to provide high-quality services, fraud, bad practice, etc) rather than a risk itself. By identifying the real risk and being specific about it, it is more likely that you will be able to mitigate against it and prevent the negative consequences happening.

Step-by-step guide to managing risk

Risk management is the process by which risks are identified, evaluated and controlled. The process does not try to fully eliminate all risks, as this cannot be achieved and would not always be cost effective. Instead, it acts to reduce the risk that remains after controls are inserted to a level that the charity is comfortable with.

There are many ways to do this, including the following tried-and-tested seven-step process. It is best to do this with a group of people, including trustees and staff who really understand the organisation.

1 Identify the risks that will stop you achieving your objectives.

2 Analyse how likely they are to happen and what the consequences would be.

3 Prioritise the risks.

4 Determine risk appetite.

5 Mitigate/control – what can you do or do you do to reduce the risk?

6 Assurance – test the controls to determine if they are working and if they are effective at reducing the risk to the planned level.

7 Monitor, review and report – who is responsible for managing each risk, who needs to know about the risks and how do you monitor them?

The following sections outline each step.

Identifying risks

A useful first stage in risk management is to explore in a systematic way key areas of uncertainty, looking at different elements of your charity's work to identify possible risks. A good way to do this is to look at your strategy and key objectives and think about the things that might stop you achieving these.

For example, your main objectives might be:

- to campaign to change public attitudes

- to provide aid in a foreign country to reduce immediate hardship

- to ensure organisational strength and excellence in finance, governance, people and systems.

The Charity Commission suggests that you review risks under the headings of governance, external, regulatory, financial and operational. Using this as a framework, you might consider each of your strategic objectives and the following risks.

- **Governance risks**: Does your board have the right skills and does your governing document allow you to do the things that you need to do to make the difference you want to make?

- **External**: Do you have the influence and reputation that you need and what are the risks to this reputation in terms of negative publicity caused by poor service or practice, your brand etc? What might change in terms of government policy that might have an impact on your ability to achieve your campaigning objectives?

- **Regulatory and compliance**: Failure to comply with legislation or reporting might result in reputational damage as well as financial damage.

- **Financial**: Are there risks to your finances that might prevent you achieving your objectives, for example are you dependent on one source of income or are your reserves low? Is there a risk of fraud in transferring money to another country that has few regulations or financial checks in place?

- **Operational**: Is the organisation set up and run in a way that allows success? Do you have the right staff with the right capabilities? Are they in the right places within the structure with the tools they need to be successful, communicating in the right way, using effective processes and with the right organisational culture?

Remember to consider a range of possibilities in each area ('things that might happen') and explore the potential positive outcomes as well as the negatives. For example, the change in government policy mentioned in the list above may offer opportunities for your organisation to work in a new way.

Analysing risks
Once a risk has been identified, you can assess:

- the likelihood of the risk happening

- the impact of the risk on the organisation if it happens.

To identify the impact of a risk, try to consider all the possible implications, some of which might not always be obvious. For example, it might be obvious that if the risk is that you cannot articulate the impact of your work then a consequence of this might be that you will see a reduction in funding. You might not identify that there is a potential for staff in the organisation to get disheartened and lose focus and passion if they cannot see the difference they are making. Spending some time thinking about this together as a board with your senior team is a valuable exercise.

It can be useful to give each risk a score for likelihood – out of three perhaps, for low, medium and high – and a score for impact, and to multiply these two scores together to give each risk a total score. You could then plot your risks on a table.

Carry out this exercise as if there were no controls in place at all – this gives you the initial risk score.

Risk map for the Fictitious Health Care Agency

	High impact (3)	Medium impact (2)	Low impact (1)
High likelihood (3)	New local authority contract Requirement for same gender care Senior staff member leaves Difficulty recruiting support staff Major health and safety breaches	Breach in appropriate user representation on board	Minor health and safety breaches
Medium likelihood (2)	Failure to raise £100,000 Shift in ethnic/gender balance of users Board unaware of funder priorities	Changes to record keeping on users required by funder Younger clients dissatisfied with service	Changes in IT/security equipment is problematic
Low likelihood (1)	Inadequacy of insurance Destruction of office Employment Tribunal claim by member of staff	Gaps in financial controls	Data protection breach

Prioritising risks

You can't manage every risk your charity will face, so use the analysis of likelihood and impact above to prioritise which risks you should focus on.

It's useful to determine a cut-off point, above which you will manage the risk and below which you won't. The cut-off point could be, for example, the top five or ten risks or risks scoring six points or more. The cut-off point will partly depend on how much time you will have to manage these risks. It's better to manage the most serious risks properly than to manage a full list weakly.

Determine the risk appetite for each of the risks

For the charity to really understand how much risk it is willing to take, it is important to understand its risk appetite. In other words, how much risk is the organisation willing to seek or accept in pursuing its objectives?

This risk appetite might change depending on the activity. An example might be where a charity provides aid in a war zone and uses charity shops to fund this work. This charity might have a low risk appetite for health and safety risks in the shops but a high risk appetite for safety risks in the war zone.

In this step, look at the top 10 risks that you are managing and determine your risk appetite and your target risk score. You should aim to get the 'residual risk' (the risk that remains after you have your controls in place) to a level in line with the risk appetite.

Mitigate/control risks

The level of each identified risk must be transferred or controlled to a satisfactory level. This will involve the board working with the people who own the risk to consider all of the things that the organisation does to reduce the likelihood of the risk occurring or the impact if it does occur. For example, if the risk is fraud then you might consider all of the anti-fraud measures in place.

List or 'map out' all of the controls that you currently have in place. Once you know the controls that you currently have you can then score each risk in terms of the residual risk.

You can then consider whether this residual risk is:

- at the right level (the same level as your target risk), so the remaining risk is accepted

- too high, so it needs more controls, existing controls need to be enforced better, the activity needs to be stopped or the risk insured against or contracted out – from this you will have an action plan that you review

- too low, which means that you might consider stopping or reducing some of the controls.

Assurance

Once the key risks have been identified, assessed and are subject to controls, it is important to get confirmation that the controls are being performed as expected. We can all think of policies that are place but are never used or not used in the right way.

This assurance can be received in various ways depending on the charity. You can ask the risk owner to confirm annually that they have checked the assurance and it is working as planned along with evidence to support this. You can ask internal auditors (if you have them) to give assurance that the controls are working or you can ask your external auditors or a non-audit external professional to do this.

Monitoring and reviewing risks

Once you have identified your key risks and decided how to deal with them, record your plans in a risk register (see page 135 for a template) along with your risk map, so that you can come back to it later. You need to decide how you will monitor and review your risks and plans, to take account of changing circumstances. Risks may come and go, or their likelihood or potential impact could change, requiring you to change the way you deal with them. It's a good idea to tie this monitoring and review process into your strategic and operational planning (see Chapter 6).

Review your risk register at least once a year, perhaps more often for large or complex projects, review the risk register if incidents happen that might indicate that the controls are not working effectively and ask that all papers that go to the board include a summary of the main risks and suggested mitigation as a matter of course.

It is often useful to take one risk at each board meeting and do a 'deep dive' on the risk so that the board really understands the risks and the controls and can get assurance that this risk is being managed effectively.

Communicating your risk-management plan

Make sure everyone is aware of their responsibilities and is supported in implementing them. Consider others who could benefit from knowing how you deal with risks. For example, users may have more faith in your services if they are aware of your risk-management policies, and potential funders will also be looking for reassurance that their money is in good hands.

Checklist

Does your board really understand the main risks that the charity faces?

Does your board have an agreed appetite for risk?

Does your board get assurance that the main risks are being controlled effectively?

Does your board regularly carry out a risk-management exercise?

Do you act on the findings of the exercise?

Do you report on risk in accordance with the SORP (if appropriate)?

Sample register

Risk
Describe the risk – be specific

Likelihood
1–3

Impact
1–3

Initial risk score
Before any controls in place – Likelihood multiplied by impact

Controls
List all the current controls

Residual risk
Likelihood multiplied by impact after controls in place

Risk target
Target risk score

Actions
Actions needed

Assurance
Assurance that controls are working (eg annual testing, internal audit, trend analysis)

9.2

Insurance

Trustees have a responsibility to act prudently and safeguard the charity's property from loss or damage. One of the ways trustees can fulfil this duty as a part of their overall approach to risk management is by maintaining adequate insurance cover.

Trustees' responsibilities for insurance

Are trustees required to take out insurance?

There has been concern in recent years about the high cost of taking out insurance, which has led to some trustees to question the need for certain types of insurance.

Some types of insurance are required by law. There may also be a duty in the charity's governing document to purchase insurance, but this is usually stated to be a power to do so rather than an obligation. Trustees should check the governing document for the necessary power.

Where a form of insurance is not compulsory, trustees should decide whether or not to take out insurance as part of their risk-management exercise and to consider their duty to protect the assets.

Further information:
Charity Commission (2011)
Charities and Insurance (CC49).
London: Charity Commission.

Can trustees be held personally liable for failing to take out insurance?

If trustees fail to take out insurance when they have a duty to do so, or unreasonably fail to take out insurance for which they have the power to do so, they may be personally liable for any loss arising. Personal liability may also arise for trustees of unincorporated organisations if the organisation cannot pay an uninsured claim made against it.

Taking out insurance is one of a number ways that trustees can manage any risks facing the charity and themselves personally. Understanding their duties and responsibilities as trustees, following good governance practice and putting sound risk-management practices in place are also key to managing risks, along with taking out insurance cover.

Insurance contracts are contracts of 'utmost good faith' meaning it is for the insured person to make sure that the insurer has all relevant information made available to them.

Types of insurance

Cover is required or recommended for a wide range of items or situations. In certain situations, charities must have compulsory insurance, for example, charities that employ staff must have employee liability insurance and those that operate motor vehicles must have appropriate third-party insurance. There is a wide variety of other insurance types that the trustees may consider, according to the nature of the charity's operations. These include insurance relating to the charity's property (such as land, buildings, furniture and computers), cash on the premises or in transit, liabilities to the public at large, liabilities for a breach of contractual obligations such as the provision of advice and insurance for fundraising or special events.

Trustees should review the insurance policies regularly to make sure the cover remains adequate and the premiums competitive. The detailed terms of the policies, such as exclusions, should be carefully considered.

In the context of the prudent management of the charity's assets, an up-to-date inventory of all property, furniture and equipment should be maintained. This will assist in obtaining appropriate insurance and managing any claim.

Compulsory insurance
Employee and volunteer insurance
Trustees are required by law to insure against any liability for personal injury or illness sustained by their employees as a result of their employment for a minimum amount of £5m. Trustees must ensure that employers' liability insurance is taken out and that a copy of the certificate of insurance is displayed at the premises. Copies of certificates must be kept for at least 40 years.

Trustees need to be aware that no distinction is drawn between paid or authorised voluntary workers under health and safety law. You should ensure that the employers' liability insurance covers volunteers to the extent that your organisation uses them. As with all insurance policies, you should check that the insurance covers the activities being undertaken.

Motor vehicles
A charity that owns or operates motor vehicles must take out insurance against third-party injury and property damage.

Property insurance
If a charity owns or occupies a building, it would be unusual for trustees to decide not to insure their interest in it or consider what the consequences would be if there were a disaster. Trustees are responsible for ensuring that there is adequate insurance cover for the following areas.

- **Buildings**: If you are the owner of the property, it is advisable to choose a policy that covers what is known as 'all risks' to the building. Trustees should take professional advice on the sum for which the building is insured.

- **The contents of premises**: An 'all risks' policy will generally cover damage to contents from most events. If the policy is not 'all risks', additional cover against damage to contents, or particular assets, from specified events or accidents should usually be taken out.

- **Consequential loss**: This covers any costs resulting from disruption to the activities of the charity, for example as the result of a fire, such as the costs of renting alternative premises. In certain instances, trustees may consider premiums too high and may decide to mitigate risks through a disaster recovery plan.

If a charitable company owns its premises, it is the charity's responsibility to insure the property. If the charity's premises are leased, responsibility for insurance will generally be specified in the lease.

Legal expenses insurance

Some charities consider taking out employers' legal indemnity insurance, which provides cover against losses related to employment matters, such as legal expenses and compensation arising from employment tribunal awards. Trustees need to balance the benefit of insured tribunal awards against the need to follow extensive procedural requirements and advice from the insurer's designated advisors compared with obtaining its own advice and retaining operational flexibility.

Some types of insurance can cover the costs of providing cover for an employee who is off sick. This type of insurance cover may be required when a charity has employees delivering work against contractually set targets that could not be fulfilled by other staff if they were off work for any significant amount of time.

Fidelity insurance

This insurance can provide protection against dishonesty by employees, volunteers and sometimes trustees, but is not a substitute for having sound financial and management controls in place. Fidelity insurance is usually provided only if the charity can show that its administrative arrangements are appropriate and proper supervision is in place.

Professional indemnity insurance

If a charity provides professional services, for example advice or consultancy, it could be held liable if those services are delivered negligently and a client suffers a financial loss or injury as a result. Professional indemnity insurance can provide protection against such claims but charities need to ensure that anyone (staff, volunteers, trustees etc) providing such services have the skills, knowledge and experience required.

Public liability insurance

Public liability insurance is needed to cover for any injury, illness or damage to property incurred by members of the public as a result of the activities of the charity. 'Members of the public' may include the charity's volunteers, as well as the trustees, and volunteers should be informed about the extent of cover provided for them by the charity.

Volunteers should be given advice about the insurance position if they drive their own vehicles in the course of their volunteering and they should be properly protected while working on the charity's premises. Some policies exclude cover for volunteers over a certain age. Volunteers should be made aware of such exclusions and of any alternative arrangements made to protect them.

Trustee liability insurance

The Charity Commission states that:

'If trustees act prudently, lawfully and in accordance with their governing document, then any liabilities (debt and financial obligations) that they incur as trustees can normally be met out of the charity's resources.'

However, if you do not act prudently, lawfully and in accordance with your governing document, for example if trustees receive unauthorised benefits or payments, you allow the charity to act outside its objects, you are negligent in managing the charity's investments or engage in unlawful political activities, you may be in 'breach of trust' and personally liable to pay any loss to the charity. As trustees act jointly in administering a charity, you and the rest of the board are jointly liable to pay any loss. The Charity Commission has powers to take proceedings in court to recover from trustees personally any funds lost to the charity because of a 'breach of trust' (see section 3.8 for more information on trustee liability).

There are no restrictions on trustees personally paying for insurance to protect their personal liability. Trustees may also use the charity's funds to insure the charity against loss to its own funds resulting from the acts and defaults of trustees.

However, the law will only allow the trustees to use the charity's funds to pay for liability insurance to protect trustees in limited circumstances including:

- acts that are properly undertaken in the administration of the charity

- acts in breach of trust, but made as a result of an honest mistake.

The law does not permit cover for acts that trustees knew or ought to have known were wrong, or for acts or omissions made in reckless disregard of whether they were right or wrong.

There is a general power in the Charities Act 2011 to allow trustees to use the charity's funds to pay for insurance to protect their personal liability, unless there is an explicit prohibition in the charity's governing document.

If you are considering taking out trustee liability insurance, you should identify the areas of your charity's activities where you may be at risk, assess how much cover you need and balance this with the number of trustees and the size of premium quoted.

Remember that it is unusual for trustees who have behaved honestly to suffer financial loss as a result of their trusteeship. There are risks, but they should be kept in proportion. When breaches of trust have been committed as the result of an honest mistake, or when trustees have been found wanting in the degree of control they exercised over staff, the Charity Commission has rarely required trustees to make good any loss. Insurance would not protect you from liability incurred as a result of breaches of trust knowingly committed. However, trustee indemnity insurance does cover the cost of legal defence and this can be valuable. Note that insurance will not generally cover claims that are made against trustees of an unincorporated charity in their personal capacity where that unincorporated charity cannot meet the claim itself.

How should trustees obtain insurance cover?
It is good practice to obtain up to three comparable quotes from insurers or brokers.

Fulfilling conditions of insurance
It is essential that trustees understand the conditions of insurance policies and ensure that they are fulfilled. This means making sure all relevant information is provided. You should also understand the exclusions that apply; failure to do so can be costly.

Checklist

Does your board need to review its procedures for ensuring that the charity has adequate insurance cover?

Does your charity hold annual reviews of its insurance cover?

Has your charity taken appropriate advice on the sums insured?

Are you satisfied that all the important conditions of insurance have been fulfilled?

Are you satisfied that your charity fulfils its legal requirements in respect of employers' liability insurance (including voluntary workers)?

Discuss the need for trustee liability insurance at a board meeting. Do you face a risk that justifies spending the charity's assets indemnifying the trustees, or are there better ways of protecting your personal liability?

If you plan to take out trustee liability insurance, have you checked your governing document to ensure that it does not expressly prohibit it?

9.3

Health and safety

Trustees are collectively responsible for health and safety within their charity. This includes the health and safety of all its employees, volunteers and members of the general public who may visit the buildings they occupy or with whom they may engage in their activities. Trustees have a duty to ensure that the charity complies with all health and safety legislation and regulations by providing the necessary policies, by risk assessing day-to-day activities and by ensuring that both policies and risk assessments are suitable and sufficient, implemented and regularly reviewed.

What are trustees' statutory responsibilities for health and safety?

The Health and Safety at Work Act 1974 is the main legislation for health and safety, but there are also other acts that govern health and safety.

Employers' legal obligations under these laws include requirements to:

- provide a written policy on health and safety (for organisations with five employees or more)

- assess risks to employees, volunteers and anyone who could be affected by the activities of the charity

- arrange for the effective planning, organisation, control, monitoring and review of preventive and protective measures

- ensure they have access to competent health and safety advice

- consult employees about their risks at work and current preventive and protective measures.

Any risk assessment carried out should:

- be 'suitable' and 'sufficient'

- be carried out by a 'competent' person

- enable trustees to set the charity's health and safety priorities.

There is a large, complex body of statutory regulation concerning health and safety and this Guide can only provide a very brief introduction.

Trustees are responsible for ensuring adherence to a wide range specific health and safety regulations. These regulations include – but are not restricted to:

- obligations about fire safety in non-domestic premises,

- the ban on smoking in enclosed public places and workplaces

- regulations about employees' working time, rest breaks and paid annual leave

- regulations about using computer display equipment

- regulations about first aid

- regulations about manual handling

- regulations about electricity

- regulations about using of machines and equipment

- regulations about protective clothing

- regulations about hazardous substances

- regulations about the reporting of certain accidents, diseases and dangerous occurrences

- other specific regulations.

This list is not exhaustive and trustees should check their obligations and ensure compliance with requirements specific to their charity.

What can trustees do to promote good health and safety?

The Health and Safety Executive with the Institute of Directors have published guidance specifically for board members and leaders.[16] The guidance underlines the important role of the board in ensuring effective health and safety management and the importance of integrating health and safety into an organisation's governance arrangements (especially around risk and internal controls). In particular, the HSE guidance includes:

- information on drawing up a health and safety policy, starting with an assessment of risks; the policy should confirm the board's commitment to leading on health and safety and set out a plan to communicate, promote, champion and monitor health and safety

- a recommendation that trustees regularly include health and safety on board agendas and consider appointing a board health and safety champion

- The need for the board to review the organisation's health and safety performance on an annual basis or more regularly as required.

Further information:
HSE Infoline

Charities Safety Group (CSG)

Institute of Occupational Safety and Health (IOSH)

Royal Society for the Prevention of Accidents (RoSPA)

Checklist

Does your charity have a health and safety policy?

Are you satisfied that your board has adequate procedures for monitoring and overseeing your health and safety policies and practices?

Do trustees ever carry out spot checks in the charity's premises, for example, checking that fire exits are not blocked or locked?

Does your board need to check that a risk assessment has been carried out and that your charity's health and safety policies comply with recent legislation?

16 Institute of Directors (IOD) and Health and Safety Executive (HSE) (2013) *Leading Health and Safety at Work: Actions for directors, board members, business owners and organisations of all sizes.* London: IOD and HSE.

10

10.1

Information technology and data

Trustees' responsibilities for information technology (IT)

How charities utilise IT should be a key strategic issue. IT presents opportunities to make an organisation's work more efficient and far-reaching but also poses threats and potential liabilities, such as the legal compliance and confidentiality issues concerned with managing data. It is important that trustees respond proactively and support staff and volunteers to maximise the benefits and minimise the risks.

Trustees have a duty to lead by example. Are there new IT solutions that would help them plan and administer board meetings, data-handling and decision-making in a more effective way? How can trustees ensure that discussions about IT developments are embedded in their governance work, and that changes come as a result of proactive exploration rather than reactive panic?

10.2

A board's approach to IT generally should be the same as the way in which it approaches any other issue it faces – create a supportive environment and ask probing questions about any new proposals or developments.

What does 'creating a supportive environment' mean?
IT costs money, both in the initial investment and the maintenance. It can't always however be viewed in terms of return on investment. A successful IT project depends on spending what is necessary, not the least possible. Trustees need to be aware of this so that IT proposals are not rejected out of hand. They must also be aware of the benefits that change can bring.

How can a board ensure the organisation benefits strategically from its IT?
The following list of questions can be used by boards to help them provide effective governance of their organisation's IT and is based on information taken from *An ICT Survival Guide for Trustees.*[17]

- Is IT included in the induction of all trustees?

- Has the organisation conducted a needs analysis for IT?

- Have we agreed an IT strategy, plan and budget?

  – Have we engaged staff, volunteers and other trustees as appropriate?

  – Have we assessed and developed a plan for risk management?

- Do we have tailored policies for all elements of IT and communications?

- Does the organisation have an asset register of all IT equipment (and passwords)?

- Does the organisation have an effective disaster recovery policy?

- Is IT considered appropriately in all project discussions?

- Is return on investment and the impact of IT considered in all project discussions and proposals?

- Are we comfortable that we are asking the right questions about IT and IT projects?

- Is the board making effective use of IT to support effective decision-making?

- Have we considered the future implications of IT on our activities?

Further information:
IT resources on the NCVO website: www.ncvo.org.uk/practical-support/it

Social media

Social media includes platforms, websites and applications that encourage users to create and share content or engage in social networking. For example, a website that allows reviews and comments is 'social', a platform such as Twitter where people can post photos and thoughts is 'social' and a private online community where people with similar interests can talk to each other from different sides of the world is also considered to be 'social'.

The open nature of social media will raise questions for trustees that should be considered as part of the organisation's overarching public relations/communication's strategy (see section 14.2) and not dealt with in isolation from the other policies and procedures (email, internet, equal opportunities, anti-bullying, confidentiality, data protection, code of conduct for trustees etc) that protect and promote your organisation.

Trustees, staff and volunteers
While some social media 'accounts' and 'identities' can be created in the name of the charity, others will be held in the name of individuals or teams. It is likely that the people who work and volunteer for your organisation will have their own personal online accounts. It is not difficult to see how lines between what is work related or personal can become blurred.

17 NCVO (2008) *From Nightmare to Nirvana: An ICT survival guide for trustees.* London: NCVO.

10.3

Many organisations will already have guidelines in place for trustees, staff and volunteers who represent or act as ambassadors for them, either in person or in writing. However, given the complexity of the ways in which an organisation and individuals will use social media to promote the work that it does, all trustees should consider the need for a social media/networking policy that applies to its use for both business and personal purposes, during or outside of working hours.

As part of agreeing or reviewing a social media policy and/or a code of conduct for trustees, the board should consider whether it is appropriate for messages or information from the meeting to be posted on social media. If trustees agree that this is an appropriate way to engage with stakeholders, detailed and comprehensive guidance should be put in place including what monitoring will be undertaken and how any breaches will be handled.

Complaints handling

Another consequence of these open forums is that complaints by beneficiaries or donors are public. If you already have a complaints-handling policy and procedure, you should consider including provision for how complaints are handled in a social media environment.

There have been many examples over the last few years of organisations that responded too slowly or without apparent respect for the person complaining, which has backfired. If your organisation is engaging with their stakeholders in an open and online environment, it is wise to consider reputational risk and how to keep up to date with best practice as part of your strategic approach to digital engagement.

Data protection

Organisations and individuals that process information about living individuals are data controllers under the Data Protection Act 1998. Information is 'processed' when it is collected, used, stored, deleted, processed or transmitted.

Certain data controllers have a duty to register with the Information Commissioner's Office (ICO) but even where they do not, they must still comply with the data protection principles under the Data Protection Act. Some not-for-profit organisations are exempt from registration if they use personal data only for certain specific purposes – such as membership records – but the exemption is quite limited and charities should check the ICO's guidance.

Special rules apply to 'sensitive personal data', which relates, for instance, to an individual's racial or ethnic origin, political opinions, trade union membership, religious belief, health, sexual life or criminal record.

Failure to comply with the Data Protection Act and the data protection principles can lead to criminal convictions and fines of up to £500,000 in the most severe cases. The ICO has begun exercising its powers more vigorously in recent years, especially where organisations, including charities, have mishandled data and particularly sensitive personal data. These have commonly involved loss or theft of unencrypted data.

The reputational consequences of a breach should not be underestimated. It is vital that trustees inform themselves of the issues and put appropriate internal procedures and policies in place.

Charities are likely to be processing personal data if they hold any data about an individual in any kind of database (including a manual database such as a card index system). This will include:

- name and address lists

- donor databases

- fundraising databases

- records about employees

- records about their service users and beneficiaries (some of which may well constitute sensitive data).

Trustees need to determine what information about individuals the charity gathers, how it uses it and whom it gives it to. It then needs to adopt a set of practices in relation to the information, which complies with the Data Protection Act.

Compliance with the Act requires compliance with what are known as the eight data protection principles. In summary, data must be:

- fairly and lawfully processed

- obtained for a lawful purpose and not then used for purposes outside those for which the individual gave consent

- adequate and relevant for the purpose

- accurate and kept up to date

- only transferred to other parties with the individual's consent

- kept secure

- kept only for as long as is necessary for the purpose for which they have given consent.

In order to be processed fairly, it is usual for organisations to seek specific consent from the individual concerned. Such consents are often contained in privacy notices on websites or in direct marketing communications. Special rules apply to direct marketing. With charities increasingly communicating with supporters via websites, running chatrooms and entering the world of e-commerce, it is vital the website's terms of use, cookie and privacy policies are comply with the Data Protection Act. Trustees should also make sure that relevant staff and volunteers have access to appropriate guidance and training in relation to the Data Protection Act and the principles.

The Data Protection Act gives members of the public the right to find out what personal information is held about them, by making a 'subject access request'. If a member of the public feels that they have been prevented from this access, they can complain to the ICO.

Further information:
ICO

Checklist

Does your charity have data protection policies and procedures that are regularly reviewed?

Is the implementation of the policy reviewed to ensure the charity complies with data protection law?

Do relevant staff and volunteers have access to appropriate guidance and training?

11

Staff and volunteers

11.1

Employment responsibilities

Staff are a key resource for charities. A well-managed diverse and effective staff group can help your organisation's public image and improve your performance overall.

Overview of trustees' employment responsibilities

If the charity employs individuals, whether full time, part time, casual or temporary, the charity is likely to be their employer. You will need to ensure that you understand and abide by current employment legislation.

Employment law is complex and changes frequently. Much of the detail of trustees' responsibilities as employers is beyond the scope of this Guide.

Employed, self employed or worker?

Are you clear as to the employment status of people who are paid to carry out work for your charity? Are you clear whether they are employed, self-employed or in the category of 'worker'?

Employees

Employment rights extend to full- and part-time employees and employees on permanent, fixed-term or annual-hours contracts.

Self-employed

Some individuals may carry out work for a charity on a self-employed basis. A self-employed person is not an employee of the charity and does not have any obligation beyond the specific piece of work for which they are contracted. There are a number of criteria to determine whether someone is self-employed. Self-employed people are responsible for their own tax and national insurance. Treating someone as self-employed, even if they say they are, can have very serious tax and employment law risks if legally they are employed. Legal advice should be sought.

Worker

A 'worker' is an individual who works for a charity who is not employed under a contract of employment, but because of the nature of their work (usually on a flexible or casual basis) has some other contract that puts them in the middle ground between employee and self-employed. Workers have some rights under employment law, but not as many as employees, for example they do not have the right to claim unfair dismissal, notice pay or redundancy pay. However, they do have the right to receive the minimum wage, not suffer unlawful deductions from their wage, receive paid holiday under the Working Time Regulations, freedom from discrimination under equality legislation and protection under health and safety law.

Employment rights for employees

In general, all employees have a right to certain benefits and conditions in the areas of equality, leave, pay and contracts/conditions. This is a complex area but, in broad terms, employees rights include the following.

- Not to be discriminated against or suffer detriment
- Equal pay
- Rights relating to work on Sundays
- Part-time workers should be treated no less favourably
- Employees on fixed-term contracts should be treated no less favourably
- Rights to take leave in certain circumstances, including maternity leave, and other entitlements, and rights around annual leave and working time limits

- Pay, including the minimum wage, not to have unlawful deductions from pay and statutory pay (eg maternity pay, sick pay etc)
- A written statement of the main terms of the employment contract
- Not to be unfairly dismissed
- Apply for flexible working
- Notice of termination of employment
- A safe system of work
- Trade union membership
- Protected employment rights when a business transfers to a new employer
- Written reasons for dismissal on request if they have two years' service
- Rights to be accompanied at disciplinary and grievance hearings
- Protection when making disclosures of wrongdoing to the employer.

Employers must:

- register with HM Revenue and Customs if they are taking on an employee
- adhere to data protection principles – employee data constitutes personal data (see section 10.3)
- check each employee's entitlement to work legally in the UK before employment commences under the Immigration Asylum and Immigration Nationality Act 2006.

Contract of employment

All employees have a contract once an offer of employment is made and accepted. This does not have to be in writing to constitute a legal contract. However, employees (including part-time employees and those on fixed-term contracts) employed for more than one month have the statutory right to a written statement of terms and conditions of employment. Under the Employment Rights Act 1996, this must now be provided within two months of starting work. The statement must include certain information, and it is important that you ensure the statement of terms and conditions includes this information.

In addition to the statutory particulars that are required to be included in all employment contracts, it is advisable for the charity to include additional clauses designed to give it further protection. For example, it would be advisable to include clauses dealing with confidentiality, disclosing conflicts of interest, agreement to the charity obtaining medical reports where there are concerns, intellectual property rights, post-termination restrictions, the right to make deductions, etc.

Employment policies and procedures

In 2013, following a great deal of critical media attention on the 'high pay levels of charity chief executives', NCVO launched an inquiry tasked with producing guidance for trustees on setting remuneration. The inquiry published recommendations, including the need for trustees of charities that employ staff to consider adopting a formal pay policy (especially if they have an income over £500,000) as a matter of good practice.

The inquiry also recommended that all charities with independently audited accounts should:

• publish an annual statement explaining their charity's ethos and policy on remuneration

• explain how this impacts on the delivery of their charitable purposes

• report the actual remuneration, roles and names of individual, highest paid staff, as defined by the charity.

Whilst the basic principles for setting pay may not have fundamentally changed over the years, the public are definitely calling for greater transparency from organisations in the private, public and charitable sector when it comes to how they reward senior staff.

Further information:
NCVO (2014) *Report of the Inquiry into Charity Senior Executive Pay and Guidance for Trustees on Setting Remuneration.* London: NCVO.

What other employment policies and procedures should we have?

Trustees should ensure that the charity has policies for the recruitment of staff, ensuring that policies and practices are in place so that applicants are treated fairly and in accordance with equal opportunities practice at all stages of advertising, shortlisting and interviewing. They should establish policies for staff appraisal, support and supervision, probationary periods and remuneration that are proportional to the size of the charity.

Employers should follow the ACAS Code of Practice on Disciplinary and Grievance in relation to disputes at work. If the charity has five employees or more, it is required to prepare a written policy regarding health and safety.

Some employers, as a matter of good practice, adopt non-statutory policies, such as an email, internet and social media policy. However, you should ensure that these policies do not form part of the employee/worker's contract. This is so that if you wish to amend the policies at a future date you do not need to obtain the employee/worker's consent before any amendments, additions or substitutions are made. You should, however, inform the employee/worker of any amendments as soon as is practicable.

All policies should be reviewed on a regular basis (at least annually).

It is likely that in small charities the trustees will be personally involved in appointing all the staff. In larger charities they may appoint only the chief executive, or the most senior staff, delegating responsibility for appointing other staff to the chief executive or other senior managers. Similarly, trustees' personal involvement in staff appraisal or review will depend on the size of the charity.

You should be aware that some staff may be bound by their own code of professional ethics, for example lawyers working for charities or medical staff working in charitable hospices or research institutes. You should respect the constraints that this may place on staff.

Trustees should be cautious about linking terms and conditions with that of local authorities (for example by placing salaries on the National Joint Council (NJC) pay scale). Although such an approach may be familiar to staff and funders, it risks tying the charity to a process over which they have no control. It is recommended that if NJC scales are adopted, it is made clear that increments are not guaranteed but are dependent on affordability and at trustee discretion.

Employment issues and employment contracts are the areas most likely to produce a situation in which the charity finds itself liable. Employment law is a fast-changing area of law and if the charity is in doubt about an employment issue, it should seek expert advice.

The chief executive

Where a staff structure is in place and a chief executive manages the staff team, the board has a direct responsibility to recruit and support the chief executive. The board takes overall responsibility for:

- setting the organisation's strategic direction and the boundaries within which staff operate

- recruiting and inducting the chief executive, setting remuneration, establishing a monitoring system

- managing and appraising the chief executive

- delegating authority, sometimes to the chair, for liaison and support to the chief executive in between board meetings

- respecting the boundaries between board and chief executive and reviewing these regularly (see Chapter 8 for more guidance in this area).

This is an important area of board responsibility and other guides exist to inform the board in this area.

Dealing with conflict

Internal conflict in a charity is not uncommon. It can be time consuming and costly, and it distracts the trustees and any staff or volunteers from getting on with the work the charity was established to do. Moreover, the resulting bad publicity can damage the charity's public image.

Trustees should be aware that employers should follow certain procedures in relation to disputes at work (see previous page).

Further information:
ACAS Code of Practice:
www.acas.org.uk

CIPD: www.cipd.co.uk

11.2

Checklist

Does your board need to review its procedures for ensuring that the charity is acting in accordance with employment law?

Does your board need to review its employment policies and procedures, including its recruitment policy and the grievance and disciplinary procedures?

Has your board adopted a remuneration policy that is in line with the purposes, aims and values of the charity and the needs of its beneficiaries?

Does your board regularly review the salaries, terms and conditions of service of the staff?

Does your board ensure that there is adequate support and supervision for staff?

Does a group of trustees agree an annual work plan for the chief executive officer and annually appraise his or her performance?

Do any of the trustees involved in appointing or appraising staff need support, for example training in interviewing?

Does the charity have any fixed-term employees and, if so, should any of them be converted to permanent employees? (After four years, employment contracts may automatically become permanent unless there is good reason for them to remain fixed term).

Should the board conduct an audit of employees on fixed-term contracts to ensure that their terms and conditions are not less favourable than for comparable permanent employees?

Should the board conduct an audit of part-time employees to ensure that they are not treated less favourably (unless it can be objectively justified)?

Volunteers

Many organisations involve volunteers to help achieve their aims – indeed, trustees are volunteers, and many organisations rely entirely on volunteers. If your charity involves volunteers, trustees should be aware of their overall legal responsibility for their management and support and, through the board's leadership, create an environment that is a supportive and positive place to volunteer.

What does good volunteer management look like?

Like many aspects of a trustees' responsibility, the way in which the board supports and manages volunteers will vary depending on the organisation's size and the extent to which it relies on volunteers. There are some key principles of good volunteer management that are relevant to most organisations and have been widely agreed as a way to ensure organisations have good volunteer management in place. A good place to start is to review how your organisation compares to the nine principles of good volunteer management that make up the Investing in Volunteers Standard, which is the UK standard for good practice in volunteer management.

Principles of good volunteer management

The Investing in Volunteers Standard comprises nine indicators.

1 There is an expressed commitment to the involvement of volunteers and recognition throughout the organisation that volunteering is a two-way process that benefits volunteers and the organisation.

2 The organisation commits appropriate resources to working with volunteers, such as money, management, staff time and materials.

3 The organisation is open to involving volunteers who reflect the diversity of the local community and actively seeks to do this in accordance with its stated aims.

4 The organisation develops appropriate roles for volunteers in line with its aims and objectives, which are of value to the volunteers.

5 The organisation is committed to ensuring that, as far as possible, volunteers are protected from physical, financial and emotional harm arising from volunteering.

6 The organisation is committed to using fair, efficient and consistent recruitment procedures for all potential volunteers.

7 Clear procedures are put into action for introducing new volunteers to their role, the organisation, its work, policies, practices and relevant personnel.

8 The organisation takes account of the varying support and supervision needs of volunteers.

9 The whole organisation is aware of the need to give volunteers recognition.

Further information:
Investing in Volunteers:
www.investinginvolunteers.org.uk

Volunteer management practice

How can our organisation put in place good volunteer management practices?

NCVO provides practical support and guidance on volunteer management and good practice. This includes a range of online resources including information sheets, quick guides and links to other helpful guidance available.

Further information:
NCVO: www.ncvo.org.uk/ practical-support/volunteering

KnowHow NonProfit provides a range of practical support on a range of topics including volunteering and supports an online community where organisations can contribute and share good practice: www.knowhownonprofit.org

Keeping it legal

It is important to make a clear distinction between individuals who are paid to work for your organisation and individuals who volunteer. Blurring the boundaries between volunteers and paid staff risks inadvertently creating an employment contract with volunteers. This could then entitle volunteers to the same rights and responsibilities of staff, which is inappropriate. You can help avoid this situation by:

- only reimbursing volunteers for genuine out-of-pocket expenses; avoid flat-rate expenses or payments over and above actual expenses, and avoid providing other material benefits that could be seen as constituting payment

- avoiding creating a relationship between a volunteer and an organisation that could be seen to be an employment or contractual relationship. Such a relationship need not have a written contract but includes consideration (the volunteer receiving something of value) and intent to create a legally binding relationship (an obligation for the volunteer to provide their services). For example, agreeing to provide training of considerable value to a volunteer that is above and beyond what is required for the role should be avoided. Training should be relevant to the role and should be available to all volunteers undertaking that role.

The use of any language that might suggest an employment relationship could exist should be avoided in the volunteer agreement and all other volunteer-related policies and procedures.

National Occupational Standards for volunteer managers

National Occupational Standards for managing volunteers set out the skills that staff and volunteers who manage volunteers should have, as well as what they should know and understand in order to do their job well.

They were developed with people who have direct experience of managing volunteers in charities as well as social enterprises, community groups and other voluntary sector organisations.

Further information:
National Occupational Standards for Managing volunteers: www. skillseffect.org.uk/products/ national-occupational-standards/ managing-volunteers

11.3

Checklist

How does the leadership within your organisation demonstrate a commitment to volunteering and volunteer management, for example by ensuring it is adequately resourced?

Do trustees need to review the organisation's compliance with the law around volunteers?

Does your organisation have an up-to-date volunteer policy and is it regularly reviewed?

Do volunteers have an opportunity to share their views on the organisation's work and to participate in decision-making?

Does your organisation regularly acknowledge and thank volunteers for the contribution they make, for example via awards or celebrations?

Relations with staff and volunteers

As trustees you are collectively responsible, along with staff and volunteers, for ensuring that good relations exist between yourselves and any staff you employ or volunteers you manage.

All too often the board–staff–volunteer relationship in an organisation can be undermined because of a lack of clarity of roles. What are the boundaries between trustee and staff/volunteer roles? Where do roles overlap?

There is no 'right' or 'wrong' answer to any of these questions. An effective relationship is built on understanding the distinction between the roles and responsibilities of the board and those of the staff and volunteers, identifying where roles overlap and paying attention to building good working relationships.

Clarifying the roles of the board and staff/volunteers

It may help to begin by clarifying the formal aspect of the board – staff/volunteer relationship – that is, the extent and nature by which authority is delegated from trustees to staff and volunteers. Are trustee role descriptions, staff job descriptions, volunteer role descriptions, policies and procedures and internal controls clear and up to date? Do they need to be reviewed?

Is there a clear and shared understanding between board, staff and volunteers as to their respective roles and areas of overlap? Has this been discussed by both parties? You could use an exercise like the one in the box as a starting point.

Remember that what is a board role in one organisation may be a staff or volunteer role in another. Where boundaries overlap – for example in the area of planning or budgeting – the respective duties of board members and staff/volunteers will vary between organisations. Even when a task is clearly the responsibility of the board, some organisations will involve staff or volunteers far more than others in helping trustees discharge their duties – for example by way of providing information, guidance or practical support.

Remember also that organisations are dynamic and change all the time. Your board should revisit the issue of board/staff/volunteer boundaries from time to time, particularly when your organisation reaches a new point in its development. It is important to take time out of the normal schedule of business to review roles (for example, by holding an away day).

Exercise – Board, staff and volunteer roles

This exercise explores the roles of the board and those of staff or volunteers. It should take about 45 minutes to complete.

Learning objectives: As a result of this exercise, participants should be able to list the complementary roles of the board and staff/volunteers and describe the areas of overlap.

Board	Staff/volunteers	Both

1) Ask individual participants or groups to identify the top five roles within each column (ie roles of the board; roles of staff/volunteers; roles of both).

2) Review the answers as a group. Is there anything participants would like to review or change, perhaps where roles overlap? Use this Guide to identify where practical changes may be needed (eg internal controls, induction of trustees).

Relationships between the trustee board and the chief executive

Many staffed organisations employ a chief executive, manager or head of staff to manage the day-to-day running of the organisation.

An important way that the board exercises its power is through the appointment, supervision and holding to account the chief executive.

Both board and chief executive are dependent on each other: the chief executive needs the authority of the board to allow them to manage the organisation and the board needs the chief executive to exercise leadership by building a successful staff and volunteer team. The chief executive needs the collective wisdom that board members can bring to decisions about the organisation's mission and plans, and the board needs the support of the chief executive to ensure precious board time is used effectively.

Above all, the chief executive is a primary source of information and advice to enable board members to agree plans and priorities, monitor the organisation's work and make effective decisions.

For practical purposes, most chief executives have a closer day-to-day working relationship with one or more individual trustees to:

- ensure there is effective and efficient communication between the board and chief executive at and in between board meetings

- ensure that board meeting agendas can be planned and papers drawn up to make best use of the board's time and most effectively utilise input from staff

- to supervise and appraise the chief executive

- in exceptional circumstances, take decisions efficiently without always having to call a full board meeting.

These day-to-day working relationships often take place between the chair and the chief executive, although not exclusively so. In some organisations, responsibility for managing the chief executive is delegated to the vice-chair or another trustee because they have greater line-management experience.

The chief executive may have some day-to-day contact with other trustees for particular purposes, such as with the treasurer for the purpose of financial oversight or to utilise the skills or advice of a particular trustee in the area of, say, marketing or law.

Developing board–chief executive relationships

The board–chief executive relationship will have a strong bearing on the way your board relates to staff and ultimately on the effectiveness of your organisation. It is important that they have a good working relationship based on a clear, agreed understanding of respective roles and responsibilities.

When can the board–chief executive relationship break down?

Just as individual board members can engage in micromanaging the chief executive and interfering in the day-to-day running of the organisation, chief executives can be guilty of not helping board members engage in the oversight of the organisation and fulfilling their responsibilities. What might be the indicators of a poor board–chief executive relationship?

- Where the board is unaware of the true financial condition of the organisation, perhaps because they do not understand financial information given to them, do not receive adequate financial information or do not take the time to read information

- Where the board is not kept informed by the chief executive about important news, and where board members find out about important news informally from staff or even from the media

- Board members who are reluctant to evaluate the performance of a strong and charismatic chief executive

- Chairs acting as a second 'chief executive', heavily involved in the day-to-day running of the organisation, with trustees and staff unclear as to who holds authority in different areas of organisational activity

- Where there is little or no contact between the board and chief executive, even via an individual such as the chair

Building healthy relationships

A healthy relationship between the board/chair and chief executive might best be described by the following two quotes:

'Close but critical, co-operative but never cosy'[18]

or

'Constructive tension tempered by mutual respect.'

What can help build good relationships between the board and chief executive?

- Clear boundaries between the roles of chief executive, board and individual trustees (particularly those who have specific roles on the board)

- Clear documentation of what delegated authority has been passed to the chief executive and honorary officers and what powers are reserved for the board as a whole

- A recognition that individual board members only act on the specific authority of the board

- Clear communication between the chief executive and the board

- Regular meeting times and agreed methods of communication between the chief executive and the chair (or other board members with specific roles)

- Agreement on the level of contact that the chair and individual trustees have with the chief executive and individual members of staff

- Where board members have contact with individual members of staff, to respect the agreed boundaries between staff and board roles

- Recognition from the chief executive that, if a decision is required between board meetings, the chair or other board members with specific roles will need to consult with other board members; this means allowing time for this in the decision-making process

- Clear systems of internal control, so that levels of authority are clear and unambiguous

- Ongoing supervision, support and annual appraisal of the chief executive

- Taking time out to review relationships

---

18 Taken from NCVO resource 'A summary of legal issues involving volunteers'.

What can be unhelpful?

- Over-involvement or interference by trustees in the day-to-day management of the organisation

- Chief executives seeking to make decisions that belong to board members and vice versa

- Poor judgement by the chief executive or board about what falls within their delegated powers

- The chief executive concealing information from the board

- Board members or chief executive seeking independent publicity

- The chief executive seeking to manipulate individual board members against each other

Trustees should be aware that the chief executive is (usually) an employee of the charity. If the relationship between trustees and chief executive does reach a serious point, for example concerning a grievance or disciplinary issue, trustees should be aware of their responsibilities concerning employees (see section 11.1). This is a complex area and if this situation occurs it is recommended trustees take appropriate professional advice.

Case study

The trustees of a patient support group have all been involved from the beginning of the group's life. Despite recruiting a chief executive, all the trustees still regularly work in the office carrying out a variety of tasks including managing some of the other staff. Board meetings are monthly and typically still involve all purchasing decisions, recruiting decisions and decisions on many other day-to-day matters.

The lessons

The new chief executive is unclear about whether they were recruited as a head of staff or as a glorified administrator. The board must decide if it is ready to let go of the day-to-day management of the organisation and set remits, limits of authority and line management structures so that the chief executive can effectively become the head of staff and relieve them of some of the burden of the day-to-day running of the organisation. Trustees need to be clear about what their governance role is and what are other roles they carry out on behalf of the charity (see the 'hats' exercise on page 159).

What helps build relationships between staff and board?

- Creating an environment in which the chief executive can comfortably raise issues that they are concerned about

- The board receiving an overview of organisational activities as well as progress and challenges against a strategic plan from the chief executive's report

- Co-ordinating strategy sessions for the board and senior managers

- Appropriate level of attendance at board and committee meetings by senior managers or other relevant staff

- Investing in trustee and board development, including an induction programme for new board members and ongoing briefings/support for all board members

- Inviting board members to informal and formal events, where they can be ambassadors for the organisation, meet staff and learn more about the organisation's activities

- The chair being prepared to deal with board members who step out of line

Relations with staff and volunteers in small organisations

If your organisation is small, you may find that it is more difficult than the above guidance suggests to distinguish between governance activities undertaken by trustees and operational/day-to-day activities.

In organisations without a chief executive and where few or no staff are employed, trustees will inevitably find it tricky to separate their strategic, governance roles and their operational roles, because much of the attention of board members will be concentrated on the day-to-day running of the organisation. Individual trustees may be involved in managing specific projects, running the organisation's services, fundraising or bookkeeping. If a very small number of staff are employed, and there is no overall chief executive, individual trustees may 'manage' specific areas of the organisation's work on a day-to-day basis. Trustees may act as board members, managers and volunteers.

However, the distinction between strategic and operational roles is still important, for three reasons.

- As an organisation grows, the activities of the board may change but the fundamental duties and responsibilities of the board – as set out in the 12 responsibilities in section 1.5 – stay the same.

- All trustee boards should be able to distinguish between governance matters – issues that trustees must deal with collectively as a board and matters relating to the long-term future or strategic direction of the organisation – and operational matters – issues relating to day-to-day operations that may in a larger organisation be delegated to staff but in small organisations may be carried out by individual board members in a non-governance role.

- The more complex the relationships between a trustee's strategic role and the day-to-day roles of trustees, staff and volunteers, so it becomes more important to ensure that respective roles are clearly understood, to avoid confusion and tension.

If the distinction between strategic and operational roles is made, even in small organisations with few or no staff and where trustee agendas tend to be dominated by operational issues, it can help trustees to keep abreast of their duty to guard the charity's long-term future as well as to deal with short-term crises. The 'hats' exercise (see box on the following page) may help trustees in understanding the different roles they may take in a small organisation.

The 'hats' exercise

As a trustee you may have several 'roles' or 'hats' in your organisations. Which of the following hats do you wear?

- **The governance hat:** this is worn when attending formal board meetings and taking board decisions. This is a collective responsibility, working with other trustees.

- **The 'specific role' hat:** this is worn when you are authorised to implement a particular decision the board has made. Your individual responsibility will be specifically delegated to you by the board.

- **The management hat:** this is worn when you are managing a specific project (usually in a small organisation where no chief executive is employed). You will be wearing the hat of an unpaid manager, distinct from your role as trustee. You may be accountable to the board or sometimes to another member of staff. Your authority only extends to that which has been specifically delegated to you.

- **The volunteer hat:** This is worn you are when involved with the organisation at other times (for example volunteering in the organisation's office). You will be wearing the hat of a volunteer, distinct from your role as a trustee. You may be accountable to an individual member of staff, who will be responsible for managing your work even though staff are ultimately accountable to the board.

Trustees in small organisations can wear many hats and the roles and relationships between the board, individual trustees, staff and volunteers can be complex and less clear-cut than in larger organisations. Identifying different 'hats' can help to distinguish between when you are involved in the 'governance' matters of the trustee board and when you are instead involved in the day-to-day running of the organisation.

Issues to consider

Staff, volunteers and trustees have distinct roles that should involve acknowledging, respecting and avoiding undermining each other. The way your board, staff and volunteers treat each other does more to affect the quality of leadership and governance in your organisation than any iron-clad agreement on proper boundaries.

The relationship between trustees, staff and volunteers is a factor you should consider when assessing the effectiveness of your board (see page 153).

There are many ways to encourage good working relationships. Some charities hold annual conferences or other social events to which both trustees and staff/volunteers are invited.

If you are not satisfied with this relationship, you could consider holding a meeting of trustees and staff/volunteers to review your roles and responsibilities. If agreement is not reached, you could consider inviting a consultant or facilitator to work with the board, staff and volunteers (see section 16.2 for further information about dealing with differences).

Checklist

Have your board members and staff/executive/volunteers carried out an exercise to review respective roles?

Does your organisation have written agreements, procedures or documents regarding the respective roles of board and staff/volunteers?

Do board members recognise the distinction between their role as a board member, with collective responsibility, their role when they act on the express authority of the board and their role when they act in some other voluntary role for the organisation?

Are you confident that the relationship between board and staff/volunteers is positive?

12

12.1

Equalities, diversity and human rights

Equality and diversity

The principle of equality is fundamental to the work of charities and should be an underlying principle of good governance.

What does equality mean?
In charities, equality means ensuring equity, diversity and equality of treatment for all sections of the community.

What is the board's role in upholding equality and diversity?

One of the principles of the Code is that the board should:

'ensure that it upholds and applies the principles of equality and diversity in every sphere of its activity, going beyond the legal minimum where appropriate.' [19]

How can the board uphold equality and diversity in practice?
In practice, boards can follow equality and diversity principles in many practical areas of their responsibility. Here are some examples.

• Agreeing organisation-wide policies that set out equality and diversity principles – these can include:

– a diversity strategy – setting out an approach to diversity and equality across the organisation, including clear plans, targets (where appropriate) and reporting arrangements

– an equal opportunities and diversity policy – setting out the principles and practice by which the charity can ensure it is open and fair to all

• As part of the strategic planning process – including the identification of needs and priorities

• Making decisions on the use of resources, grants or services

• The accessibility of services, activities and premises

• Policies around purchasing goods and services

• Monitoring and evaluating services and activities

• Staff and volunteers – recruitment, training and management

• Accessibility of meetings and communications within the organisation

• Communicating with stakeholders and the public

Equality and diversity – legal responsibilities

The Equality Act 2010 aims to protect people who share certain characteristics and prevent discrimination. Current protected characteristics include:

• age

• disability

• gender reassignment

• marriage and civil partnership

• pregnancy and maternity

• race

• religion and belief (including lack of belief)

• sex

• sexual orientation.

All trustees are required to comply and ensure their charity complies with the Act. Trustees must always take expert advice if they do not have this expertise on the board.

While discrimination in employment is a key concern, the duty to avoid discrimination also extends to the provision of goods, services and facilities.

In the case of disability, trustees are required to take reasonable steps to adapt their services and premises.

Some charities are treated as public bodies and have a stricter duty to promote equality not just prevent discrimination. Many other charities adopt this principle as a matter of good practice.

19 NCVO (2010) *Good Governance: A code for the voluntary and community sector.* London: NCVO.

12.2

What if our charity serves a specific section of the community?

Exceptions in the Act allow charities to target their services to certain protected groups. However, this is not a blanket exception and trustees should ensure the charity complies with the restrictions in the Act and is still meeting their general duty to provide public benefit. This can be a very complex area and advice will often be required.

Human Rights Act

As with equality, human rights are often a core part of a charity's ethos and principles.

The Human Rights Act 1998 codifies the protections in the European Convention on Human Rights into UK law. All public bodies (including courts, police, local governments, hospitals, publicly funded schools) must comply with the Act. This may apply to other bodies carrying out public functions, such as charities delivering public services on behalf of government or a public body.

The Act sets out the fundamental rights and freedoms that individuals in the UK have access to, including:

- right to life
- freedom from torture and inhuman or degrading treatment
- right to liberty and security
- freedom from slavery and forced labour
- right to a fair trial
- no punishment without law

- respect for your private and family life, home and correspondence
- freedom of thought, belief and religion
- freedom of expression
- freedom of assembly and association
- right to marry and start a family
- protection from discrimination in respect of these rights and freedoms
- right to peaceful enjoyment of your property
- right to education
- right to participate in free elections.

As with the Equality Act, trustees should consider seeking professional advice on the application of the Human Rights Act to their charity if they deliver public services.

Further information:
Equality and Human Rights Commission

Equality, diversity and the board itself

The board can also follow equality and diversity principles within its own role and functioning, for example concerning:

- **board recruitment practices**
  – creating an inclusive board, for example by encouraging user involvement at board level

- **board codes of conduct**
  – ensuring that equity and fairness are part of the values and behaviours expected of trustees

- **attention to board meetings**
  – including the timing, location and accessibility of meetings, the format of board papers and language and jargon used in papers and during meetings

- **creating an inclusive wider decision-making process**
  – for example, ensuring board business is open and accountable (unless confidentiality restricts this), creating opportunities for user involvement in advisory groups or working groups and making annual general meetings inclusive and accessible.

Checklist

Does your charity have an equal opportunities and diversity policy?

Does your charity have a diversity strategy or plan that is regularly monitored and reviewed?

Are your trustees aware of their legal duties concerning discrimination?

Are your trustees aware of their legal duties concerning human rights if they deliver public services?

Have trustees considered how the functioning of the board can be made more inclusive and diverse?

12.3

Inclusion and involving users

Whatever the purpose of your charity, it is likely to benefit a group of people: your 'users' or beneficiaries. Depending on your charity's purpose, users may be a specified group or groups of individuals referred to in the objects clause of your governing document. You may also have a range of 'secondary users' who benefit indirectly from your work.

Why involve your users?

Many charities involve users in the planning or delivery of their work as a way of better meeting their mission. Indeed, the benefits of involving service users in activities are increasingly being recognised by organisations as a way of being more effective and more 'inclusive'. Government, regulators, charitable trusts and corporate funders also recognise the importance of user involvement.

Instead of having a one-way relationship with users in which a charity provides services or activities 'for' users, it is possible – and increasingly common – for organisations to develop a two-way relationship with users, in which users take an active part in decision-making, planning and evaluation. Involving users in this way can generate new ideas, challenge the assumptions of the trustee board and ensure an organisation's services are as relevant as possible users' needs. Involving users can also empower them to use their expertise and allow them to better 'own' the organisation.

Many charities see the involvement of users as an essential element of the additional value they provide.

13

Making a difference

Once your policies and plans are in place, how do you know whether your charity is making a positive difference? Only by tracking and evaluating its progress can you understand how effective your charity has been in achieving the changes you are aiming for.

Charities use a range of terms to describe the various elements to be considered when measuring the difference their work makes.

- Outputs are the products or services a charity delivers, for example training courses, advice sessions, publications, a user survey, a helpline or a website.

- Outcomes are the benefits, changes and other effects that happen as a result of your work. Your planned outcomes should relate to your charity's strategic plan (see Chapter 6). Often, they can be less tangible and therefore less countable than outputs, but there are tools and techniques to help you capture evidence of these 'soft' outcomes.

- Impact is harder to define. Most understand it as the broad, more long-term effects of your work. Others take it to mean summing up all the changes resulting from an output, including intended as well as unintended effects and negative as well as positive changes. But 'impact' is also often used more generally and interchangeably with 'outcomes'. You'll need to decide what it means to you. The important distinction is that 'impact' and 'outcomes' refer to the difference you make, as opposed to 'outputs', which cover the work that you do.

Other elements of your work include:

- inputs – the resources that contribute to a programme or activity, such as income, staff, volunteers and equipment

- activities – what an organisation does with its inputs to deliver its outputs, such as HR procedures, running an office, devising a service, etc, as well as the other activities you need to do to deliver that service, such as promotional work.

This table depicts the logic of how outcomes and impact are created by your work and resources.

Inputs	Activities	Outputs	Outcomes	Impact
People, income, assets, materials, etc	The actual work that happens using the inputs	The products, services, etc resulting from activities	The benefits to users resulting from outputs	The broad or long-term effects of your work

13.1

13.2

Planning the difference you want to make

Through the strategic planning process (see Chapter 6), the board will lead the charity to define the changes it exists to make.

Many organisations represent these planned changes and the anticipated causal links between their outcomes and their outputs with a 'theory of change'. This usually takes the form of a diagram that sets out your overall desired impact, the specific outcomes that will happen along the way and in what order and how each will be delivered by your outputs.

The process requires you to define clearly your impact and outcomes before deciding on the work that you will deliver to achieve these. This helps to ensure that planning is led by the difference you aim to make and not by individual preferences, a funder or how things have always been done.

Having a clear 'theory of change' helps staff, volunteers and board members to understand and be motivated by the overall difference your charity will make and to see where their individual contribution might fit. It can also be useful to share with funders and partners who may need to know what your organisation wants to achieve and how it plans to do that. It will help you to know which areas of your work and impact to measure. After all, if you don't know where you're going, how will you know when you've got there?

How boards should monitor and evaluate

Boards should have a good idea of what the charity is achieving and how this compares with the strategic or operational plan (see Chapter 6). This means ensuring that the charity has in place a system to collect regular data about its achievements (both outputs and outcomes) and to provide summary information to the board so it can assess progress.

As a board, you need to decide what information you require to form judgements about progress, rather than relying on the chief executive or staff, if you employ them, to present the information they think you need. If you have a staff team, you should delegate to them the actual design and implementation of the monitoring system.

You should also ensure that the monitoring and reporting requirements of any funders are built into your system to avoid duplicating work by creating different data for different people. Where duplication seems to be happening, it may be worth negotiating with funders to ask them if you can streamline reporting requirements, for example by offering to provide them with reports in the same format as the report to the board, rather than creating multiple reports.

The process of actually measuring your work and the difference it makes requires the following information.

- **Indicators:** Signs that tell you if the planned outputs and outcomes are actually happening, often described in terms of quantity, proportions, frequency or quality. For example, indicators could include the number and frequency of courses, the number of participants or the percentage of students achieving accreditation. You could also include satisfaction levels too.

- **Targets:** A particular level of output, outcome or satisfaction an organisation aims to achieve over a set period, for example, six courses every quarter, 20 participants on each course, 50% of participants achieve level two, 75% of tutors are satisfied with the level of administrative support, etc.

- **Data:** This includes both countable information (quantitative) and descriptive information (qualitative).

- **Monitoring:** The systematic process of collecting and recording your indicator data.

- **Evaluation:** The process of drawing together your data and making judgements about progress against targets at the end of a project or at certain points along the way. It can be useful to collect baseline information early in a project to help you make before-and-after comparisons.

How much activity should trustees monitor?

You are responsible for monitoring all areas of the charity's activity. However, in larger charities, it is worth taking time to consider the level of detail that should be reported and how much operational monitoring is best left to staff.

Too many detailed reports of activity will weigh down your board or tempt it to interfere with the management role of staff; too few could lead to the charity's programme going seriously off course before action can be taken.

In larger charities, an audit committee and internal audit reports can play a useful role in helping you to execute your responsibilities for monitoring (see page 104).

Key indicators
Identifying a list of the key indicators across the most important areas of your charity's work is crucial. This should cover your services (eg a key indicator about the number of counselling sessions run) and the difference they make (eg a key indicator about the mental health of service users). They could also include some warning indicators for the health of the charity, for example the number of staff resignations (see section 9.1).

Taylor Reveley, a writer on governance, observes that key indicators are an opportunity for the board to:

'think seriously about what really matters to the organisation...determined efforts must be made to find simple, intelligible methods of tracking performance, watching closely for warning signs, and then utilising the information needed to make decisions in a timely way.'

Evaluation
Evaluating the work of your organisation encourages you to question whether you are:

- carrying out your aims and objectives and making the difference you intend to

- meeting the needs of your beneficiaries

- providing the appropriate quantity and quality of service

- using the resources you have to the greatest effect or in the most efficient manner

- working within the organisation's policy framework.

At the planning stage, your board needs to make sure that you or your staff decide on indicators and, where appropriate, set targets. There should be processes in place to collect information about both of these, so that when it comes to the stage of evaluation, the necessary data is available.

Evaluation of the organisation's outputs and outcomes will usually take place fairly regularly, for example every quarter or every six months. It can also take place at key stages in a project and after work has been carried out.

There is a huge range of tools and techniques to help charities evaluate their work. If your board of trustees is having difficulty finding the most appropriate way to monitor and evaluate your charity's work, you should seek advice.

Deciding what caused a change
Establishing cause and effect can be difficult: how do you know that a particular activity and output was the cause of the change? For example, how do you know that the recent governance review carried out by the board was the cause of the improvement in your charity's services? Three things can help with this.

1 Don't worry too much about 'proof'. 'Reasonable evidence' is what you need. After all, there is no burden of absolute proof in the legal system; people are sent to prison for life on the basis of 'reasonable evidence'.

2 You can sometimes track the cause from the effect. For example, you could ask the staff and managers who improved the charity's services about the role that the governance review played in these improvements. It might have been the staff who actually made the changes, but perhaps it was the board that saw the need for them and insisted upon them happening.

3 It's sufficient to say you contributed to the outcome and to identify the other factors you think have played a part.

Full value

NCVO recommends that organisations adopt a comprehensive approach to assessing their effectiveness, by exploring the full range of their value, much of which is often hidden. An organisation's full value includes:

- all the outcomes you bring about for your users or cause and for other stakeholders and your operating environment, such as staff, neighbours of users, tenants in your building, the local economy or sector policy development

- the satisfaction your services bring – the 'feel good' factor that your users and other stakeholders get through their contact with you.

This approach is introduced in: NCVO (2008) *True Colours: Uncovering the full value of your organisation.* London: NCVO. The approach has been developed as an alternative to two other concepts: full cost recovery, which focuses boards and staff on the costs of their work rather than its impact and the idea of the voluntary sector's 'added value', which has no clear meaning and has been criticised for being too crude to be really useful.

The impact of campaigning

Practical tools that organisations can use to assess the extent to which their campaigning or advocacy work is making a longer-term impact are included in: NCVO (2008) *Is Your Campaign Making a Difference?* London: NCVO. This might include changes to policy, practice and behaviour, or empowering people and communities.

Checklist

Are you clear about what difference your charity wants to make?

Do you regularly evaluate your charity's progress in delivering its outputs and outcomes?

Do you need to improve the way in which information is presented to the board?

Are planning, monitoring and evaluation integrated with each other?

Do you need to seek advice on monitoring or evaluation methods?

Once you have evaluated your charity's work, you need to make use of the findings in two ways: feeding your learning into future planning to make improvements and communicating your impact.

13.3

Reporting your impact

What is impact reporting?
'Impact reporting' means communicating whether and how you are achieving the change that you seek. Few charities will thrive if they fail to do this.

- There are many reasons why an organisation of any shape or size might need to demonstrate its impact to various audiences.

- Funders and commissioners are increasingly asking for evidence that a programme has achieved its outcomes.

- The role of the voluntary sector in the delivery of public services means that voluntary organisations are keen to demonstrate their value (see previous page).

- Donors are becoming more discerning in their choice of causes to give to and organisations are keen to demonstrate that they are using funds in an efficient and effective way to bring about a positive impact on their cause or the lives of beneficiaries.

- Measuring and communicating impact can be a very powerful way to motivate staff and volunteers – and your own board – by showing that their work is making a difference. It can encourage the whole team to build on successes to achieve even more for users or the cause.

- The board, staff, volunteers and partners can be clear on what is working well and what may need improving to achieve the greatest possible impact.

- Charities are accountable to a range of stakeholders.

Three things are crucial in impact reporting.

1. Clarity: Do not underestimate the power of being specific. It is as important to be accurate about your achievements as it is to be accurate about your organisation's finances.

2. Success: To make the most of opportunities to sell your organisation's achievements, consider its full value (see previous page)

3. Honesty: To give credibility to your organisation's communications, you must display real humility about what you don't know and straight honesty about things that haven't gone to plan that will be improved.

Five steps to successful impact reporting

1. Identify why your charity wants to engage in or improve its impact communications.

2. Decide the priority audiences for your impact communications, what you want them to know and how you want this knowledge to influence their behaviour. Don't forget your internal audiences, including the board itself.

3. Agree the general formats, content and channels for the different impact communications you will produce.

4. Check what information you will need, consider what you already collect and, where necessary, fill in the gaps in your monitoring systems.

5. Create and communicate your messages.

13.4

An improvement culture

Unfortunately, not everyone will be receptive to the idea of measuring your progress. For example, it may be difficult to convince some funders that assessing outcomes is a worthwhile (and fundable) activity. You may also encounter internal resistance: staff may see outcome measurement as a waste of resources that should be spent on frontline services or as a threatening activity that will assess their individual performance.

However, creating a culture of continuous improvement is an essential element of all truly successful organisations. Introducing and then fostering this attitude is a crucial role for the board. It can sound like hard work, but staying open to new ideas and possibilities and honing our practices should allow us to achieve more without necessarily doing more.

The role of monitoring and evaluation

Ensuring that there is a sound monitoring and evaluation process in place is a key starting point to encouraging an improvement culture. The board can help to ensure that insights and learning are drawn out of the review process and fed into future strategic planning by prompting, asking questions and acting as a 'critical friend'. It's important to show how the findings from evaluation ultimately lead to better services for users and to make sure that the results of this cycle of improvement are clear to everyone contributing to your organisation.

Benchmarking

Benchmarking is the process of comparing your organisation's performance with other organisations. By taking a look at how other people do things and the results they achieve, benchmarking can save you from unnecessarily repeating work. It also shows what is possible and can help to promote an organisational culture that is open to new ideas. Benchmarking provides organisations with reassurance and enables them to celebrate by showing where they perform well.

You can benchmark any aspect of your charity's operations, for example comparing numerical information, such as the cost per user of providing a service or the average length of time served by trustees. Alternatively, you can compare how things are done, for example the way an organisation plans strategically or the way its accounts are presented.

Quality

You can use the concept of 'quality' to improve the way you do things. A quality service means doing something that is:

- needed by users to a standard they require

- well run

- assessed and improved

- shown to make a positive and measurable difference to users

- continuously improved in order to achieve the very best results.

It is an excellent mechanism for embedding an improvement culture.

Since the 1990s, there has been a significant increase in interest amongst voluntary and community organisations in using the concept of quality. Many funders are now keen to see organisations adopt quality systems and the implementation of certain quality standards or frameworks has become a requirement of some funders and statutory commissioners.

Quality assurance systems

A quality assurance system is a systematic way of ensuring your organisation undertakes a continuous process of learning, developing and reviewing, usually by aiming to meet an agreed level of performance. It's possible to devise your own quality system with your own standards and to do your own self-assessment, but there are also ready-made standards or frameworks available, with or without kite marked assessment, such as:

- PQASSO – the Practical Quality Assurance System for Small Organisations

- Investors in People

- EFQM Excellence Model

- Social Auditing and Accounting

- Investing in Volunteers

- Quality Mark.

There are also quality marks for specific kinds of work or organisations (eg for advice services).

What is the board's role in quality improvement?

Because your board is able to step back and take a more strategic overview of its organisation, it is in an ideal position to take the lead in choosing and committing to a quality assurance system. The decision to implement a particular quality assurance system is one that should be made by trustees. The board is also able to ensure the overall process is balanced across the organisation and the priorities for quality improvement are the 'right' ones for the charity's long-term future.

Engaging in quality improvement

Your first step is to consider which areas of your charity you want to quality assess. You may have particular priorities, such as the management of your volunteers or your human resources processes, or you may want to take a holistic approach to help you identify the areas of your organisation that most need improvement.

Once you have a list of topics or areas, you need to decide on an approach to quality improvement. The following three possibilities provide a starting point.

1 **Devolved approach:** This involves giving responsibility for each area to people with specific roles within your organisation. Individuals would be expected to check and compare their practices with any identified standards. In small charities, many of the core topics such as strategic planning, recruitment and external relationships can fall to the chief executive or to individual trustee(s) who may need support from the rest of the board to assess current practice and suggest improvements.

2 **Centralised approach:** This involves establishing a working group to take forward quality improvement. Depending on the size of your charity, the working group may consist of, for example, a few managers, frontline staff and board members and is typically led by a named individual. The group considers all areas in turn, talking to those who have a particular stake in each area. Improvements are identified by the working group and reported to the board, although sometimes working groups have decision-making and reviewing powers. This approach introduces a stronger element of 'challenge', which can be useful where some topic areas have been neglected or where the culture of improvement needs strengthening.

3 **External approach:** This involves getting an external agency to assess your practices, rate them and suggest alternatives. This external validation of the way your charity is run, perhaps with a kite mark for the successful, can be useful with funders or potential partners. However, it focuses more attention on assessing and recognising your existing standards than on improving them. You may still need a working group to facilitate the process, especially the collection of data for the assessor.

The process you adopt will need to reflect your charity's existing culture and attitude to improvement, as well as the state of your existing practices. It will also be dependent on the time you have available and the financial costs involved, for example purchasing an off-the-shelf system or buying in advice or external assessment and/or accreditation.

Both the centralised and external approach require investment of considerable energy over a sustained period.

Some would argue that the devolved approach is the ideal that you should aim for, because it is sustainable and involves a self-generating culture in which people across the organisation enjoy taking responsibility for continuous improvement, albeit with the support and encouragement of their managers and the board. However, in order to get to the devolved approach to quality improvement, you may need to use the centralised or external approach at least once, and work hard to ensure that both the specific learning and the broader attitude of improvement 'sticks' within the organisation.

Useful tips

- If you employ a chief executive, they can support the board to ensure that it is ready to take on quality improvement. This can involve skills development, recruitment, communication, information and clarifying boundaries between the board and staff.

- Be sensitive to workloads if you are expecting a large investment of time from staff or, in smaller charities, from individual board members.

- Decide who from the board will be involved and how you will monitor and review the process.

- Communicate across the organisation. A quality improvement system will only work if people within the organisation are committed, which means raising awareness of what you want to achieve and feeding back on progress and outcomes.

How can quality improvement help trustees?

Structured checking mechanism

A quality system helps you to make sure your organisation is performing as well as possible and meeting the right needs in the right ways.

Improving board–staff communication

Involving boards in a quality improvement initiative can help to develop a shared understanding about the organisation's current and future position, such as what is working well, what can be improved and what role the board can take in leading the process and setting direction.

Board performance

The performance of the board itself is a vital stepping stone to continuous improvement. The quality improvement process can include evaluating the board's own role in the organisation; some approaches, such as the Code, focus specifically on the role of the board (see Chapter 22).

Further information:
NCVO (2013) *The Code of Good Impact Practice.* London: NCVO. This was created through the Inspiring Impact Programme and provides broad, agreed guidelines for focusing on the outcomes and impact you create. It sets out a cycle of planning, assessment and review and a series of high-level principles to follow.

Checklist

How do you report on your charity's impact?

Is your charity committed to a culture of improvement?

Have you considered implementing a quality assurance system in your charity?

14

Accountability

Trustees are accountable for the way in which they carry out their responsibilities and the decisions they take. 'Accountability' takes place in a number of different ways.

- Being held 'to account' for decisions taken and work carried out: This might take place at an annual general meeting when members or other stakeholders question the activities of the charity, or in the way an organisation reports back to a funder on money spent.

- 'Giving an account': This might take place in an annual report, where trustees set out an account of their work over the previous year.

- It can also mean 'holding others to account': To be accountable, trustees will need to hold to account those to whom they delegate the work of the charity, like staff, volunteers, committees or other trustees.

14.1

14.2

To whom are the trustees of a charity accountable?

For almost all charities, there is a need to be accountable to multiple parties. These parties are sometimes known as 'stakeholders' because they are thought to have a stake or interest in the charity, either formal or informal. They include:

- those who give the charity money – private donors, other funders such as government, local authorities, trusts, foundations or corporate donors

- regulators, for example, the Charity Commission and Companies House

- members in membership organisations

- beneficiaries, clients or service users

- partner organisations

- staff and volunteers

- the general public.

Accountability in practice

The Code recommends that the board should make:

'accountability real, through genuine and open two-way communication that celebrates successes and demonstrates willingness to learn from mistakes, helps to build trust and confidence with stakeholders and to demonstrate legitimacy when representing them.'[20]

In practice, trustees can be accountable in different ways.

- Ensuring that the organisation upholds principles of equality and diversity in every sphere of activity.

- Communicating with private donors on the use of the charity's funds.

- Reporting to funders, such as a trusts or foundations, in line with terms and conditions. This may involve completing monitoring reports setting out how the money has been spent and the benefits of the funding. If such reporting is delegated to staff, trustees remain ultimately responsible and should have a system of reporting to ensure that staff and volunteers are accountable (in the 'holding to account' sense) to their managers and ultimately to the board of trustees.

- Complying with regulatory requirements.

  - Charities must comply with their requirements to report to the Charity Commission. The requirements vary depending on the size and status of a charity (see pages 86–87).

  - Companies limited by guarantee must comply with their requirements to report to Companies House concerning an annual return, reports and accounts (see page 86), along with other requirements including registering ongoing changes to the company's directors, secretary and registered office.

  - You may be required to report to other regulatory bodies, depending on your activities, services or legal structure.

- Involving members – in a membership organisation, your annual general meeting is an opportunity for members to receive a report on the charity's work, formally consider specific issues (motions or resolutions) and elect the trustee board.

- Producing your trustees' annual report and accounts, a key method by which you can inform stakeholders about your charity's work and achievements. An annual report is often a regulatory requirement. Many charities produce a formal trustees' annual report and accounts and then a shorter or more accessible version for wider public distribution (see page 85).

20 NCVO (2010) Good Governance: A code for the voluntary and community sector. London: NCVO.

- Being open and responsive to beneficiaries or service users, which could take place in a variety of ways, for example, involving service users at board level and ensuring communications are accessible and available in a variety of forms and languages (see Chapter 12).

- Consulting with stakeholders as part of planning, decision-making and evaluation. Stakeholder representation on trustee boards has been seen as a useful mechanism for accountability. However, muddling the 'holding to account' role of a stakeholder with that of a trustee can lead to both being handled badly.

- Making sure that stakeholders have the opportunity to hold the board to account and know how to do it appropriately.

- Being open and responsive to feedback and criticism via a proper complaints procedure. All charities should have a complaints procedure in place (see box).

The Code also states that the board can demonstrate that it is open and accountable by:

'recognising and acting on broader organisational responsibility towards communities, wider society and the environment, in so far as this does not divert the organisation from achieving its objects.'[21]

21 NCVO (2010) *Good Governance: A code for the voluntary and community sector.* London: NCVO.

22 Charity Commission (2006) *Cause for complaint: how charities manage complaints about their service* (RS11). London: Charity Commission.

23 NCVO (2010) *Good Governance: A code for the voluntary and community sector.* London: NCVO.

Dealing with feedback and complaints

One way in which an organisation can demonstrate that it is being open and accountable, both internally and externally, is by handling complaints constructively, impartially and effectively. A Charity Commission survey in 2005[22] found that only 30% of charities surveyed had a complaints procedure in place. The Commission's regulatory study on charity complaints highlighted the importance of charities having in place a complaints procedure that is understood by everyone working in the charity. The study found that 'an effective complaints management system is a proven way of maintaining and building relationships with the people on whom the charity depends'. The Commission's report uses best practice examples to illustrate the benefits of a complaints procedure.

The Code states that an effective board will provide good governance and leadership by:

'demonstrating that the organisation learns from mistakes and errors and how that learning is used to improve organisational performance and internal decision-making. This could be by having clear and effective complaints procedures, implementing them constructively and using the process as a valuable source of management information.'[23]

Checklist

Have you taken stock of all the stakeholders to whom you are accountable?

Does your board comply with its statutory obligations to account to the Charity Commission?

Does your board comply with its statutory obligations to account to Companies House?

Does your board need to review how your organisation accounts to donors, funders, staff and volunteers, perhaps by producing more popular versions of reports prepared to meet statutory requirements?

Does your board need to review how staff and volunteers are held accountable?

Does your organisation have an effective complaints policy and procedure in place?

How does your board ensure that complaints and other forms of feedback are used to improve organisational performance and internal decision-making?

Public relations

Public relations (PR) is the way organisations, companies and individuals communicate with the public and media.[24]

Raising the profile of your charity and creating a positive public image is a prerequisite for raising the funds needed to develop and grow. This is just as important for small, local charities as it is for large, national ones.

As trustees, you are responsible for ensuring that your charity develops an effective public relations/ communications strategy. You are uniquely placed to bring perspective or spot media opportunities when they arise.

A media policy

An organisational media policy should spell out how media enquiries will be handled, who may speak to the media and how an organisation's position is decided.

As part of your public relations strategy, you may wish to create or review your charity's logo, house style and the way you present yourself to your members, funders and the outside world. Some organisations even change their name to update their image or to reflect more clearly the nature of their work. Macmillan Cancer Support (formerly Macmillan Cancer Research) and Action on Hearing Loss (formerly Royal National Institute for Deaf People – RNID) have both done this.

If you represent the charity in public or in the media you must follow the public relations strategy agreed by the board and you should be given any necessary training. An effective public relations strategy will also include procedures to limit damage should the charity ever come under public criticism and you should be aware of this. When speaking to the press, always give the charity's agreed position rather than your personal opinion.

Getting celebrities and famous or influential people to acknowledge publicly their support for a charity can support your public relations strategy. Such people are unlikely to have sufficient time to act as trustees, but you could ask them to act as patrons. It may be best to ask them to act as patron for a fixed period, say five years, in case they fade from the public eye or their own reputation becomes tarnished.

Checklist

Do you have an agreed public relations/communications strategy?

Does the strategy:

• state who is authorised to make public statements?

• outline the process for agreeing press releases?

• explain on what occasion staff should contact the trustees about PR?

Does the name of your charity adequately reflect the work you do?

Does your board need to review your logo and house style?

If certain trustees speak to the media, do they have proper training?

15

Collaborative working

All charities should consider seriously and imaginatively whether there are ways in which they could do more for their beneficiaries by working together. While every charity has its own distinctive contribution to make to society, an effective charity explores whether collaboration or partnership with other organisations or merger with other charities could improve efficiency, the use of funds and the delivery of services to current and future beneficiaries. We encourage trustees to look at this regularly.[25]

25 Charity Commission (2009) *Collaborative Working and Mergers: An introduction* (CC34). London: Charity Commission.

15.1

In recent years charities have increasingly explored collaborative working as a way to improve organisational efficiency and effectiveness or take advantage of funding and commissioning opportunities. As a trustee, examining how to further the charity's objects, and assessing the environment in which the organisation operates, may involve looking at working with other organisations.

Working in partnership can bring substantial benefits, including cost savings, greater credibility, sharing good practice and improved services for beneficiaries.

However, it is also important to understand the risks involved. Will the work still be within your charity's objects? Will it enable you to further your mission? What legal implications will arise from joint ventures? Is the organisation ready for joint working or will it cause disruption? How will it be perceived by stakeholders?

The final decision on any collaborative working arrangement rests with trustees. It is the trustees' role to see that the decision-making process covers all angles to make the most effective use of funds. Trustees must ensure their organisation acts legally and that professional advice is taken where relevant. The key question should be: will engaging in joint working provide greater outcomes for beneficiaries now and in the future?

Types of partnership

The term 'joint working' covers a wide spectrum of activities. These include:

- networks and alliances
- formal partnerships
- joint ventures
- mergers.

Informal networking
Attending events and conferences can be a worthwhile way to keep your charity 'visible' and to share information. Joining a membership organisation can be a valuable way of accessing information and support.

Resource sharing
Staff, back office functions (eg payroll or IT support) or office space can be shared between charities to reduce duplication and save costs and time. A key consideration is whether there are VAT implications to sharing services. Professional advice may be required.

Outsourcing services
Here, a charity's service or services are provided by another charity (or non-charitable organisation) in an outsourcing agreement.

Providing joint services
Many charities work in partnership to provide services jointly. Sometimes one organisation is a lead partner that takes overall responsibility backed up with an agreement between the other partners. Other models include the creation of a new organisation or 'special purpose vehicle' (SPV) to deliver the purposes of the partnership.

As a trustee, it is essential to clarify where overall accountability lies. If it is with your organisation as lead partner, then your board will take overall responsibility. Are there proper procedures in place to ensure that this does not become too big a risk? If it is with another organisation, what agreement is in place with the lead partner?

Federal and branch structures

Organisations with a national body and local groups can work together in a variety of ways, providing a balance between national presence and grassroots involvement. A federal structure involves a national body and a number of independently constituted local groups. Organisations in a branch structure constitutionally form one legal entity, with local branches sharing the national body's governance and charitable purposes.

Group structure

A group structure normally consists of a parent body and one or more subsidiary bodies in which the parent has a controlling interest. Group structures can be complex because they do not form a legal entity of their own. They are a collection of entities which enter into a legally binding agreement to work together that, usually, is not time limited. Groups can be formed with the parent body, which has overall control, providing a strategic role and in many cases having a central servicing function for other members of the group. The group can involve a charitable or non-charitable body becoming a subsidiary of another organisation (eg a non-charitable trading subsidiary).

One of the advantages of a group structure is that a subsidiary organisation can retain its existing legal structure, avoiding some of the issues involved in the process of full merger. With a non-charitable trading subsidiary it can allow commercial trading to take place outside of your charitable objects (see Chapter 2). It can also allow a struggling organisation to be sustained whilst retaining its own structure. Professional advice is recommended for such arrangements.

Mergers

A merger involves two or more charities becoming one organisation. This could involve two charities merging to set up a new body (eg the merger of Cancer Research Campaign with Imperial Cancer Research Fund to form Cancer Research UK). Alternatively, it can involve an organisation transferring its staff, assets and activities to another organisation and then winding up. Which option is chosen can depend on a number of factors, including whether the organisations involved are keen for it to be seen as a merger of equals or whether one organisation has a defined benefit pension's scheme and all parties are keen to avoid a situation where a pension debt could be triggered.

Mergers can bring advantages but can be time consuming and have legal implications. Transferring staff or assets may bring problems because of the restrictions placed on sources of income or TUPE arrangements under employment law. It is important to take the time to consider the pros and cons of such a venture and it is essential to take professional advice if your charity is considering this route.

There will be governance and management implications and undertaking a thorough due diligence process is essential. What form will the board of the new organisation take? Who will sit on the board? Will the new organisation be able to develop an effective governance and management relationship?

Checklist

Do trustees regularly consider whether the needs of their beneficiaries, now and in the future, would be better served if the charity worked in partnership with others or whether another organisation could do the job more efficiently or effectively?

Is collaborative working permitted in your charity's governing document (objects and powers)?

Will there be measurable benefits to service users and beneficiaries?

Is there a danger of 'mission drift' (losing sight of your mission, eg because of an attractive funding opportunity)?

What are the legal implications?

Will collaborative working 'add value' to your organisation's work that justifies the time, effort and money invested in the collaboration?

What will you lose by working on your collaborative project?

Is it cost-effective?

Will the structure of your organisation be affected by the change and, if so, how will you deal with the long-term implications?

Will collaboration change your organisation's other existing relationships?

Who is liable for the partnership if things go wrong?

If a trustee of your organisation is sitting on the board of a partnership, however constituted, have you considered the difference in roles (between being a trustee and being a member of the partnership) and any potential conflicts of interest?

Are there VAT implications?

If the work involves transfer of staff, there will be TUPE implications?

Would a working group or committee of trustees (and staff) be useful to scrutinise any joint working proposal in sufficient detail?

16

Handling change and conflict

16.1

Managing change

Every charity will face change. The question is whether trustees will steer the charity to a desired future or let the pace and direction of change go unmanaged.

Reasons for change

There are a number of reasons why your charity may be changing or will need to change. The causes of change can come from within or outside your charity.

External causes of change might include changes to the law, new funding opportunities, changes in government policy or increased competition from other organisations. To help identify these causes before they happen, you could use a tool such as a PEST (political, economic, social and technological) analysis.

The need for change can also come from within. You may have carried out a review of your performance, such as assessing your progress against plans and targets, or comparing performance and practice with other charities or against an established quality standard (see section 13.3).

You may have experienced changes in key individuals, such as the departure of a chief executive or chair of the trustee board, or undergone a sudden crisis such as a disaster or dispute.

Types of change

Changes may be planned or unplanned, major or minor and fast or slow. You may be looking at a long-term office move, a short-term restructuring, a loss of premises or sudden departure of a key person.

All these factors will affect how you will respond to change. The sooner the change or the need for it is identified, the earlier you can start managing it. The size of the change will affect the timescales and resources you will need and decisions about who to involve and to what extent. The nature of the change will determine how it will affect different elements of your organisation such as its purpose, relationship with key stakeholders, ways of working and culture. Remember that changes in one area will often mean changes in another.

Key principles for managing change

The role of a trustee can involve making difficult decisions. Remember that the charity's overall purpose (as ultimately set out in its charitable objects, see section 2.2) and the needs of beneficiaries now and in the future should be at the forefront of the decision-making process.

In managing a process of change, bear in mind the following principles.

Lead, but don't go it alone

Above all, managing change requires clear leadership from the board. This includes creating and communicating a clear vision for the change by answering some key questions: Why does this change need to happen now? What will the organisation look like afterwards? And who will it affect and how?

This doesn't mean the board should try to manage change on its own. You should involve others in your organisation to help you manage a process of change – this could include your chief executive, if you employ one, and perhaps advisors and other external stakeholders.

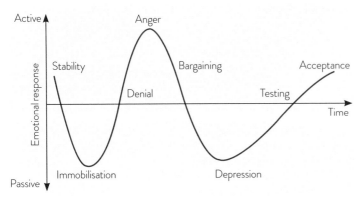

The Kubler-Ross Coping Cycle states that people go through the following stages.

- **Shock:** initial paralysis on hearing the news
- **Denial:** trying to avoid the inevitable
- **Anger:** venting frustration
- **Bargaining:** seeking to negotiate an alternative outcome
- **Depression:** realisation of the inevitable
- **Testing:** seeking realistic solutions
- **Acceptance:** finding the way forward

To overcome resistance, you can use allies in different parts of the organisation, engage with people to address their objections and provide third-party support. This support could include training to help people learn new skills or ways of working or opportunities to talk about their feelings and experiences.

Choose the right approach

Reflect on your organisational culture – the way things usually happen in your organisation and the way people behave and interact with each other. Managing change will be more successful if you choose an approach that fits with the way you generally do things. For example, a change approach in which the board makes decisions without much consultation may work if that's how things usually happen, but it is less likely to work if your organisational culture is more democratic, involving staff at all levels in decision-making.

Also, certain approaches to change might be more appropriate to particular situations. For example, it may be difficult to involve a range of stakeholders if change needs to happen rapidly.

Anticipate how people might respond

Understanding and anticipating people's reactions to change can help you support them to accept and adapt to new circumstances. Organisational change can be very stressful for people for a number of reasons. Some may be reluctant to shift from their comfort zone. They may fear that their job is at risk, or that their role or working environment will become unfamiliar. Others may worry that they lack skills or expertise needed for new systems or ways of working.

You might find it helpful to think about the stages people go through when experiencing change.

Communicate consistently and honestly

It is vital to communicate clearly and honestly during a period of change. This does not mean telling everyone everything all of the time – use your judgement to decide what's useful to say to whom and when and who should say it. If there are legal implications, particularly employment ones, take early advice.

16.2

Planning your communications can ensure you give the right messages to the right people, in the right format, at the right time. First, identify your stakeholders, then think about what they need to know or understand and when. For each group, think about specific messages and which communication channel will best meet their needs. For staff and volunteers, options might include face-to-face meetings or briefings, emails, staff newsletters or extranets. For external communication, you could use newsletters, events, emails, websites and press releases. Make sure your communications are two way, giving people an opportunity to speak to you and ask questions.

Embed the change

It is important to ensure that changes are sustained and become part of the lifeblood of the organisation. A model that can help with this uses the idea of unfreezing, moving and re-freezing. The idea is that, in order to change, people need to:

- **unfreeze** – give up old ways of doing things

- **move** – accept the need for change and use the support offered to them to learn new ways of doing things

- **refreeze** – adopt and become comfortable with new ways of working.

Refreezing tactics could include removing old ways of working, rewarding people for embracing new working practices and building change into existing management systems and structures.

Handling conflict

When things go wrong
Every board will face periods of conflict from time to time – between trustees and staff, between individual trustees or between factions or cliques on the board.

The first thing to acknowledge is that conflict is not inherently unhealthy; it can be a source of creativity and can revitalise the work of the board. Many community organisations function as a forum in which tensions and disagreements are addressed and resolved. However, there is a difference between this situation and the type of conflict that negatively affects the ability of the organisation to fulfil its mission.

Whatever the cause, it is important that disagreements are acknowledged and addressed before they become serious disputes and cause damage not only to internal relationships but also to the external reputation of the organisation.

Conflict on the board

Working collectively is what boards are about, but it is not always easy. Human nature means that we can be ambitious or energetic – strong characteristics in many walks of life but they can lead to tension in the boardroom. Common scenarios include:

- ignoring boundaries (see case study on page 188)

- monopolising meetings

- reticent or 'sleeping' trustees

- the 'loose cannon' trustee

- belittling others

- withholding information

- factions and inner circles

- outside agendas

- the 'founder syndrome'

- refusing to prepare for meetings

- lacking respect for diversity

- resisting compromise

- inability to think strategically.

Case study

A new trustee who was previously a volunteer has been upsetting staff by going into the office unannounced, bossing staff around, countermanding the director's orders, demanding confidential information and generally meddling in day-to-day affairs.

The lessons

Boundaries have clearly been stepped over in several ways. This is an example of someone not only confusing which hat they are wearing and when, but also disregarding what is acceptable behaviour in terms of respect for others. Hold a board development session and complete the 'hats' exercise (see section 11.3) during which attention can be drawn to the importance of the board acting collectively and that a trustee has no power individually except that which is specifically given to them by the trustee board. Remind the trustees of the organisation's values, the trustees' code of conduct and their employment law responsibilities and clarify what responsibilities have been delegated by the board to the chief executive. In addition, a one-to-one meeting between the chair and the new trustee will provide an opportunity to explore these issues in more depth.

Conflict between board and staff

Conflict between the head of staff (chief executive/director) and the head of the trustees (chair) arises all too frequently, often because of a lack of clarity about their respective roles and boundaries.

A key question at the root of the conflict is 'who leads?' (and consequently 'who follows?'). There are many models of board–staff relations, but it is vital to remember that the distinction between governance and management is a dynamic one.

A chief executive who has become used to taking the lead and even expects their board simply to act as a rubber stamp to their ideas will resist the efforts of a new chair who starts to set the agenda. Conversely, a board that is passive and allows staff to lead the organisation may feel uncomfortable with a new chief executive who expects the board to take a more active role in leading the organisation and setting policy.

A founder who becomes chief executive needs to accept that at some point the board may set the organisation in a new direction. That is the role of the board and, provided the decision is reached in a considered way, the founder must respect the board's decision.

Practical steps to avoid staff–board conflict

- **Clarify roles:** Who is responsible for taking which decisions? Tempers can flare when the board treads on what staff regard as their territory or vice versa. Board policies and a code of conduct can help, as well as making sure that any authority delegated by the board to others is in writing and understood by all concerned.

- **Induction of staff and board members:** When recruiting a new chief officer be clear and realistic about what they will be able to achieve and ensure that their understanding of their role is the same as the board's. Introduce new trustees to the management team and encourage them to ask questions.

- **Foster good personal relationships:** Build in time for social interaction.

- **The chair–chief officer relationship is key:** If they don't get on, the whole organisation is affected. They should commit to regular contact, including one-to-one meetings, having considered each other's availability, to share information and identify and address any potential conflict.

- **The board should also get to know the staff and volunteers:** No one likes the idea of being ruled by a distant, faceless entity. For example, you could include site visits in your induction, invite staff to board meetings or hold an 'open house' where staff members and volunteers can meet and mingle with board members.

Section 11.3 contains more information about board–staff–chief executive–volunteer relationships.

Disagreements between trustees

A board of trustees will often be made up of people from diverse backgrounds who may have different reasons for being on the board and be new or long serving. They may have been nominated by another organisation or by a local branch of the national organisation. They may be a user or a specialist in their daytime profession. This mix can provide valuable knowledge and expertise but can also lead to individuals taking entrenched positions on matters being discussed.

Leadership from an experienced chair should ensure that trustees work together productively and appropriate challenge, as well as teamwork, is part of the mix. If there is a personality clash between the chair and another trustee, this may require the intervention of a neutral person respected by both the board members. In some circumstances the vice-chair can be the facilitator; in others it may be the president or a patron. It is not appropriate for a staff member to play this role. Having a grievance procedure in place for the trustees help to prevent disagreement resolution requiring external help.

Dealing with internal conflict

Understanding motivations and being clear about expectations on both sides from the beginning can help lessen conflict or prepare for when it happens.

You should:

- ensure that the organisation has an appropriate induction process in place for all volunteers, staff and trustees

- ensure that the boundaries between different roles – board, individual trustee, staff and volunteer – are defined, clearly communicated and understood by everyone

- rely on a confident, perceptive chair to make sure that factions or individual disruptions are not detrimental to the work of the board

- make sure that the chief executive understands the particular board–staff relationships that exist in your organisation

- focus on the organisation's purposes and its mission, not personalities

- refer to your board's code of conduct, which sets out the values that trustees need to adhere to in order to fulfil their duty (a code of conduct usually sets out the procedure to be followed if it is breached)

- bring in outside help (to mediate or inform) if conflict cannot be resolved internally – the involvement of someone neutral from outside may help people to communicate more freely and to find a resolution

- consider mentoring for the chair and the chief executive – finding that others may have had similar problems and hearing how they dealt with them can diffuse tense situations

- be prepared to remove trustees and check your governing document to see what it says about disqualification or removal. There are certain statutory disqualifications in law, and governing documents sometimes include clauses such as failure to attend meetings without consent.

Conflicts in membership organisations

Many charities have a formal membership. Usually, relations between members and trustees are positive. However, tensions can sometimes occur, which can, if unchecked or poorly handled, lead to dispute and affect the charity's ability to govern well.

The relationship between trustees and members can be positive if members feel their views are represented and they can exert influence. But a perception amongst members that they are ignored or undervalued can risk leading to conflict and dispute. Often the breakdown in relationships can result from inappropriate governance structures combined with a lack of communication and consultation with members. Tensions between trustees and members can occur when the distinction between governance (the control of strategy and policy by trustees) and representation (the influence members exert on strategy and policies and how trustees take account of this) is not fully understood.

Attention to good governance practice can help to create good member relationships, in particular:

- attention to board election/ appointment methods (Chapter 1)

- decision-making structures (Chapter 21)

- accountability (Chapter 14)

- conduct of annual general meetings (Chapter 21)

- periodic governance reviews (Chapter 22).

Sometimes, changes to governance structures can be the most effective way of improving trustee–member relations (see Chapter 21 for examples). Remember that change can be controversial in itself and restructuring governance arrangements may involve consultation, communication and, ultimately, the support of members.

Dealing with external conflict

Trustees have a responsibility for ensuring that conflicts between the organisation and its beneficiaries, partners or service providers are dealt with efficiently to protect the reputation of the organisation. A dispute may involve one of the trustees, but not in their role as trustee.

Reference to the organisation's complaints policy, a contract or service agreement may provide the answer, but trustees must ensure they obtain the best possible advice to resolve the matter, possibly from a lawyer or an accountant, and identify when neutral external mediation is necessary.

Preventing conflict

Whether internal or external, disputes can be avoided by:

- clarifying areas of responsibility
- ensuring expectations are mutually understood
- avoiding making assumptions
- being aware of personal perceptions and prejudices
- respecting the views of others
- respecting confidentiality
- making time for informal discussion
- obtaining the best possible advice where professional expertise is needed
- setting achievable targets and timeframes
- above all, listening, and asking questions when a situation is not clear.

Conflict and the role of the Charity Commission

The Charity Commission will not get involved in a dispute or conflict if there are properly appointed trustees in place. It is the responsibility of the trustees to ensure any disagreements or disputes are addressed by following any 'disputes clause' in their governing document and getting independent, external help if required. The Charity Commission will become involved in a dispute or conflict if there are no trustees or no correctly appointed trustees and all other methods of resolving the dispute have failed.

According to the Charity Commission, if you don't have any properly appointed trustees, it may step in to help you recruit the number of trustees you require. If it finds evidence of misconduct or mismanagement that could put your charity's funds and users at risk, it will step in and provide advice and guidance. Even after it gets involved, you and the other trustees will need to be able to show that you can work together to come up with a solution. The Charity Commission states that:

'If we think a solution will not be reached, we may withdraw our help. If we suspect an agreement will not be reached, your charity may have to cease operating and wind up.'[26]

26 Charity Commission 'Disagreements and disputes within charities' www.charitycommission.gov.uk/trustees-staff-and-volunteers/trustee-board/disagreements-and-disputes (accessed August 2014).

The Charity Commission is very clear in its guidance that it will not get involved in disputes about decisions taken by trustees or policies they have put in place.

If there are serious regulatory concerns, the Charity Commission may open a formal inquiry (under section 46 of the Charities Act 2011).

Further information:
Charity Commission 'Disagreements and disputes within charities' www.charitycommission. gov.uk/trustees-staff-and-volunteers/trustee-board/disagreements-and-disputes (accessed August 2014).

Part Three:

Developing the board

Introduction

The board of trustees is ultimately responsible for everything your charity does. Good governance demands that trustees set clear aims and objectives, establish priorities, safeguard the charity's assets and use them effectively and exclusively for the benefit of the charity's beneficiaries.

The changing environment within which charities operate requires organisations to have in place a knowledgeable and committed board that is sufficiently aware of these developments to respond to change.

As trustees, it is essential that you feel confident that you can direct your organisation as well as possible. This involves using and developing your existing skills and acquiring new skills as appropriate. It is your knowledge and experience that makes you uniquely capable and valuable as a trustee.

Remember that the role of a board member is a collective one – you are not expected, individually, to have expertise in all areas – but it is important to ensure that the combined skills, qualities and knowledge of your board meet the organisation's needs, or that you know where the gaps are and where to access advice.

How can your board achieve this ideal balance? The first element you need is a group of trustees with the right mix of skills, experiences and backgrounds. Add to this the support and development they need to carry out their responsibilities.

Next, ensure that your board has in place the processes and decision-making structures to enable trustees to perform effectively. Finally, examine the personal and professional motivations of trustees – are your board members engaged in their work? If not, what can be done to harness their potential and tap into their experience?

Throughout this journey, keep a focus on the big picture. What does your board need to support and develop your organisation in an ever-changing environment?

17

17.1

What makes a good trustee and an effective board?

What makes an effective trustee?

The Trustees and Management Committee National Occupational Standards (Trustees NOS) set out the skills, knowledge and qualities that trustees and board members should possess in order to carry out their role effectively. They set out the type of information trustees will need to be able to access, and identify their key areas of responsibility. The Trustees NOS can also be used to help develop trustee role descriptions, ensure regulatory compliance or design trustee training sessions.

17.2

Trustees and Management Committee National Occupational Standards

- The Trustees NOS cover four units.
- Safeguard and promote the values and mission.
- Determine the strategy and structure.
- Be effective, responsible and accountable.
- Make sure that the board of trustees functions effectively.

Further information:
National Occupational Standards for Trustees and Management Committee Members, available from Skills for Health.

What skills and competencies do trustees need?

The Trustees NOS sets out a list of 'qualities' that it is felt all trustees should be able to draw on in order to fulfil their responsibilities. It says that trustees should:

- be committed to the purpose, objects and values of the organisation
- be constructive about other trustees' opinions in discussion, and in response to staff members' contributions at meetings
- be able to act reasonably and responsibly when undertaking such duties and performing tasks
- be able to maintain confidentiality on sensitive and confidential information

- be supportive of the values (and ethics) of the organisation
- understand the importance and purpose of meetings and be committed to preparing for them adequately and attending them regularly
- be able to analyse information and, when necessary, challenge constructively
- be able to make collective decisions and stand by them
- be able to respect boundaries between executive (staff or day to day) and governance functions
- be able to assess the environmental impact and efficiency of the organisation and recognise the impact of climate change on users and communities.

17.3

What specialist skills might trustees need?

As well as having the competencies that are set out in the Trustees NOS , it is important that an effective board of trustees should be able to draw on a diverse range of skills and knowledge. These may well include:

The 'hard' skills such as:

- charity law and governance
- financial management
- human resources (including a knowledge of employment law)
- media and public relations
- marketing
- legal
- information technology
- income generation including fundraising
- campaigning
- property and estate management
- monitoring and evaluating organisational performance.

The 'soft' skills such as:

- team working
- problem-solving
- independence of thought and judgement
- being able to challenge appropriately
- decision-making
- negotiation
- listening
- making people laugh!

The lists are not exhaustive, and the level of knowledge and understanding will be different for different organisations. If you are a trustee of a small community organisation, your financial knowledge will not need to be as high as if you are a trustee of, say, a large housing association.

Remember – each trustee does not need all of the above skills and knowledge. It is, however, important to identify what skills at what level are required by the board as a whole to ensure your organisation works well and then to identify which trustees have which skills and where any gaps may be.

What are the collective skills and competencies needed by a board?

Good governance is a collective responsibility, so any consideration of the skills and qualities needed by trustees should consider what the board as a whole needs to be effective.

What are the specific skills that make trustee boards effective? Researchers Richard Chait, Thomas Holland and Barbara Taylor[27] suggest six key areas – or dimensions – where board competence made a measurable difference to organisational performance.

1 **Contextual**
   You need a profound understanding of your organisation's mission coupled with an up-to-date knowledge of the threats and opportunities posed by the organisation's environment.

2 **Educational**
   You should continue to learn and train, assess and evaluate your own performance and identify your strengths and weaknesses.

3 **Interpersonal**
   You shouldn't let individual personalities – no matter how brilliant – dominate the governance process. Instead, encourage group decision-making, teamwork and a sense of shared purpose.

27 Taylor BE, Chait RP and Holland TP (1996) 'New Work of the Nonprofit Board.' *Harvard Business Review*, September/October 1996.

17.4

4 **Analytical**
Cultivate your analytical skills so you can stand back, take the long view of difficult situations and suggest appropriate actions to better serve the overall mission.

5 **Political**
One of your primary responsibilities to the organisation is to develop and maintain healthy relationships among key constituencies such as members, volunteers, clients, government agencies and community groups.

6 **Strategic**
As a board member, you are part of the strategic engine behind the organisation. As such, you must eventually take responsibility for the organisation's long-term success or failure.

How can our board identify its skills needs?

Your board was set up when your organisation was at the start of its life. As the organisation has grown or developed, it is inevitable that different skills will be required from board members. A good starting point would be for current board members to identify the skills, knowledge and experience that will be required by the board collectively during the next three to five years and then to use the information to conduct a skills audit of current board members.

This will identify:

• the skills, knowledge and experience of current trustees

• what gaps exist between the skills etc of current trustees and those that will be required going forward

• what the training and development needs are for current board members and whether this will fill the gaps identified

• what new or prospective new trustees can offer.

A skills audit avoids assumptions being made about why a trustee has joined the board and what they can offer. Some join out of commitment to the organisation's work and its beneficiaries, others bring a particular technical or professional skill and others may see board membership as a way of gaining valuable work experience.

There are a number of ways in which a skills audit can be conducted but the most frequently used method is for trustees to be asked to complete a self-assessment questionnaire. In order to achieve the most accurate picture of your board's current strengths, and therefore to identify what gaps exist, board members should be asked to 'rate' their capabilities and to explain how they have gained any particular skills or abilities they profess to have, for example professional qualification, in-work training etc.

The Charity Commission recommends that all charities carry out a skills audit and ideally the process should be carried out at regular intervals, as your trustee board and your organisation changes. Remember to ask all new board members to complete a skills audit when they join the board.

Example trustee skills audit

Name: _____ Date: _____

Please use this questionnaire to rate your own capability:
1 = expert/substantial, 2 = competent and 3 = no relevant skill, knowledge or experience

Skill/knowledge/experience (examples only)	1 2 3	Please provide evidence of how you have gained the skill/ability eg professional qualification etc
Example		
Charity and company law and other relevant legislation		
Charity governance and regulation		
Financial management and cost control		
Accountancy/bookkeeping		
Strategic planning and implementation		
Policy development		
Monitoring and evaluating organisational performance		
Organisational development/change management		
Income generation including fundraising		
Property and property services		
Operating environment		
Voluntary or community sector		
Public/private sector		

Skill/knowledge/experience (examples only)	1 2 3	Please provide evidence of how you have gained the skill/ability eg professional qualification etc
Profile raising		
Campaigning		
Social media		
PR and media relations		
Human resources		
HR/employment law and practice		
Training and professional development		
Equal opportunities and diversity		
Volunteer recruitment/management		
Skills and abilities		
Leadership		
Setting and implementing priority plans		
Questioning and challenging (critical friend)		

Please give further details:

1. What other skills, knowledge or experience do you feel you have to offer?

2. What motivated you to become a trustee?

3. How long have you been a trustee?

4. Are there areas in which you would like further training/information?

5. On the whole, do you feel stretched, stimulated and satisfied in your role as a trustee?

    – If your answer is 'No' then please provide further information, especially in relation to how your experience of being a trustee could be improved.

18

Learning and development

A skills audit of your board can help identify learning and development needs. All board members should be encouraged to keep their existing skills and knowledge up to date and develop new ones where appropriate.

18.1

Learning methods

Trustees come from all walks of life, so everyone will have different support and development needs and will want to meet these needs in different ways.

In addition to formal and informal training, there is a wealth of practical and up-to-date information available to trustees. These include books and magazines, email newsletters and websites. Here are a few ways in which trustees can meet some of their needs.

- Join an action learning set or network: become part of a small group of other trustees to address real-life problems, develop solutions and take action (see case study on page 204). Alternatively, is there a trustee network in your area, or nationally, that you can join to meet other trustees, access mutual support and share experiences?

- Use the information from the skills audit: many skills audit questionnaires help trustees to gain insights into their own strengths and abilities and to identify their support and development needs.

- Access a coach: an individual development relationship with a coach can assist a trustee to recognise their potential by helping them to identify their goals and overcome barriers.

- Benchmark yourself against a competency framework: this will help to establish a frame of reference for organisational good practice and individuals' competence. See Part Four for ideas on how your organisation's governance and your individual role as a trustee can be reviewed.

- Seek guidance from a mentor: mentors can help trustees to think through their ideas and support their professional development. Some organisations offer new trustees the opportunity to be mentored by an existing trustee or a trustee from another charity based in the same locality or operating environment.

- Take time out: carve out time away from work and/or other commitments to learn, reflect and network. Many boards arrange away days/weekends to provide trustees with 'quality' time to reflect, plan and tackle the big/strategic issues away from the normal business of the board.

- Research your needs and direct your own learning: taking responsibility for finding, managing and assessing your own learning builds confidence.

- Attend a workshop, master class or conference: this allows trustees to learn about specific topics and provides them with opportunities to get information, develop skills and learn from others. These could be small or large scale: for example, NCVO holds an annual Trustee Conference or workshops could be provided in house if there is a particular need across the board.

It is important to remember that you have much to learn from other trustees, volunteers and staff.

Further Information:
Trustee matching service, Small Charities Coalition: www.smallcharities.org.uk/trustee-matching

Case Study – Housing Association

A housing association offers all board members access to traditional training and opportunities to attend conferences. In addition, a 30 to 60-minute update session is organised before each board and committee meeting. The update sessions cover issues that affect the organisation – changes in legislation, for example – or provide an opportunity for trustees who have been on a course/conference to pass on their learning.

Case Study – Chair of a village hall management committee

The chair of a village hall management committee said, 'I had been chairing my village hall for three years and I was beginning to lose heart. Despite having very committed colleagues on the committee, I felt the onus was on me, especially as many of them are older or have other commitments. And I didn't really know where to go for help.'

Then came a timely offer. The chair was invited to join an action learning set of chairs of local village halls, who would come together to share and learn from each other's experiences.

The group of six chairs was led by a facilitator and met three times. The group used an 'action learning' approach. People took it in turns to share an issue and, with the help of targeted questions by the rest of the group, take a fresh look at the issue and the options they have to deal with it.

The chair used her turn to explore how to get more people to use the village hall. 'I got so many good ideas. What really surprised me was that I wasn't alone – other people were dealing with the same challenge.'

The chair suggests: 'Be open-minded. Action learning helps you challenge not just your own ways of looking at things but other people's too. Some of the questions I was asked made me think "Of course I can do that, why didn't I think of that before?" The questioning techniques also encouraged me to challenge others and so help them find the answers they needed themselves.'

18.2

Do you have a budget for trustee development?

Trustees need to feel confident that they have the skills, knowledge and experience required to fulfil their roles. Every charity should therefore strive to allocate at least some of their resources (time and/or money) to support its trustees to develop their existing skills and acquire new ones.

For those organisations that believe supporting trustees in their learning and development could be considered to be a 'waste of charitable resources', it is worth noting that, depending on the size and complexity of the charity, the trustees' annual report should include information about how trustees are appointed and the policies and procedures adopted for the induction and training of trustees. *The Accounting and Reporting By Charities: Statement of recommended practice* (revised 2005) explains that this information is required 'in order assist the reader to understand better how the charity's decision-making processes operate'.

Enthusiasm, desire and commitment for continuous learning should be considered a very desirable characteristic in any trustee. No one knows everything, and everyone has something to learn to help them in their role. By being systematic in identifying the needs of the organisation, the skills of existing trustees and the training needs and recruitment priorities that will help fill any gaps, you will improve your own, the board's and the organisation's performance.

Checklist

Have you carried out an assessment of the skills, qualities, knowledge and perspectives trustees bring to the board?

Are all trustees offered the opportunity to develop their skills further via appropriate learning opportunities?

Do you have a budget for individual trustee development?

19

Building the board

Many charities, especially smaller ones, experience difficulties in recruiting trustees and struggle to find trustees with the appropriate skills, knowledge and experience they require. According to research carried out by the Charity Commission amongst organisations seeking registered charitable status:

- One third (34%) of respondents were seeking to recruit new trustees and a quarter (26%) had faced some difficulties.

- Trustees were most commonly recruited from amongst the organisation's existing staff, volunteers and members (53%), personal connections (46%) or by word of mouth (39%).[28]

Surveys have also found that trustee boards do not reflect the population, with less than 1% aged under 25[29] and black and minority ethnic groups being under-represented.

28 Charity Commission (2012) *Birth of a Charity: Governance of organisations seeking registered charitable status.* London: Charity Commission.

29 Charity Commission (2005) *Start As You Mean To Go On: Trustee recruitment and induction* (RS10). London: Charity Commission; Charity Commission (2001) *Trustee Recruitment, Selection and Induction* (RS1). London: Charity Commission; Charity Commission (2010) *A Breath of Fresh Air* (RS23). London: Charity Commission.

19.1

The Charity Commission has recommended that poor recruitment and induction procedures for trustees can lead to problems such as:

- lack of clarity about duties and responsibilities

- failure to recognise where advice should be taken

- failure to manage conflicts of interest

- vesting control in an 'inner core' instead of the whole board.

Board recruitment, induction and support are not things to be left to chance.

This chapter outlines the methods your organisation could adopt to find new board members with the appropriate skills and to help ensure trustee opportunities reach a wide group of people.

Five questions for building a happy board:

1 Why are we recruiting new trustees?

2 Are we ready to bring in new people?

3 What skills, knowledge and experience are we looking for?

4 How do we attract and select people?

5 How do we keep trustees motivated once they have joined?

19.2

Preparing the ground

Decide who will lead your recruitment programme
Who will take forward your trustee recruitment activities? Decide on one individual or small group – perhaps the chair, vice chair or small working group – who will take responsibility for sustaining the process. Your board may decide to call this group a nominations committee with a specific remit to recruit new trustees. Or the group may be a governance or board development committee with a wider remit to improve the organisation's governance.

Devise an action plan
The first step is to draw up an action plan setting out what you will do at each stage of the recruitment process. It is also helpful to have a timetable. Does the board and do potential new trustees know how long it is likely to take between an individual expressing interest in a vacancy and being formally appointed or elected as a trustee?

Use the headings in this chapter as the basis for your action plan.

Further Information:
NCVO (2006) *Good Practice in Trustee Recruitment (Toolkit)*. London: NCVO.

NCVO (2014) *Trustee Recruitment for Small Organisations*. London: NCVO.

Who are you looking for?

Start with your governing document
Your governing document (which may be called a constitution, trust deed, articles of association or another name – see Chapter 1) is your rulebook for the way your charity is governed. This should be the first place to look for 'terms of office', 'eligibility', 'procedures for election' and so on. For example, some charities have the power to co-opt people on to the board, which is a useful way of complementing the skills and experience of your elected trustees.

Why do you want to recruit?
Ask yourself what skills, knowledge and experience your organisation needs in order to improve the effectiveness of the board. Does it have the right mix of skills or experience to oversee new areas of service delivery? Could it better reflect changes to the ethnic or age profile of the beneficiaries? Does it need an injection of 'new blood' in preparation for existing, more experienced trustees reaching the end of their term of service?

Nationally, surveys have shown that trustee boards do not reflect the population as a whole, with minority groups and young people in particular being under-represented in trustee roles. The tendency for many charities to recruit only using word of mouth also inevitably limits the number and diversity of people who can access trustee opportunities. For this reason, many organisations have looked at how their recruitment practices can help create a more inclusive and diverse trustee board.

19.3

Is your board ready to recruit new people?

All boards should pause and reflect before embarking on a trustee recruitment campaign to ensure that they are alert to the issues or board practices that might need to change in order to attract people with the skills, knowledge or experience the organisation needs.

Questions that trustees should consider individually and collectively are listed here.

- Is the board prepared to reconsider times, length and frequency of board meetings?

- Is the board prepared to reconsider the venue for board meetings?

- Is the board able and willing to offer appropriate support to new board members?

- Is the board prepared to reconsider its approach to the payment of trustee expenses, eg do current trustees claim expenses or do trustees consider it inappropriate for trustees to claim expenses?

- Does the trustees' expenses policy allow trustees who are responsible for providing care to reclaim the costs incurred when they attend meetings etc?

Creating an inclusive and diverse trustee board

What do we mean when we talk about an inclusive and diverse trustee board? An inclusive trustee board can have many characteristics.

- It can be more responsive to the community it serves, because trustees will have actively worked to see how board membership reflects the wider community.

- It can bring fresh perspectives to the way the organisation is governed by bringing together people from different backgrounds and with different perspectives.

- It accesses a wider pool of talent and skill – if you openly promote your board vacancies to a wide group of people you are more likely to attract people with the skills your organisation needs.

- It is more inclusive in the way its mission is fulfilled, by involving a range of people and interests.

- It sets an example about inclusion 'from the top'. If your organisation has a commitment to diversity – typically, in a policy – then an inclusive and diverse board is an ideal way to demonstrate that your organisation is acting on its policy.

- It is inclusive and accessible in the way it operates – whether it is the venue for meetings, the format of papers or the culture in the boardroom.

Some misconceptions about board diversity

- **A diverse board is not one that simply looks diverse.**
  Appointing a trustee on the basis of their age or ethnic background alone, without considering what they can offer by way of skills or knowledge or how they can contribute to the organisation's worth, can risk being a token gesture.

- **A diverse board is not one that automatically expects an individual to represent their entire community.**
  Everyone has something to offer as a trustee, and it may not be what you expect. A finance expert brings other skills beyond financial expertise (and they may not want to simply carry on their day job!). A person who has a disability does not automatically 'represent' all people with disabilities. Have you considered what the board expects from its new trustees, and how the board is perceived by the new board member? Make sure expectations on both sides are matched.

- **A diverse board is not about the democratic representation of interests around a board table.** Creating a large board with a large number of different groups being 'represented' risks creating an unwieldy decision-making process and, perhaps more seriously, can create a perception that trustees are appointed only to represent particular sectional interests. It is better to think first about how you want to include diverse views in the decision-making process and then look at how this can happen – through board membership? Through advisory or working groups? Through consultation?

Questions to consider in creating an inclusive and diverse board

- Are you confident that the strategy and performance of the organisation that you are responsible for matches the charity's mission and is keeping up with a changing environment?

- Could your board better reflect more of society, your beneficiaries and stakeholders, and could it harness people's talents more effectively?

- What skills, knowledge and experience are missing from your board?

- What would be the ideal composition of your board?

- Have you already identified people who could join your board? Are there people already in the organisation who could become involved at board level?

- What will be the challenges and the benefits to the organisation of a diverse and inclusive board?

- Is trusteeship the best way to involve people in the decision-making process? Are there other forms of involvement (committees, forums, advisory groups) that could involve people more effectively?

- Are you ready to involve more people in the governance of your organisation?

- Are potential trustees ready to be involved and aware of the responsibilities they will be taking on if they join the board?

- Why are you looking at the diversity of your board? Do you want to improve the work of your organisation and board, or do you, or does someone else, think it will 'look good'?

Practical steps to creating an inclusive board
Identify the obstacles to diversity

The following exercise, from NCVO's *Good Practice in Trustee Recruitment (Toolkit)*, can be carried out by your board to examine the obstacles to diversity and some of the measures to overcome them.

What prevents a broader range of people from joining our board?	What can we do to overcome these obstacles?
Lack of awareness of the organisation and its relevance	• Go on a publicity drive specifically with this group of people • Organise events, or attend events held by minority ethnic groups, young people or people with disabilities (depending on who it is you are trying to recruit)
Lack of interest in our organisation	• Build relationships with the under-represented group to demonstrate that your organisation is relevant to them • Consider partnerships with organisations that do have good links already
Time and place of meeting (inconvenient and inaccessible)	• Review the time and place of meetings and be willing to change
Use of jargon	• Adopt a Plain English approach
Lack of confidence among potential candidates	• Offer training and getting-to-know-us sessions • Invite people to get involved in other activities first • Offer to provide a mentor
Lack of appropriate support (eg information in large print, availability of interpretation, lack of Plain English in our documents)	• Seek advice from organisations like Action on Hearing Loss, RNIB and People First on the services available • Remember however not to make assumptions about what any individual needs – ask them
We don't know what prevents people joining	• Ask them • A well-considered consultation exercise with a community can be an excellent way to build relationships, provided you are committed to following through on the results

19.4

Review board recruitment methods
An inclusive approach to board recruitment benefits everyone. Use the suggestions later in this and the next chapter to help you plan your recruitment, selection and induction programme to best meet the needs of your prospective and new trustees.

19.5

Preparing the vacancy

Before promoting a trustee vacancy, it's vital that the role is clearly agreed, set out in writing and understood by all. It would be a shame if keen prospective board members were put off because they didn't understand what they were being asked to do and what would be expected of them.

First, check that board members clearly understand the formal duties and responsibilities of trusteeship and any specific roles attached to the particular vacancy.

Next, plan to put together a pack of information for potential trustees. This should provide the applicant with basic information about the role and the organisation but should not include too much detail, as more can be provided later on in the process. As a minimum, you should include:

- a role description setting out the duties, responsibilities, expectations (especially time commitment and any additional duties), eligibility criteria and an expenses policy (see Chapter 4)

- background to the organisation

- sufficient information to be able to apply – an application form or instructions on how to apply or be nominated

How do you attract new trustees?

The Code encourages boards to use (where permitted by the governing document) *'a range of ways to recruit board members (such as advertising) to encourage diversity; including formal recruitment procedures and making appointments based on merit, objectively measured against the agreed skills audit and role description'.*[30]

Making the approach
Remember to sell trusteeship: emphasise the positive and rewarding contribution that trustees make to society. But do be realistic about the time commitment and responsibilities; for example, it would not be suitable to say, 'Well, it's only a few hours every three months.' The role of an honorary officer, in particular, may in practice be much more time consuming than the formal business of meetings because of their additional duties.

Inform your members
If your trustees are drawn from membership, you could circulate information about the skills required in advance of elections and circulate biographies of candidates during the election process. Within the organisation, advisory groups or similar bodies can be good 'training ground' for potential trustees.

30 NCVO (2010) *Good Governance: A code for the voluntary and community sector.* London: NCVO.

Promote to the wider public

Promoting your vacancy to the wider public helps you to be transparent and reach as wide a pool of potential trustees as possible. The following methods can be used.

Advertising or news features

Advertising (paid or free adverts) or features about your organisation in a newspaper (sometimes called advertorials) can help promote your message to the public and include reference to your trustee vacancy. Try advertising in newspapers (national or local), professional magazines, websites or, locally, in community centres, surgeries or other public places.

Trustee brokerage services

A number of agencies offer specialist trustee recruitment services. NCVO has its own trustee recruitment portal, Trustee Bank, which allows any individual and all voluntary sector organisations to view trustee vacancies. NCVO Members can sign in or create an account and post trustee vacancies for free.

Specialist recruitment agencies

Recruitment agencies can find and select trustees, chairs and treasurers. While the costs involved may be high, it can be a useful way of recruiting to key positions and matching your specific role requirements.

Trustees Unlimited – a joint venture between NCVO, Bates Wells Braithwaite and Russam GMS – is a recruitment service that helps organisations recruit trustees and non-executives from across the private, public and voluntary sectors.

Case study
Conservation charity in Yorkshire

The organisation

Conservation charity was established in the 1990s and its activities range from conserving the environmental and heritage features making up the landscape to issues such as supporting local communities and encouraging sustainable development. Following a period of rapid growth, the trustees identified significant skills gaps on the board, including in the area of human resources and financial expertise.

The charity tried to recruit new board members through voluntary sector networks and organisations in their area but this produced no new skilled trustees.

The board then agreed to publicly advertise new vacancies in a similar way to recruiting staff. Drawing on ideas and methods from other organisations, an advertisement was placed in the local newspaper:

'We are seeking to recruit people with business experience to become members of our Board of Trustees. We are especially interested in those professionals who have human resource, financial management or fundraising skills and knowledge. Individuals with varying backgrounds in business who are interested in a volunteer leadership role in the community are encouraged to apply. Your experience may be varied, but a practical approach and the capability to contribute to strategic direction and financial management is essential.'

Fifteen people, all meeting the professional criteria, responded to the advert and following a shortlisting and interview process three new trustees were appointed to the board. The charity felt that the process worked extremely well and helped to recharge and regenerate its board, gaining enthusiasts with relevant skills. It laid the groundwork for sound development of the organisation's governance – subsequent activities included strategic planning and developing more robust financial procedures.

19.6

Selection and appointment of trustees

By now you should have one or more potential trustees. They may have applied through your advertising process, or they may have been formally nominated via your organisation's rules.

Check who is making the final decision on appointment or election. Is it a decision made by members at an annual general meeting? Can the trustee board decide between themselves? Is the appointment made by an outside organisation (see Chapter 1)?

When trustees make the final decision
If trustees make the final decision, you may decide to go through a selection process to narrow down applicants and create a shortlist.

Start by agreeing the 'must have' qualities from the trustees' person specification and then agree how you will assess them. Make sure those conducting interviews and making the decision understand the role and the key qualities needed.

When you have made your decision or recommendation, remember to thank everyone who applied – not just the successful candidates. Think about how you can say no in a positive way. If you have followed a systematic process then make it clear to trustees that you are looking for specific skills and experience. Before you turn people down consider whether there are other ways of involving them in the organisation?

When members make the final decision
If members make the final decision, it is likely your governing document will specify the way in which trustees are elected. Make sure you carefully follow your procedures.

In addition, some organisations help members choose between the candidates, for example by asking candidates to produce a biography for circulation to members at the annual general meeting.

Some organisations go further by involving the board in selecting candidates or identifying recommended candidates.
For example:

• a committee of the board shortlists candidate(s) who are then nominated by trustees and put to members; members may have the right to put forward alternative candidates

• a list of candidates is 'recommended' by the board, but other candidates may be entitled to stand for election too if they wish.

Remember to ensure that any method is consistent with your governing document.

Keep it legal
• Make sure you carefully follow the procedures for the appointment or election of trustees as set out in your organisation's governing document.

• Have you checked that trustees are eligible to serve? Information about trustee eligibility should have been included in the application pack. Use the Charity Commission's Charity trustee: declaration of eligibility and responsibility' as a checklist for eligibility.[31]

• Make sure you ask trustees to sign a declaration that they are eligible and willing to serve.

• Trustees should also make use of official registers that record the names of people who are disqualified from acting as charity trustees: the Individual Insolvency Register maintained by the Insolvency Service; the register of disqualified directors maintained by Companies House; the register of all persons who have been removed as a charity trustee either by the Charity Commission or by an Order of the High Court since 1 January 1993, which is maintained by the Charity Commission.

31 Charity Commission (2013) *Charity Trustee: Declaration of eligibility and responsibility.* London: Charity Commission. www.gov.uk/government/ publications/confirmation-of-charity-trustee-eligibility

19.7

- If your charity works with young or vulnerable people, make sure the trustees seek any necessary disclosures from the Disclosure Barring Service (DBS). The Charity Commission strongly recommends that 'trustees of charities that work with children or vulnerable adults and that are eligible to obtain DBS (CRB) checks do so, to ensure both that the person they wish to appoint as a trustee is eligible and to ensure the safety of the charity's beneficiaries'.[32]

- Comply with HM Revenue and Custom's (HMRC) 'fit and proper persons' test when vetting new trustees.

It is also seen as best practice to:

- take up references including from current employer, if appropriate

- carry out identity checks

- verify relevant academic and professional qualifications.

Recruiting to specific roles (chair, treasurer etc)

Check the legals

Sometimes organisations have separate rules for the appointment or election of trustees with specific roles, so make sure you carefully check your governing document and other rules and incorporate them into your plan and timescale.

Clarifying the role

Have you reviewed the role and specific duties of the post to which you are recruiting? It may be, for example, that the existing post holder has been in office for some years, during which time the role may have evolved to suit their particular skills and the organisation's life cycle.

Don't make assumptions about the duties of a post holder – check 'Who's who in the boardroom' in Chapter 4 as a guide. If you don't ave a role description or if it needs updating, check yours against the model role descriptions in Chapter 4.

Recruitment methods

Are there specific avenues that might help you attract a candidate with specialist skills? For example, some trustee brokerage services advertise vacancies to people from particular professional backgrounds, like that operated by the Charity Finance Group – useful if you are looking for a treasurer.

Selection and election/appointment

You may decide to have a different – perhaps more formal – process for selecting candidates for the role of an honorary officer. Remember to ensure that any process complies with your governing document.

32 Charity Commission (2012) *Finding New Trustees* (CC30). London: Charity Commission. www.gov.uk/government/ publications/finding-new-trustees- cc30/finding-new-trustees

19.8

Planning the next recruitment campaign

Continuous improvement of the selection and recruitment process should make it easier for an organisation to find the right person for the role. Get feedback from trustees who have gone through the process; this can be collected after an initial period on the board or at exit interview stage. Find out what worked, what didn't and what else could have helped.

19.9

Succession planning

The trustee cycle
Once a successful board mix has been achieved, it should be constantly reviewed and refreshed to ensure that the balance is maintained.

Part of this is about creating a culture of trustees moving on: trusteeship is not necessarily permanent, but the needs of the organisation – and the needs of the board – change over time. And there will always be people who really do need to move on.

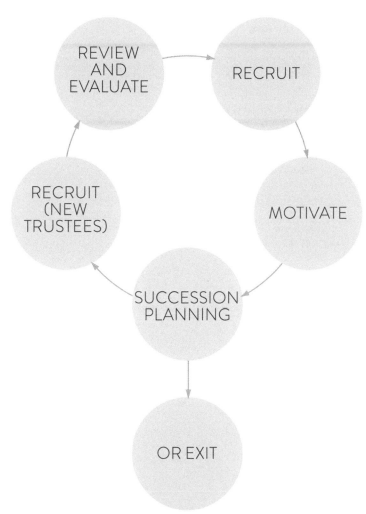

Succession planning – key issues

For board development

- How to convince people that they need to move on – both for themselves and for the organisation – without giving rise to feelings of failure and rejection.

- How to make leaving a positive event that recognises the individual's past contributions and successes (how can the trustee still remain involved in the organisation – as adviser, as vice-president?).

For the individual trustee

- Understanding that there is not an automatic right to stay and be retained, just because you have given successfully in the past.

For both trustees and trustee boards

- Moving on is a positive strategy – understand the positive advantages of the rolling board, maintaining continuity and encouraging new people to join.

- Create a culture of new blood within the organisation.

- Recognise that individual and organisation do not necessarily grow in parallel, at the same pace or in the same direction. What were valuable skills and approaches at one time may not be what the organisation and individual need right now or in the future.

Checklist

Do you have a plan to recruit new board members that fits in with your board recruitment cycle?

Have trustees discussed the benefits and challenges of an inclusive and diverse board?

Do you need to review your board recruitment practices and, if necessary, the provisions in your governing document?

Do you ensure opportunities to join the board are promoted as widely as possible within the terms of your governing document?

Are new board members eligible to serve and properly elected or appointed?

20

Induction

20.1

Induction – getting it right from the start

Induction is a key part of making your trustee board effective. For trustees, it provides an opportunity to learn about their new role and about different aspects of their new charity. For existing board members, induction is a way of identifying the needs of the new trustee and finding ways to support them.

Induction programmes need not be lengthy or expensive. If your organisation has a limited budget for induction, there are many resources available that can be tailored to your own needs; some are included in this guide and there are others online. These include model role descriptions, skills audits, hints and tips and induction checklists.

Charity Commission guidance

The Charity Commission emphasises that new trustees are more likely to feel welcome in the charity, and start making a positive difference sooner, if they have immediate access to the charity's aims and objectives and are given a working knowledge of the way the charity operates from the outset.

The Charity Commission recommends that all trustees receive some form of induction, with the aim of ensuring new trustees have a clear understanding of their roles and responsibilities. All trustees should have access to the charity's governing document.

20.2

Planning the induction programme

Tailoring induction to the individual's needs

Every trustee brings their unique experiences to the board, so each will require particular support or training. Some trustees may value personal development opportunities and have time to carry them out; others may feel that a lifetime's experience in the workplace equips them for their role. Some believe passionately in the cause but feel they lack skills or confidence. Sometimes trustees elected to specific roles have other needs – new chairs may need support if they lack previous chairing experience, or may find it useful to be mentored by an existing chair of another charity.

Yet, all trustees require certain skills and qualities to carry out their role, and all trustees certainly need information and clarity about their duties and responsibilities. Any induction programme should aim to cover the following four areas.

- The key responsibilities – providing factual information to ensure trustees understand their duties and responsibilities, the charity's governing document and the legal structure of the organisation.

- Understanding the role – going beyond the role description or written induction pack and ensuring new trustees have a very clear understanding of their prospective role.

- Getting to know the organisation – learning about the history, culture, values, traditions and issues facing the organisation.

- The trustee's own development – ensuring the new trustee settles into their role and can access support and development opportunities.

To try and meet the needs of different organisations, this guide sets out a range of suggested activities for a new trustee's induction, divided into 'essentials' and 'options'. When new trustees join the board, try discussing the range of suggested activities below with them and decide which will best meet your charity's and the individual trustee's needs.

Inducting trustees into specific roles

Individuals taking on specific roles – honorary officers such as the chair, secretary, treasurer or other specific role on the board (see Chapter 4) – will need an induction programme tailored to their needs.

To start planning an induction into a specific role, begin with the role description itself. What are the skills and qualities required in the role description or person specification? Next, how does the new post holder feel about the skills and qualities required? Are there gaps? How do they feel they can learn about their new role? Use the planning table below as a starting point (the example given is for the role of chair).

Planning inductions

Specific role	The skills required include	Possible induction activities
Responsibilities as a charity trustee	Objectivity Working as a team	Observing the board Attending training / briefings Joining a trustee network
Chairing trustee board meetings	Listening Timekeeping Summarising issues	Meeting and observing the outgoing chair Being a board member or serving as a Vice Chair before becoming Chair Attending training Being mentored by another chair
Other roles (see role description)		

Many of the suggested activities below can be adapted to the needs of a board member in a specific role. For example, a new treasurer could arrange to be mentored from someone in a similar position in another charity or they could shadow the outgoing post holder. They may need a longer or more in-depth induction into their role and more meetings with trustees and staff.

20.3

Induction activities

Essential elements of a trustee's induction

The induction pack can be provided electronically or in hard copy, whichever is most appropriate for the trustee. As a minimum, all trustees should receive:

- a written statement of their responsibilities (often called a role description – if you do not have one, see Chapter 4 for an example)

- a pack of essential information (an induction pack).

The pack is the basic part of any induction; a trustee should be given one to keep. The pack should be reviewed every year (a good time to do this is before your annual general meeting if you hold one).

The pack may contain a lot of information and should highlight how it can take time and a variety of different activities to get to grips with the role. Don't just rely on an induction pack. The pack should include, as a minimum:

- governing document/(s) including any standing orders, by-laws etc

- an annual list of dates for board and committee meetings, annual general meeting, away days etc

- sets of recent board papers and minutes

- a list of board committees including details of membership and terms of reference

- a list of working or advisory groups and their terms of reference and make-up

- annual reports and accounts for the previous three years

- policy documents including health and safety, investments, performance management, reserves, risk, safeguarding and financial controls

- profiles of trustees and their contact details

- chief executive/head of staff's job description if you employ one

- diagram showing management structure.

You should also consider including:

- guidance about the organisation:
  - its history
  - vision, mission and values statements
  - structure (committees, user groups, staff and volunteers)
  - any offices or buildings
  - newsletter/other marketing materials

- formal documents about the organisation:
  - details of how the organisation approaches staff appraisal
  - business plans/strategic plans/ work programme
  - risk register

- documents about the organisation's governance:
  - task descriptions of other trustees and honorary officers
  - a manual giving guidance on trustee roles and responsibilities of trustees
  - code of conduct for trustees and other relevant policies including conflicts of interest policy and procedure, confidentiality, expenses policy and procedure for claiming, whistleblowing etc
  - self-assessment form to indicate skills, experience, interests and support needs

- other useful information and guidance:
  - Charity Commission (2012) *The Essential Trustee: What you need to know* (CC3). London: Charity Commission; Charity Commission (2008) *Hallmarks of an Effective Charity* (CC10). London: Charity Commission.
  - *National Occupational Standards for Trustees and Management Committee Members*, available from Skills for Health.
  - NCVO (2010) *Good Governance: A code for the voluntary and community sector.* London: NCVO.

Induction pack checklist

An induction pack should provide, as a minimum, enough information for a new trustee to be able to list the following.

- Who the trustees and honorary officers are and what they do.

- How long trustees serve for.

- Frequency, dates and length of trustee meetings.

- The number and names of the board committees.

- Date of the next annual general meeting (if applicable).

- A brief background to the organisation (history, funders, staffing, achievements).

- The board's current priorities.

Getting to know other trustees

New trustees should be made to feel welcome, valued and part of the team. At their first board meeting, the chair should formally welcome a new trustee and invite them to:

- introduce themselves

- say why they wanted to become a trustee

- say something about how they feel they can contribute to the work of the trustee board.

Some organisations ask new trustees to write a short CV or biography for circulation with the board papers.

Existing members of the committee should introduce themselves to the new person and describe briefly their involvement with the organisation.

Tip: New trustees could attend a first meeting in an observer role before they are appointed or commit to the position.

Options and ideas for trustee inductions

Use trustee inductions as a refresher for all trustees

When new trustees join a board, it's a good opportunity to refresh all trustees on governance and trusteeship essentials. This could be followed by a social event when trustees have an opportunity to get to know each other. The session may include:

- a briefing on the charity's history

- review of important documents such as the governing document and other organisational policies

- discussion of the duties and responsibilities of trustees

- discussion of the skills involved in an effective board.

Hold an induction workshop

It's vital that new trustees spend some time with the chair and key staff, if applicable, to get a really good understanding of the charity and what will be involved in the role.

You could offer this on a one-to-one basis over a drink or lunch, or, if your organisation is large or if you have an influx of several new trustees, this could form a group discussion and combine with a discussion about trustee roles and responsibilities (see above).

Use the suggested topic areas below as prompts for the meeting.

- The charity's structure or activities. This could include presentations from key staff if your organisation is large enough.

- The role of the board.

- The time commitment involved in being a trustee.

- Conduct and behaviour expected of a trustee (eg a discussion about conflicts of interest).

- Skills and interests new trustees could contribute to the organisation.

- The board's relationship with staff.

- Any support or training opportunities available.

Mentoring or buddying a new trustee
It's useful to offer a new trustee the chance to learn informally about the role from somebody else in a similar position. You could team up each new trustee with an existing board member or a new trustee may prefer to be mentored by a trustee from another charity.

Essential reading for trustees includes
- Charity Commission (2012) *The Essential Trustee: What you need to know* (CC3). London: Charity Commission.

- NCVO (2010) *Good Governance: A code for the voluntary and community sector.* London: NCVO.

- *National Occupational Standards for Trustees and Management Committee Members*, available from Skills for Health.

- NCVO (2006) *Good Practice in Trustee Recruitment (Toolkit).* London: NCVO.

Local organisations should try contacting their local support agency (sometimes called a Council for Voluntary Service) to find out about support available nearby. Some areas organise a local trustee support network; see www.navca.org.uk for details of local support agencies.

Reviewing or appraising the role of a trustee
A review meeting – often with the chair of the board – a couple of months after a new trustee has joined can help clarify any aspects of the new trustee's role that are unclear and find out whether further training, development or support (formal or informal) is required.

Some charities provide trustees with the opportunity for an 'appraisal' – a review of their role, usually every 12 months – where there is an opportunity to reflect on their role and performance as a trustee. You may consider setting this up for your organisation – if so, it is important to think about this at induction stage.

Identifying learning and development opportunities
See Chapter 17 for guidance on helping trustees identify their skills and development needs and Chapter 18 for guidance and ideas on learning opportunities available for trustees.

Checklist for new trustees

Provide copies of the checklist below
for new trustees: they can use it to
record progress and ensure that their
induction process covers all essential
aspects of the role.

Activity	✓	Comments
Have you received an induction pack including the organisation's governing document and annual report and accounts?		
Have you been offered an induction programme?		
Do you have a statement of your roles and responsibilities as a trustee?		
Have you identified what skills, experiences and knowledge you can offer?		
Do you have a copy of any trustee documents and policies (eg a code of conduct)?		
Do you know when the organisation was set up and its history?		
Do you know the aims of the organisation?		
Do you know about the activities of the organisation?		
Do you know how your organisation is funded?		
Do you know about the key issues facing the organisation?		
Do you know about future projects or activities planned?		
Do you know about other organisations or people your organisation has networks or special relationships with?		
Do you understand the structure of the organisation and your role in it?		
Do you understand the staff and volunteer structure and your relationship with staff and volunteers?		
Do you understand your role and responsibilities and expected duties as a trustee?		
Have you met with trustees and the chief executive (if there is one) and had a visit to premises or activities?		
Have you met and got to know the other trustees and got their contact details?		
Do you know how the work of the organisation relates to initiatives undertaken by other organisations?		
Do you have support or training needs and are they being addressed?		
Do you feel you are ready to take on your role?		
Do you think the board needs to review its induction programme?		

21

Effective meetings and decision-making

A board can only carry out its role effectively if it maintains strong decision-making processes and procedures. The 12 responsibilities of the board outlined in Part One require trustees to act collectively, with the board meeting as the main focus of discussion and decision-making.

21.1

Board meeting basics

Types of meetings

Trustees are typically involved in the following types of meetings:

- Board meetings – formal meetings of the charity's trustee board as required by the charity's governing document, where trustees discuss business and take decisions.

- General meetings – meetings of the charity's membership (if it has company law/constitutional members) as required by the governing document, where members discuss issues, receive reports and take decisions.

- Committee meetings – committees of the trustee board as set out in the governing document and/or as agreed by the board or membership.

- Advisory or working groups – other groups of trustees, staff, members, users or stakeholders – usually advisory – that provide information or advice for trustees or carry out detailed work.

- Other meetings – social, fundraising or other meetings for a particular purpose that trustees typically attend but that are not directly related to the governance of the organisation.

Remember that trustees may wear different 'hats' at different meetings. For example, at a trustee board meeting, trustees will be expected to act collectively and take formal decisions in their role as a charity trustee. At committee meeting, however, trustees that attend the meeting will be in a different role, expected to act within the terms of reference of the committee; their duties and responsibilities as a member of the committee will be as set out in the terms of reference. For a discussion about the different role trustees can play or 'hats' they can wear in an organisation, see section 11.3.

How many people should be present at a trustee board meeting?

The quorum is the minimum number of voting members who must be present for a meeting's decisions to be valid. This should be set out in your charity's governing document.

Who should chair the meeting?

The chair of trustees is responsible for chairing the meetings of the trustee board. Your governing document may set out procedures governing what happens if the chair is not present. The chair should:

- understand their responsibilities in chairing the meeting and any formal procedures that govern the conduct of the meeting – these may be set out in the charity's governing document or other procedures

- understand the issues to be addressed in the meeting – such as the charity's financial position and any advice that is to be considered

- ensure that a proper agenda has been drawn up, in consultation with all relevant parties

- keep discussions focused, stimulate discussion and draw out quiet members

- be clear as to the status of participants at a board meeting – trustees, staff, advisors or observers

- recognise a potential decision when one arises

- ensure that decisions are clearly minuted.

21.2

Can our trustees meet by telephone or video conference?

Participants in a meeting must be able to see and hear each other for the decisions at the meeting to be valid, unless your governing document specifies otherwise. Video conferencing is a valid form of meeting (unless prohibited by your governing document) but telephone conference is not (unless it is allowed by your governing document).

If you regularly conduct board meetings using video conference facilities, the Charity Commission recommends that all trustee boards hold at least one physical meeting of all trustees per year.

> **Further Information:**
> Charity Commission (2012)
> *Charities and Meetings (CC48).*
> London: Charity Commission.

Running a board meeting

The agenda

As a rule of thumb, efficient meeting agendas include two or three substantive items at the most. These are the decision-making and monitoring issues that your trustee board must consider. Incidental information – which doesn't require discussion or a decision by the board – can be studied outside of meetings.

A typical board agenda

1 Apologies, welcome and agenda review

2 Minutes of last meeting

3 Matters arising not covered elsewhere on the agenda

4 Declaration of conflicts – interest and loyalty

5 Chief executive's report (including staff matters and performance against strategic/business plan)

6 Financial report

7 Strategic matters

8 Review/approve board policies

9 Compliance issues

10 Reports from committees

11 Activities or issues specific to this meeting

12 Review of meeting

13 Any other business

14 Dates of future meetings

Improving board agendas

The main focus for most voluntary and community sector boards is their regular schedule of meetings where they act collectively to fulfil their responsibilities for governing the organisation. For most boards the time available to them is limited and the importance of agendas cannot be overstated and should not be overlooked.

Well-crafted and structured agendas can make all the difference to whether a board uses its time productively which will ultimately improve the performance of the organisation as a whole. It is therefore vital for all boards to have a forward plan for agendas which ensures that over twelve months the board will be able to fulfil all of its duties and responsibilities eg sufficient time is allocated to – setting strategy; reviewing and approving board policies; monitoring organisational performance; ensuring legal and regulatory compliance etc.

Agendas should also clearly state why each item is going to the Board eg for discussion, for scrutiny, for decision etc.

Board papers and information
John Carver, a management consultant, describes three types of board information:

- Decision information: used to make decisions, such as agreeing the organisation's strategic plan. This type of information looks to the future and is designed to measure performance.

- Monitoring information: enables the board to assess whether the organisation's plans are being met. It looks to the past and provides a specific survey of performance against criteria. An example is the annual review of an organisation's strategic plan.

- Incidental information: for the general information of the board and not related to board action. Committee reports may fall into this category.

The following is an example of a schedule for circulating information to board members:

Two weeks before the board meeting
- Agenda

- Information categorised as being either for discussion, information or decision

- Financial information

At least two weeks before the board meeting at which it is discussed
- Annual budget

- Audit report

- Strategic plan

After each board meeting
- Minutes

- Notice of next meeting.

Monthly
- Financial report

- Significant published articles about the organisation.

Quarterly
- Financial report

Regularly, when appropriate
- Memo from the chief executive or chair summarising current activities, accomplishments and needs

- Updated material for the trustee board handbook

- Advance copies of publications, brochures or promotional material

Taking and using minutes
The minutes are a formal, legal record of what has happened at a board meeting. Minutes are an invaluable source of information for those at the meeting as well, as for those who could not make the meeting. Minutes may also be examined by the regulators, courts or police if something goes wrong in a charity.

Charitable companies must maintain minutes of all trustees' meetings for at least 10 years from the date of the relevant meeting. It is, however, also argued that the minutes of all charities, irrespective of their legal form, should maintain the minutes of all trustees' meetings for the lifetime of the charity and beyond.

Taking minutes is not an easy skill, so make sure your minute taker has support and training if necessary and has a general awareness of the topics to be discussed.

Good minutes should be an accurate record of:

- advice taken

- risks considered

- decisions made

- actions required

- actions taken

- main points of discussion.

Draft minutes should always be circulated as quickly as possible to allow all trustees to review them and agree they are an accurate record or suggest where changes need to be made. Usually, the minutes of a meeting are formally agreed at the next meeting of trustees, signed by the chair and filed in a minute book as a formal record of decisions taken. The minute book should be kept in a safe place.

21.3

Improving board meetings

Participating in meetings

All board members, not just those who are new, should regularly remember the following points.

- Read all of the papers and be well prepared for the issues that are going to be discussed.

- Do not use mobile phones or other electronic devices for unrelated activities.

- Do not pass messages to others or carry on side conversations during the meeting.

- Think before you speak.

- Speak clearly and be brief.

- Do not be afraid to speak.

- Be reasonable and listen attentively to other people's points of view.

- Let go – even if you disagree with a decision, in the end you may have to let go if there is a broader consensus of opinion.

Essentials of good decision-making

Good decision-making is generally the result of a systematic process. The main stages of decision-making may be summarised as follows.

- Clarify – gather the facts and be clear about the proposal. A decision may have to be deferred whilst further clarification or advice is sought.

- Debate – get a broad cross section of viewpoints. Allow all the alternatives to be aired.

- Decide – try to achieve consensus but do not delay unnecessarily. If necessary, put it to a vote and make sure all decisions are accurately recorded, including who is responsible for implementing them.

- Inform – report board decisions to those who will be affected by them.

- Reflect – make sure that the board reviews the implementation of its decisions.

Decision-making checklist

The Charity Commission published guidance on how charity trustees should approach making decisions affecting their charity: Charity Commission (2013) *It's Your Decision: Charity trustees and decision-making.* London: Charity Commission. The guidance states that when trustees make a decision they must:

- act within their powers

- act in good faith, and only in their charity's interests

- make sure they are sufficiently informed, taking any advice they need

- take account of all relevant factors

- ignore any irrelevant factors

- manage conflicts of interest

- make decisions that are within the range of decisions that a reasonable trustee body could make in the circumstances.

Electronic communication

Email, telephone conferencing and the internet have opened up many new possibilities for improving the information systems of boards. These include:

- circulating board agendas by email

- using web 'chat' facilities for informal discussions

- emailing draft funding applications for comment

- web pages containing latest information and updates about the organisation

- video conferencing, which reduces the costs of involving overseas participants.

Protocols are key and it's important to note the following points.

- Know the legal restrictions over conducting virtual board meetings (see page 226).

- Email is convenient but beware of excluding trustees from discussions or information just because they don't have access to email.

- Will trustees want to print out lengthy reports on their home computers?

- Does your expenses policy cover the cost of internet connections and the cost of paper and printing materials by trustees at home?

- Don't be tempted to shorten deadlines for sending out papers just because they are being emailed.

21.4

Better meetings checklist

- Start and end meetings on time and assign time limits to agenda items.

- Schedule meetings for times when most participants can make it. Don't assume participants can take time off work or devote weekends to meetings. Remember school holidays and religious festivals.

- Hold meetings in a place that is convenient, secure and accessible for all participants.

- Provide transport and/or reimburse legitimate travel expenses.

- Circulate the agenda at least a week in advance with papers.

- Offer refreshments.

- Schedule in breaks.

- Prepare the meeting room in advance providing supplies, such as name tags, flip charts, overhead projectors, pens, paper and video equipment.

- Make sure that seating is comfortable and that all participants can see, hear and be seen by each other.

- Appoint a secretary or individual who will 'service' the meeting by providing administrative support – preparing meeting rooms, circulating necessary papers and taking minutes (see page 227). This is sometimes carried out by more than one person.

21.5

Other meetings

General meetings

Membership organisations will hold general meetings of all members as required by the organisation's governing document. Such meetings are held so that members can carry out their formal responsibilities as set out in the governing document. Annual general meetings often include the election of trustees, and these and other general meetings may, for example, be called to approve changes to the governing document. The specific responsibilities of members and the procedures for holding meetings will vary depending on your organisation's legal structure and the content of your organisation's governing document.

Committee meetings

The rules governing committees may be set out in your organisation's governing document or in associated standing orders, by-laws or rules. You may also have agreed terms of reference for committees. See below for more information.

Best practice

Much of the best practice concerning better board meetings can be adapted to other meetings, but remember to ensure any procedures you adopt are consistent with your governing document and with regulatory requirements.

Effective governance structures

The size and composition of a trustee board, and the way it relates to other parts of the charity's governance structure (members, committees, advisors and so on) can have a major impact on how efficient and effective trustees are in carrying out their duties.

It has been increasingly common in recent years for charities to review governance structures to ensure that the structure and composition of the board is effective and best meeting the charity's needs.

21.6

Board size

Research into the largest 500 charities (by income) carried out by Compass Partnership in association with Centre for Charity Effectiveness, Cass Business School in Delivering Effective Governance, 2012, found that: *'It is noteworthy that 10% of boards have more than 20 members and a quarter have more than 16 members, although many of these did say that they wanted to reduce their board size.'*

The report went on to note that the trend for large organisations to reduce the size of their boards had been identified in previous research and: *'appears to be linked to the increased demands on governance and the consequent need for boards to have tighter discussions and for all board members to have sufficient "air time" to be fully engaged and feel responsible for ensuring top quality governance.'*

Boards need to be large enough to bring in a range of skills and backgrounds and have enough people to carry out the work but be small enough to work effectively as a team. The consensus of opinion favours smaller rather than larger boards and suggests an optimum number of between eight and 12.

Dangers of...
...too large a board?
- A dominant inner core and the marginalisation of some individual trustees

- Trustees feel less personally responsible for governance decisions

- Inefficient discussion and decision-making.

...too small a board?
- Overload of work on a small number of individuals

- May not bring enough skills and perspectives

- May not be seen as 'legitimate'/'democratic' in representing the diversity of stakeholder perspectives

Questions to consider

How can your board attract the 'right' number of people with the right skills, knowledge, experience and perspectives to join the board? (Note: what is right for one organisation and its stage of development may not be right for another.)

Are there ways of utilising the skills and experience of individuals other than using them as members of the board? (For example, experts, co-option on to board committees (if governing document allows), advisory groups.)

If there is a 'two-tier board' – for example, a large board of trustees and a smaller executive committee – is it time to review the composition and effectiveness of the board and its committee to avoid the risk of an 'inner circle' dominating or undermining overall authority of the trustee board?

In a large board (eg in excess of 19 members), how can effective governance and good team working be enhanced?

21.7

Board composition

Trustees with specific roles

As organisations change and develop, so too do the roles of specific board members, particularly those usually known as 'honorary officers' (see Chapter 4), such as in the following examples.

- The duties of a chair may include responsibilities agreed as a matter of custom and practice or because of the skills a particular individual can bring.

- As an organisation grows in size, the duties of a treasurer are likely to change from a 'hands-on' individual involved in bookkeeping to a role more focused on financial oversight, providing advice and reports to the board.

- The role of secretary can change with an organisation's legal structure. For example, companies limited by guarantee were until recently required to appoint a company secretary. In larger organisations, the role (or the responsibilities) is often taken by a member of staff.

- The role of vice-chair is one that can be useful, either as a deputy for the chair or as a position for an incoming or outgoing chair.

It is good practice to review periodically the role and contribution of honorary officers or other trustees with specific roles, to ensure that the range of positions and their duties best meet the needs of the charity. See Chapter 4 for guidance on the duties and responsibilities of trustees with specific roles and Chapters 19 and 20 for guidance on recruitment and induction.

Trustees appointed by outside organisations

Some organisations give the power to appoint certain trustees to outside organisations (see Chapter 1). It is good practice to review periodically the role of trustees appointed in this way.

- Do trustees appointed by outside organisations fully understand their role as a charity trustee?

- Do potential conflicts of interest and loyalty between a trustee's role and their external role exist?

- If so, do trustees follow a conflicts of interest and loyalty policy?

- If so, are any such conflicts manageable (this may be particularly significant if there is a funding relationship between the charity and the organisation making the appointment)?

- Does the inclusion of appointed trustees improve the governance of the charity?

- Would it be more appropriate for such appointments to be made to non-voting positions in an advisory capacity to the board?

Remember that any changes you make must be consistent with your governing document and should involve consultation with the organisation that makes the appointment. It is quite likely that any change will require a change to your governing document.

21.8

Board relationships

Board committees

Board committees play an important role in the lives of boards. They can help the board save time by dealing with the detail of board issues separately from the main meeting and are a valuable training ground for new board members and future chairs and a mechanism for utilising the specialist skills of trustees and external people, where allowed by the governing document.

However, too many committees can mean that the board loses overall control and that decision-making and delegation are not clear. Or committees may find themselves starved of any authority or resources by an over-controlling board.

Advantages of board committees

- They are an effective way of utilising the expertise of board members and external people, where allowed by the governing document.

- They help to foster good working relations with staff.

- Potential trustees and advisers can usually be invited to join board committees.

- Chairing a board committee is a good training ground for a future chair.

Disadvantages

- The board may lose its oversight of the charity.

- There could be confusion over the respective roles of the board, committees and staff.

- The board may be unwilling to challenge the decisions of 'expert' committees.

- Decision-making process can become lengthy.

- There could be an overload of meetings.

- They can have an indefinite lifespan.

Key principles

- Committees serve the board, not the other way round.

- They should not take decisions on behalf of the board unless it has been explicitly authorised.

- Where committees replicate internal management divisions, there could be confusion between board and management roles.

- Take a flexible approach that allows your board to create committees when the need arises and to disband them when the need is fulfilled (try changing terminology and calling committees 'working groups' or 'advisory groups' and see how they are then perceived).

- All committees need to have written terms of reference setting out role and powers (see below).

- Know which 'hat' you are wearing – trustees who serve on a committee should also be able to distinguish between their role as a board member and their role as a committee member.

Working parties

Working parties are an alternative to committees and are typically task oriented – (they focus on one particular topic) – and time limited – (they finish as soon as work is complete). An example of a working party is a group set up to oversee a governance review (see Part Four).

Advisory groups

An advisory group – council, committee or assembly – is often a representative grouping of users or stakeholders that provide advice and feedback to trustees. Such a council may be formally elected by members, and the council in turn may elect some or all of the trustee board, although the exact relationships vary. Some councils are purely advisory and are set up informally.

The creation of such councils has been increasingly popular in recent years, particularly for boards with a large, elected structure, as a way of involving users and stakeholders but without making the trustee board too large and unwieldy (see following page).

Terms of reference

All committees, working parties and advisory groups need terms of reference that give a clear indication of what is expected and to whom the group is accountable. Terms of reference should include the following:

- name of the committee/group

- membership – including office where appropriate (eg the honorary treasurer and three trustees) and voting rights

21.9

- purpose – brief statement of why the committee exists

- function – what the committee's main duties are

- delegated authority – whether it has decision-making powers or is purely advisory

- frequency – how often meetings are to be held

- duration – maximum length of meetings

- chair – the name or office of person acting as the chair

- serviced by – person acting as secretary or minute taker

- reporting procedure – the committee or board to whom it must report

- quorum – the minimum number of people who must be present at a meeting including any officer (eg five members of the committee including at least three trustees and either the chair or vice-chair).

Remember: terms of reference must be consistent with your governing document.

Some models of board size and composition

The large representative board
One model that used to be common in large membership organisations is the large, elected trustee board (with, say, over 20 members), where trustees are elected from membership, often from different sections of the membership based around geographical areas or other groupings. This model has become less popular in recent years, often because it is felt that such boards are too large to work effectively. A number of organisations have opted to move away from this type of model towards a small, skills based board/advisory council model.

The small 'skills based' board
Another model of governance – often used by those without a large membership structure or where the only members are the current board members – comprises a small trustee board (with, say, fewer than 10 members), with trustees appointed by the board based on an assessment of the skills, experiences and perspectives required by the board.

The advisory council
A trend in recent years, particularly for boards with a large, elected structure, has been to create a smaller trustee board (see previous point) backed by a larger, representative advisory council, group, committee or assembly. This development is often based on a recognition that effective governance needs a careful balance between the need to bring in the perspectives of users and stakeholders (which tends towards a larger decision-making structure) and the need to ensure that trustees discharge their legal responsibilities via efficient and effective governance (which tends towards a smaller decision-making structure).

In these cases, the responsibilities of the advisory group can vary: some are elected by members; some are partly appointed by outside agencies; some have the responsibility of electing some or all of the trustee board.

Checklist

Do you hold board meetings as required by the governing document?

If you hold 'virtual' meetings by telephone or video conferencing, do they comply with your governing document and regulatory guidance?

Do trustees receive information in advance of board meetings that is timely and in a format suitable to make decisions?

Do you need to review your current board and committee structure and composition to assess if it is currently serving the governance needs of your organisation?

Do all board members have a clear understanding of your organisation's committee structure and their involvement in it?

Do all your committees and working parties have written terms of reference that are reviewed on a regular basis?

Are all your committees and working parties clear about the extent of their delegated powers and to whom they report?

Have you reviewed your board's size and composition to ensure it is fit for purpose?

Part Four:

Improving governance

22

Carrying out a governance review

The Code recommends that boards take time out periodically to review their own effectiveness and the effectiveness of the organisation. It is becoming increasingly common for charities to carry out governance reviews and there are now a number of different tools and approaches available.

A governance review is a systematic way of improving how your charity is governed and reviewing how effectively your board carries out its responsibilities.

A governance review can take place for many reasons and take many forms. A review may take place to explore how well the board works together, or may be part of a wider assessment of the way the charity is run. A governance review could be carried out as a self-assessment, via an informal discussion, via a one-to-one appraisal of trustees or via a quality system.

22.1

Why should organisations review their governance? What are the benefits of carrying out a review?

- **Strategic focus** – better governance can help an organisation be healthier and make more robust long-term decisions.

- **Risk focus** – better governance can help trustees anticipate future risks and be better placed to make the most of new opportunities.

- **Mission focus** – better governance can help ensure an organisation is using its resources to best meet its mission.

- **Reputation focus** – better governance gives people confidence that your organisation is well run and effective.

- **Relationship focus** – better governance helps ensure that the many voices in your organisation – users, staff, volunteers, funders and others – can input into decision-making.

- **Learning focus** – finally, better governance can help develop a more creative organisation that learns from experience and can respond to new challenges.[33]

Reviewing your governance – getting started

Why do you want to carry out a governance review?
A good place to begin a governance review is to consider the motivation behind a desire to improve governance and to consider the practicalities of how you would like to take the process forward. Use the questions in the box below to help frame your approach. The answers should help you choose the most suitable approach to your governance review.

33 Parker M (2006) *Better Governance: An introduction to measuring and improving board effectiveness.* London: Governance Hub, NCVO.

Governance review questionnaire

Use the questions below as a guide to help choose which approach to a governance review will best meet your charity's needs.

1   Why do you want to review and improve your governance? What changes do you want to make?

• We want to look at the effectiveness of your board – its role, the way it works together as a team and how it makes decisions.

• We want to look at the effectiveness of individual trustees – their role and performance.

• We want to be sure our board and organisation is operating well with sound, up-to-date policies and procedures and sound governance arrangements.

2) How do you want to carry out the review?

• Using a comprehensive approach looking at governance within the context of the whole organisation.

• Using an approach that can be externally checked or accredited.

• By comparing our organisation with other similar organisations.

• By comparing our organisation to a sector-wide standard or set of principles.

• By using an off the shelf system that we can adapt to our needs.

• By using a self-assessment method.

• By using a questionnaire.

• Informally, perhaps via an 'away day' discussion with board members.

3   How much do you want to commit in terms of time and resources?

Budget
• We have a reasonable budget to do this – we could engage a consultant or pay for an accredited system.

• We have little or no budget to do this – we prefer to do the work in house or choose an approach that is low cost or doesn't take a lot of time.

Time
• We want to invest a considerable amount of time over a longer period.

• We want to invest a lot of time over a short period.

• We can only commit to a small amount of time, perhaps one or two meetings.

Governance review tools
Specialist governance review tools
There are a number of toolkits or frameworks that can help a charity specifically review its governance arrangements and the effectiveness of its board.

The Code provides a systematic method of assessing how an organisation's governance compares to the principles set out in the Code. Since 2005 the Code has been widely used and promoted as a framework against which voluntary and community sector organisations can evaluate the effectiveness of their own governance arrangements. The Code consists of six high-level principles (see Chapter 5), each accompanied by a series of detailed good governance characteristics. The characteristics set out why the overarching principles are essential for good governance.

The Trustees and Management Committee National Occupational Standards (NOS) is also a framework for reviewing the effectiveness of an organisation's governance. The NOS are particularly useful for reviewing the role and contribution (or 'appraisal') of individual trustees (see Chapter 17).

There are also other governance review tools developed by a variety of different organisations. For example, building on the Code, NCVO has created the Governance Wheel – a diagnostic, development and evaluation tool. The Governance Wheel provides a clear framework against which boards can measure their performance and demonstrate that their charity is well run and effective. There are also more informal governance review methods that your board can adopt, for example checklists or questionnaires that can be used as a basis for discussion. See section 22.2 for examples and section 22.4 for suggestions.

Individual trustee reviews/appraisals

You may want to look specifically at the role, performance and support needs of individual trustees. These tools are sometimes called 'trustee appraisal' tools. An example of a framework that looks at the skills and competencies of individual trustees is the National Occupational Standards for Trustees and Management Committee Members. These approaches are explored further in Chapter 23.

Benchmarking

Benchmarking is the process of comparing your organisation's performance with that of other organisations. You can benchmark governance in the same way that you can compare other aspects of your organisation's operations. An example of a benchmarking service that specifically looks at governance is Boards Count.[34] Benchmarking can also form part of a wider governance review.

A governance review as part of a quality system

A quality assurance system is a systematic way of ensuring your organisation undertakes a continuous process of learning, developing and reviewing, usually by aiming to meet an agreed level of performance. Systems look at the quality of an organisation's governance alongside other areas of the organisation. An example of a quality assurance system that includes governance is PQASSO (Practical Quality Assurance System for Small Organisations).

34 TransForm Mgmt Consultancy
Partnerships Ltd

Governance review comparison table

Type of review	What is it?	Examples of tools	Useful when...	More information
Governance review	A periodic process of reflecting on the effectiveness of the board and the organisation's governance arrangements	The Code	You want to look specifically at the role and effectiveness of the board, and how the board is organised and supported	Chapter 22
Trustee appraisal	A process of reviewing the role, contribution and support needs of individual trustees	Trustees and Management Committee National Occupational Standards	You want to look specifically at the individual trustee's role and needs	Chapter 23
Benchmarking	A process of comparing an organisation's governance with other organisations	Boards Count	You want to compare your practices with another organisation	Chapter 13
Quality system	A framework covering all aspects of an organisation's work, usually completed via self-assessment and often with an option of externally accreditation	PQASSO	You want to reach a consistent standard across the organisation (including its governance)	Chapter 13

22.2

22.3

Governance reviews – meeting your needs

A governance review can be a large or a small piece of work depending on the needs of your board and the resources available. How much time can you commit to a governance review? Here are some ideas:

Ten or 20 minutes
Reflection: your board may take a few minutes at the end of a meeting to consider the following questions.

- How effective have we been?

- Were there areas we lingered too long over?

- Did we get too side tracked at any point?

- Do the decisions we reached seem to be the right ones?

- How could the meeting have been improved?

If you only have a short amount of time, try dipping into the Code to discuss one or two of its principles. NCVO, through the work of the Governance Hub, published a pack of 26 cards, each including simple, illustrated explanations of some terms used in governance. The cards include questions or exercises aimed at helping you and your organisation reflect on how you operate as a board.[35]

One or two hours
Try dipping into the Code to review your board's practices against one of its high-level principles. After discussing the ways in which you meet the good governance characteristics and what gaps exist, formally agree and record the actions you plan to take as a result of carrying out the exercise.

A longer period
The Code can be used over a longer period of time to carry out a comprehensive review of every aspect of your charity's governance.

See below for guidance on how to structure a bigger review.

Organising the process and accessing support

Using working groups
A small working group could be established to oversee the governance review process.

The group's duties could involve: recommending an overall review process; carrying out detailed reviews of specific areas of the board's work; auditing documentation such as policies and procedures and the governing document; gathering evidence or administering a questionnaire; reporting back to the board with recommendations; or planning a board discussion or away day.

35 NCVO (2006) *A–Z of Good Governance*. London: Governance Hub, NCVO.

22.4

Accessing external support

Some organisations find it useful to hire an external consultant or facilitator for all or part of a governance review process. External input offers the advantage of providing outside expertise and an 'objective' perspective. It can be useful if the organisation's staff or trustees have limited time to invest in the more detailed aspects of the process. It also allows participants to be equally involved in discussions, because the management of the process or specific discussion sessions can be left to the facilitator. This can be particularly helpful for the chair, who may otherwise take on, for example, the role of chairing an away day.

On the downside, your organisation may not be able to afford the cost of a consultant. And your board may not be happy or comfortable with a person from 'outside' being involved in analysing what may be sensitive issues.

Gathering information

A governance review involves building up a picture of how effectively your charity is governed. How, in practice, you create this picture will depend on the size and scope of your review and the information required.

Questionnaires

A common way of carrying out a governance review is to ask each board member to comment on the board's performance via a questionnaire or completion of a survey. The results are then collated into a report and discussed collectively. The advantage of this approach is that it can encourage trustees to be more open because of the confidential nature of the process. The disadvantage is that trustees may not want to fill out formal questionnaires and the process can be time consuming.

The Code can be used as the basis for a questionnaire survey.

Audit of documents

A governance review will usually include a 'desk' review of documents, for example board and committee meeting minutes and policies and procedures. Such a review can help you identify evidence of good practice, as well as being an opportunity to identify where governance practices do not meet the required standard and to review the accuracy and consistency of policies and procedures, such as in the following examples.

- Are key board policies and procedures in place? Can you find up-to-date role descriptions for trustees, a board conflicts of interest policy and a trustee induction pack? Have you compared the induction pack against the sample list of contents in Chapter 20

- Are there up to date and accurate terms of reference for committees? Have you reviewed the governing document and compared it with terms of reference to ensure both are consistent?

Group discussion

A group discussion can be a valuable way for the board to reflect on its role and performance. Collective discussion of responsibilities and relationships can help trustees gain a greater insight into their role and help achieve a consensus in identifying priorities and action points for a governance review.

Group discussions can take place in a variety of ways. For some organisations, their governance review might take place entirely within a short group discussion – for example, reviewing the 12 responsibilities (see exercises on pages 245–247) and agreeing action points. Other organisations may carry out an audit or questionnaire and use the findings as the basis for a carefully planned away day.

A slot at each board meeting could be used to discuss one or two aspects of good governance. Or, one longer board meeting each year could incorporate a board review. Some organisations take a few minutes at the end of each meeting to reflect on the board's performance.

An away day (see box) to review your board's performance can be productive. It has the advantage of taking board members out of the meeting room environment and allowing time for in-depth discussion of board progress.

Planning an away day

1 Prepare

Advance preparation helps set the agenda for the day and helps the board gain ownership of the agenda. Individual questionnaires can be a way of identifying topics for discussion or a discussion at a board meeting, perhaps using one of the shorter questionnaires (see Exercise 3), could also help prioritise topics.

2 Plan

A small working group can meet to decide on the topics for the day, based on information gathered. The group can consider practicalities, including the following examples.

- Do we need a facilitator?

- Should we invite a guest speaker?

- Should we break into small groups to discuss each topic?

- Is the day for the board only or should senior staff be invited to attend?

  A clear and agreed structure will avoid the day being bogged down in discussions that can't be resolved on the day. And remember the golden rule: don't try to cover too much in a day.

3 On the day

Make sure you leave space at the end of the day for agreeing next steps and closure.

Be realistic about what can be agreed in a single day – many issues will need further consideration at future meetings, so try not to make expectations too high.

Your away day should:

- have clear and meaningful objectives

- enable all trustees to participate

- involve activities to encourage trustee input

- include a facility for feedback and further action

- be fun!

Local infrastructure organisation

A local infrastructure organisation that had been through some difficult and challenging times found itself with a new chief executive and board chair in 2012.

Together, the chair and chief executive soon recognised that the organisation had lost strategic focus and was becoming increasingly irrelevant to the individuals, groups and organisations it was meant to serve. The board was small and was overly focused on operational issues. The trustees felt their role was to represent the views of members and the memorandum and articles were unduly restrictive in terms of trustee and membership recruitment. Trustee meetings were often dominated by one or two individuals, and the quality of papers, strategic oversight and decision-making was extremely poor.

On the basis of their organisational diagnosis, the chair and chief executive agreed that a governance review would enable the trustees and senior staff to review strategically the way in which they were operating and crucially to agree where improvements needed to be made. It was also agreed that the organisation's practices and processes would be reviewed against the Code and, more importantly, it would be used to explore the attitudes and behaviours that were having a negative impact on the way in which the board was operating.

The review included a number of steps – completion of questionnaires, interviews with trustees and senior staff, desktop research, production of a report and facilitation of an away day. During the facilitated session, the board were made aware of their roles and responsibilities as trustees and company directors and an analysis of the governance findings. The rest of the session was spent discussing and debating the findings and agreeing the way forward.

The action plan that was created as a result of the governance review set out steps that would: improve their strategic focus; ensure they developed a greater understanding and concentration on the management of risk; place greater importance on the protection of their reputation; and earmark ways in which they could become more mission focused. Other actions included: amending their articles of association; developing an effective committee structure; establishing a delegated authority framework; improving decision-making processes; and engaging board members with their strategic responsibilities.

One year later in 2013, the chair and chief executive provided their reflections on what the organisation had achieved in a relatively short period of time:

'Better relationships have been developed on the board and there is a greater sense of a shared mission as well as a clearer understanding of roles and responsibilities. Trustee recruitment processes have been improved with the provision for co-option of trustees from outside of our membership. This means the skills, knowledge and experience of trustees are paramount rather than representation of a particular interest group. As a result of these changes, and using the Code of Governance, a much more collective approach to decision-making has emerged. Our organisation is now much clearer and more confident in its offer and strategic role in supporting the local voluntary and community sector. As a consequence membership has increased by 15% over a 12-month period.'

Example governance review exercises

Exercise 1

A governance review using the summary Code

The Code has six overarching principles, with a number of supporting characteristics under each heading. You can use the overarching principles to carry out a short assessment of your governance or the detailed characteristics to carry out a more in depth assessment.

The example exercise below uses Principle 1 of the Code as an example of how it can be used as the basis for a governance review questionnaire or board discussion.

Principle 1: Understanding the role of the board – how satisfied are you that...	Very satisfied	Satisfied	Not satisfied	Comments
The board accepts ultimate responsibility for the way the organisation is directed and run in meeting its purposes				
The board is alert to those matters that cannot be delegated to individual board members or others				
The board takes a considered, proportionate and balanced approach to risk management				
The board establishes and periodically reviews – in consultation with the organisation's stakeholders – statements setting out the vision, mission and values of the organisation				
The board understands and ensures independence of board decision-making and action and puts the needs of beneficiaries ahead of any other interests				
The board follows proper and formal arrangements for the supervision, support, appraisal and remuneration of its chief executive				

Exercise 2
Short board assessment
The table below can be used as the
basis for a quick board assessment.
It is based on the '12 essential
board responsibilities' – see pages
11–12 for a fuller description of
each heading.

Area of responsibility	We do this by	We can improve this by	Action points
Set and maintain vision, mission and values			
Develop strategy			
Establish and monitor policies			
Ensure compliance with the governing document			
Ensure accountability			
Ensure compliance with the law			
Maintain proper fiscal oversight			
Respect the role of staff/volunteers			
Maintain effective board performance			
Promote the organisation			
Where staff are employed:			
Set up employment procedures			
Select and support the chief executive			

Exercise 3

Sample board self-assessment questionnaire

This short questionnaire can be completed by trustees or used as a basis for discussion:

- Does your board set clear objectives for the organisation?

- Does your board establish the organisation's priorities?

- Has your board got procedures for ensuring that assets are used effectively and efficiently?

- Does your board monitor the work of the organisation?

- Does your board monitor compliance with legislation, such as charity and company law?

- Does your board monitor whether reporting to donors, staff, volunteers and other stakeholders is carried out?

- Does your board appraise the performance of the chief executive and his/her management of the work of the staff?

- Do all members of your board attend meetings regularly and prepare thoroughly for them?

- Does your governing document give you the power to delegate to committees and if it does can you delegate decision-making or merely the implementation of decisions taken by the board?

- Are your powers of delegation adequate? If not, do they need revision?

Checklist

Does your board periodically carry out a governance review, either formally or informally?

Do you act on the findings of the review?

23

Trustee review or appraisal

Part Three highlighted the importance of reviewing with new trustees the contribution they are making and any support needs they have. This principle could be extended to all trustees.

An individual assessment is a way for trustees to evaluate their own personal contribution. It could highlight individual strengths and weaknesses, support needs and areas where trustees could use their own skills, experience and interests additionally to benefit the charity. Such an assessment can be carried out via an 'informal review' or a more formal 'appraisal'.

A sample list of questions designed to help individual trustees to reflect on their performance as a trustee is provided at the end of this chapter. A trustee's own development needs are also important – the following questions should be considered.

- What development needs do I have?

- What kind of support do I need from the board?

- What motivates me in my role as a trustee?

- What would I like to be done differently?

- What enriches my experience as a trustee?

- How would I like to contribute to the board?

23.1

Trustees and Management Committee National Occupational Standards

The Trustees NOS set out the functions and responsibilities of individual trustees. It provides a way of assessing the performance of individual trustees and the knowledge and understanding they need to carry out their role.

The Trustees NOS is a useful framework to help review and support an individual trustee's contribution.

Ideas for carrying out individual trustee reviews

Questionnaire

A simple questionnaire could be sent out to trustees once a year asking for each trustee's comments on their own performance (see Exercise 1 for an example).

Review meeting

A meeting with the chair once a year would allow a trustee to reflect on their experience as a board member. If a more formal appraisal system is to be used then this meeting could refer back to action points set the previous year or at the beginning of their term of office.

Code of conduct

At a basic level, all trustees should have a role description and many agree a code of conduct (see Chapter 3). A review of a trustee's role and contribution can reference these and provide an opportunity to highlight where issues may have occurred (for example, in conflicts of interest).

Appraisal

Some charities now appraise the performance of board members and that of the chair. The approach taken varies. It can take the form of an informal discussion, often between the chair and each trustee. Alternatively, a pre-meeting questionnaire can be drawn up for the trustee to identify their strengths, areas of improvement, support needs and where they would like to develop in the future. It is important that whoever conducts the appraisal is skilled in giving feedback because of the sometimes sensitive nature of the topic.

One approach to appraising the performance of the chair would be for the deputy chair to speak informally to each trustee about the chair's performance and then feed this back in a session with the chair.

Linking review or appraisal to learning and development

A review or 'appraisal' – of whatever format – is a good opportunity to explore individual trustees' learning and development needs. See Chapter 18 for more information.

23.2

Individual trustee review exercises

Exercise 1
How do you contribute?
Ask each trustee to complete the questionnaire. Use it as the basis for a one to one with each trustee and the chair, or collate the results for a board discussion.

1 I understand the organisation's mission.

2 I support the mission.

3 I am knowledgeable about the organisation's major programmes and services.

4 I follow trends and important developments in areas related to the work of the organisation.

5 I read the organisation's financial statements.

6 I understand the organisation's financial statements.

7 I act knowledgeably and prudently when making recommendations about how the organisation's funds should be invested or spent.

8 I advise and assist the chief executive when asked.

9 I have a good working relationship with the chief executive.

10 I have a good working relationship with other board members.

11) I recommend qualified individuals with relevant skills and experience as possible nominees for the board.

12 I prepare for and participate in board and committee meetings as well as other activities of the organisation.

13 I willingly volunteer and use my special skills to further the organisation's mission.

14 I complete all assignments in a responsible and timely manner.

15 I keep an eye on the organisation's public image in the media and among members of the community.

16 I take advantage or opportunities to enhance the organisation's public image by speaking to individuals, business and community leaders about the organisation.

17 I speak for the organisation only when authorised to do so.

18 I respect the confidentiality of the board's executive sessions.

19 I suggest agenda items for future board and committee meetings.

20 I focus my attention on long-term and significant policy issues rather than short-term administrative matters.

21 I avoid burdening the staff with special requests for favours.

22 I see to it that my communications with staff below the chief executive never undermine the relationship between the chief executive and his or her staff.

23 I avoid in fact and in perception conflicts of interest that might embarrass the board or organisation and disclose to the board in a timely manner any possible conflicts.

24 My opinions are heard and considered in the boardroom.

25 I find serving on the board to be a satisfying experience.

Exercise 2
Quality checker
Individual trustees can complete this questionnaire to reflect on what qualities and skills they bring to the board (it is based on the Trustees and Management Committee NOS).

Quality	I can demonstrate this by	I can learn more about this by
Be committed to the purpose, objects and values of the organisation		
Be constructive about other trustees' opinions in discussions and in response to staff members' contributions at meetings		
Be able to act reasonably and responsibly when undertaking such duties and performing tasks		
Be able to maintain confidentiality on sensitive and confidential information		
Be supportive of the values (and ethics) of the organisation		
Understand the importance and purpose of meetings, and be committed to preparing for them adequately and attending them regularly		
Be able to analyse information and, when necessary, challenge constructively		
Be able to make collective decisions and stand by them		
Be able to respect boundaries between executive and governance functions		

Checklist

Do you provide an opportunity for individual trustees to reflect on their role, contribution and support needs as a board member?

Part Five:

Further information and support

Action with Communities in Rural England (ACRE)

www.acre.org.uk

ACRE is the national umbrella body for the 38 Rural Community Councils that make up the ACRE Network. The ACRE Good Practice Quality Standard (The ACRE Standard) is endorsed by the Charity Commission.

Advisory, Conciliation and Arbitration Service (ACAS)

www.acas.org.uk

ACAS aims to improve organisations and working life through better employment relations. ACAS supplies information, independent advice and training.

Association of Charitable Foundations (ACF)

www.acf.org.uk

ACF is the UK-wide support organisation for grant-making trusts and foundations of all types.

Association of Charity Independent Examiners (ACIE)

www.acie.org.uk

ACIE is an association for people who carry out independent examinations. It gives support to independent examiners and provides information relevant to their examination work.

Charities Aid Foundation (CAF)

www.cafonline.org

CAF works to create greater value for charities and social enterprise by transforming the way donations are made and the way charitable funds are managed.

Charities Evaluation Services (CES) (part of NCVO)

www.ces-vol.org.uk

CES offers training, consultancy, external evaluations and publications to help voluntary and community organisations strengthen the quality of their work and achieve better outcomes for service users. CES also publishes the PQASSO (Practical Quality Assurance System for Small Organisations).

The Charity Commission for England and Wales

www.charitycommission.gov.uk

The Charity Commission for England and Wales is established by law as the regulator and registrar of charities in England and Wales. Its aim is to provide the best possible regulation of these in order to increase charities' efficiency and effectiveness and public confidence and trust in them. The Charity Commission website contains a range of publications and online guidance.

Charity Finance Group (CFG)

www.cfg.org.uk

CFG is a membership organisation specialising in helping charities to manage their accounting, taxation, audit and other finance related functions.

Community Matters

www.communitymatters.org.uk

Community Matters is the National Federation of Community Organisations. It publishes the VISIBLE Operating Standards for community organisations.

Compact Voice (based at NCVO)

www.compactvoice.org.uk

The Compact is an agreement between government and the voluntary and community sector in England. It recognises shared values, principles and commitments and sets out guidelines for how both parties should work together.

Companies House

www.companieshouse.gov.uk

The main functions of Companies House are to incorporate and dissolve limited companies, examine and store company information delivered under the Companies Act and related legislation and make this information available to the public. The Companies House website includes useful guidance for companies, directors and company secretaries.

Co-operatives UK
www.uk.coop
Co-operatives UK promotes and develops co-operative enterprises for an increasingly successful and sustainable co-operative economy.

Directory of Social Change (DSC)
www.dsc.org.uk
DSC provides information and training to voluntary and community organisations.

Disclosure and Barring Service (DBS)
www.gov.uk/government/organisations/disclosure-and-barring-service
DBS helps employers make safer recruitment decisions and prevent unsuitable people from working with vulnerable groups, including children. It replaces the Criminal Records Bureau (CRB) and Independent Safeguarding Authority (ISA). DBS is an executive non-departmental public body of the Home Office.

Funding Central
www.fundingcentral.org.uk
Funding Central is a free website for charities, voluntary organisations and social enterprises that provides access to thousands of funding and finance opportunities, plus a wealth of tools and resources supporting organisations to develop sustainable income strategies appropriate to their needs.

Fundraising Standards Board (FRSB)
www.frsb.org.uk
FRSB runs a self-regulatory scheme for fundraising in the UK. Membership is voluntary and charities that join are asked to adhere to the Codes of Fundraising Practice and the FRSB's Fundraising Promise. The FRSB aims to be a mark of reassurance for the public for fundraising. The FRSB handles complaints from donors about fundraising issues.

Good Governance: A Code for the Voluntary and Community Sector (The Code)
www.governancecode.org
The Code is a framework to support good governance in voluntary and community sector organisations. It contains principles that are easily understood and applied within organisations. The Code is not a set of rules or a checklist.

Health and Safety Executive (HSE)
www.hse.gov.uk
HSE is the national independent watchdog for work-related health, safety and illness. HSE conducts and sponsors research, promotes training, provides an information and advisory service and submits proposals for new or revised regulations and approved codes of practice. The website is a useful source of information about how organisations can manage health and safety.

HM Revenue and Customs (HMRC)
www.hmrc.gov.uk/charities (charities webpages)
HMRC is responsible for collecting most taxes.

Financial Conduct Authority (FCA)
www.fca.org.uk/firms/firm-types/mutual-societies/industrial
FCA is an independent non-governmental body, given statutory powers by the Financial Services and Markets Act 2000. It is also the registering authority for societies that register under the Industrial and Provident Societies Act 1965.

Information Commissioner's Office (ICO)
www.ico.gov.uk
ICO is the UK's independent authority set up to promote access to official information and to protect personal information. The ICO website includes guides to data protection and good practice notes.

Institute of Chartered Secretaries and Administrators (ICSA)
www.icsa.org.uk
ICSA is the leading professional body for company secretaries and senior administrators across all sectors. ICSA's website includes guidance, publications, good practice information and example and specimen documents.

Institute of Fundraising
www.institute-of-fundraising.org.uk
The Institute of Fundraising is the
professional membership body for
UK fundraisers. Its aim is to promote
the highest standard of fundraising
practice.

Investing in Volunteers (IIV)
iiv.investinginvolunteers.org.uk
IIV is the UK quality standard for all
organisations that involve volunteers
in their work. IIV is delivered in
England by NCVO.

LawWorks for Community Groups
www.lawworks.org.uk/
community-groups
LawWorks is an initiative of the
Solicitors Pro Bono Group. LawWorks
for Community Groups offers free
legal advice, mediation and guidance
to small charities, not-for-profit,
voluntary and community
organisations and social enterprises
in England and Wales.

Media Trust
www.mediatrust.org
Media Trust works in partnership with
the media industry to build effective
communications for the charity and
voluntary sectors. Services include
media and communications training,
consultancy and media production.

National Association for Voluntary
and Community Action (NAVCA)
www.navca.org.uk
NAVCA is the national voice of local
support and development
organisations in England. NAVCA's
website lists contact details of
member organisations that support
the development of local charities
and community groups.

NCVO
www.ncvo.org.uk
www.knowhownonprofit.org.uk
NCVO champions the voluntary
sector and volunteering by
connecting, representing and
supporting voluntary organisations.

Our services include training,
consultancy, information resources
and toolkits on governance,
sustainable funding, collaborative
working, campaigning, strategy
and impact.

NCVO's main website for practical
information for voluntary and
community organisations is
KnowHow NonProfit.

National Housing Federation
www.housing.org.uk
The National Housing Federation
represents and supports 1,300
not-for-profit housing associations
in England and campaigns for better
housing and neighbourhoods.

Northern Ireland Council for
Voluntary Action (NICVA)
www.nicva.org
NICVA is the umbrella body
for voluntary and community
organisations in Northern Ireland.

Office for Civil Society
www.cabinetoffice.gov.uk
As part of the Cabinet Office, the
Office for Civil Society leads work
across government to support the
environment for a thriving third sector
(voluntary and community groups,
social enterprises, charities, co-
operatives and mutuals), enabling
the sector to campaign for change,
deliver public services, promote social
enterprise and strengthen
communities.

Sandy Adirondack legal update
www.sandy-a.co.uk/legal.htm
Sandy Adirondack's legal update
for voluntary organisations provides
general information for management
committees/trustees and staff of
voluntary organisations about legal
changes over the past year and
forthcoming changes.

Scottish Council for Voluntary
Organisations (SCVO)
www.scvo.org.uk
SCVO is the national body
representing the voluntary sector in
Scotland. SCVO seeks to advance
the values and shared interests of
the voluntary sector.

Trustees Unlimited
www.trustees-unlimited.co.uk
Trustees Unlimited – a joint venture
between NCVO, Bates Wells
Braithwaite and Russam GMS – is a
recruitment service that can help you
recruit high quality trustees and non
executives in a rigorous and yet cost
effective way from across the private,
public and voluntary sectors.

Wales Council for Voluntary Action
(WCVA) Cyngor Gweithredu
Gwirfoddol Cymru (CGGC)
www.wcva.org.uk
WCVA is the voice of the voluntary
sector in Wales, representing
and campaigning for voluntary
organisations, volunteers and
communities.